Heresy Out Loud

Paths for Way-Walkers

By

The Rev. Dr. Carl R. Gillett

"For last year's words belong to last year's language
And next year's words await another voice.
And to make an end is to make a beginning."
T.S. Eliot

Acknowledgements

I wish to thank many people who have encouraged me to present this work. Sarah Gorman was an insistent presence urging me to publish the sermonic material found herein. Without her help, I would never have gotten the project underway. Sheree Clark Lovell has helped me appreciate the importance of the theological content in the second part of the book. Lisa McIlvenna encouraged my theological explorations; Grant Soosalu has been an enthusiastic influence. Without Grant's help, I would be unaware of the significance of mBraining. The many people who have listened to the sermons have helped me appreciate the importance of sharing this effort. Many of my psychotherapy and coaching clients have helped me value my own work and find the energy to translate it into print. My beloved wife, Marilyn, encouraged my vision, validated my weird wonderings, and supported my dream. She has also endured my preoccupation with the process and been a tireless editor.

I owe a special debt of gratitude to Dr. Carl Lovell who literally saved my life as he got me through my bout with sepsis. He has enabled me to live to write this book.

I give thanks to the Godding presence that has sustained me through illness and distractions. May my work be a credit to my supporters, an act of praise to the Godding Creator and an invitation to others to explore more deeply their own intuitions about how to speak "faithing" in a doubting world.

Carl Gillett, Eastertide 2018

Table of Contents

Part 2: Heresy Out Loud

FOREWORD

It was tempting to subtitle this book: "Ways Way-Walkers Walk." This phrase refers to a historical fact that in the earliest days of Christianity, the adherents of this new faith were called people of the Way; the Way being the style and quality of life that Jesus had promulgated in his teaching. The members of the early Christian community, as frequently attested in the Acts of the Apostles, were known as followers of the Way. The structure of the Way was in flux, and there was no central authority to settle issues or advocate for a standard (aka orthodox) system of belief. Using "ways" without the article "the" emphasizes that there have always been many ways to walk the way. Repeating the word "walk," emphasizes that way-walkers do act. Way-walking is more than an intellectual exercise; it involves embodying the faith of the walker in the world. Nevertheless, all those "W's" seemed to be clumsy rhetoric, so I settled on "Paths for Way-Walkers," which seems to preserve the essential meaning of my original idea.

In the beginning time, there was no such thing as a Christian Bible. In fact, the New Testament didn't even exist. There was a variety of written materials in circulation with many of these apparently associated with communities which existed in certain cities or perhaps in the houses of early followers of the Way. Some of these documents would eventually be accepted as official expressions of the new church and would find their way into the New Testament and become part of a book the church would eventually call the Holy Bible. Many of these early documents would get ignored, and a few may even have been suppressed as being subversive writings. Many of the suppressed documents are gone and some survive in fragments. For materials to be labeled as expressions of heresy, other materials must be endorsed as orthodox—but that was quite a while coming, about 300 years after the crucifixion of Jesus.

During this early period, there was no common agreement about what the Way was all about. It seems that different people had different ideas about how to follow the Way. Describing the modern followers of the teaching of Jesus as "Way-Walkers" can help to escape the splendid confusion of all the various people, who while laying claim to the title of "Christian," continue to affirm a worldview in keeping with the heliocentric perspective of the late middle ages. Way-Walkers might wander or meander; they might wonder or even wish as they work at articulating a faith perspective that modern people, deeply immersed in a scientific worldview, would find appealing and useful. By talking about *Ways* Way-Walkers Walk, we can affirm that there are in fact many understandings about what it means to affirm allegiance to the teaching of Jesus of Nazareth. By stating that Way-Walkers *Walk* I am pointing out the fact that these people's faith involves actions expressed in a lifestyle. This idea also invites us to dig into the early origins of the Way-Walking process as a way of shedding the excess baggage history has loaded onto the "Christian" title.

This book contains two major parts. There is a collection of sermons which I preached during the first 17 years of the 21st century. The sermons are grouped into a handful of categories, and the sermons in each category are arranged in chronological order. The logic behind this arrangement is to invite the reader to follow the developments in my thinking. This part of the book is titled "Story-telling: A Work in Progress" which alludes to the way themes in my intellectual life develop over the opening years of the 21st century. The reader will encounter some repeated allusions or comments because they are markers along the way. The second major part is called: "Heresy Out Loud: A Perspective on Doing Theology." This portion is an attempt to distill my thinking about several theological issues into a form that I believe will make sense to 21st-century people. I hope by offering this material in this particular way that I will invite people outside the contemporary church to take a fresh look at Way-Walking approaches to spiritual life and invite those within the church to refresh their own thinking.

THE STORY-TELLER
The 'who am I' part of all this

Preaching and teaching are forms of story-telling. The person of the story-teller is a major factor in the shaping of those processes. Therefore, it seems important that my readers know something about the man who is telling this story so I will share a brief "history of me."

I am a heretic. In fact, I deliberately cultivate the role of being a heretic. In the world of religion, especially Christianity, there is something called "orthodox teaching." The word "orthodox" derived from Latin roots, means a straight opinion or right teaching. Curiously, the existence of orthodoxy requires the existence of heresy. To know what's right, one must inevitably know what's wrong. The word "heresy" is derived from Greek and means "to make a choice." If orthodox teaching is to evolve and stay current with the growth of knowledge and wisdom, it must be challenged. If orthodoxy is not challenged, it is likely to become moribund and irrelevant. We might well name moribund orthodoxy as fundamentalism (in any faith tradition). The source of the challenges to orthodoxy must be a vigorous and well-defended heresy.

Before I dig into the details of my heresy, I would like my readers to know some things about me and how I happen to be where I am now. Of course, I am a son but also a husband, father (of two sons) and grandfather (of five grandchildren). I am a seminary educated and ordained clergyperson in the United Church of Christ. My professional career falls into three unequal divisions: I began as a parish pastor and pursued that chapter for 22 years; the next chapter which lasted about 26 years, was as a psychotherapist; the most recent chapter, which is also the shortest, has found me doing life coaching for about eight years. My undergraduate degree was in philosophy, and that has encouraged me to be philosophical about my various personal and professional endeavors. This thread in my life has urged me to challenge many traditional teachings that I encounter, whether elements of Christian orthodoxy or key concepts of Freudian orthodoxy. Along the way, I collected (in addition to my seminary degree) a master's degree in Counseling and a Doctor of Ministry with a concentration on connections between hypnosis and spirituality. The title of my doctoral dissertation is *The Use of Milton Erickson's Therapeutic Style to Correlate Pastoral Therapy and Spiritual Direction.*

I have had a curiosity about my origins since I was a child. I had a great-grandmother who told stories about being related to Scottish royalty. I had a piano teacher (when I was about eight years old) who did serious genealogy work and told me one day that she had determined we were 42nd cousins! A friend who does genealogy studies in a very serious manner gave me a brief synopsis of my genealogy, which seems to indicate I had a relative who came to this country on the Mayflower.

Recently, I got the DNA program that Ancestry offers. I had surmised that I was mostly English. The Gillett surname was quite frequent in the Manchester, England area. There were interesting surprises in the report I got back. There was confirmation of the English history: my ethnicity report shows me as 58% Great Britain and 33% West European. However, there were some surprises: I have a significant European Jewish link. There are connections to Italy and Greece. There is also a link to the Middle East (think Turkey, Saudi Arabia, Yemen, perhaps Egypt, Iran, and Iraq). Then there is a link to Ireland, Finland, and Northwest Russia. I got to thinking about the dominant religious faiths in those places: Judaism, Roman Catholicism, Eastern Orthodoxy and Islam. Of course, the folks on the Mayflower were Protestant Christians.

It was not surprising that there were no links to Native Americans. You see, I am an immigrant. I am an ecumenical immigrant with at least five of the major religions in human civilization as part of my DNA. Every immigrant is my brother or sister; every faith is part of my heritage. The psychology folk sometimes talk about subpersonalities or dominant motifs (like introvert and extrovert). But I, by myself, am an ecumenical congregation. When I pray, my spiritual ancestors join me and whisper petitions to the Godding we all know by a variety of names

I was a volunteer firefighter for 16 years during my life as a parish pastor. I mention this because the experience gave me more close encounters with death and disaster than I prefer to remember; and deep memories of fatal fires and accidents. First responders are often the first to know about a death and the first people to encounter survivors. It has been 34 years since I answered my last alarm, but I can tell you much about those tragedies which come alive in my memory sometimes without conscious bidding on my part. The link between many of those deaths and the poverty and the wretched housing that often goes with it feeds my concern for justice for the marginalized. There is more detail about this in the sermon titled "Committed Witnesses." [on p. 167]

Another transformative experience is more recent. In the spring of 2015, I contracted a severe urinary tract infection which eventually led to sepsis. I was forced during my hospitalization to confront and contemplate the reality that I was very close to death. There was one very long, dark, sleepless night during which I found myself knowing that I might die and actually saying that out loud. I was pleasantly surprised that I wasn't afraid. However, it also seemed very clear to me that I didn't want to die. And so, with a certain vehemence, I declared out loud in the darkness of my hospital room: "Maybe not!" By what I can call the Grace of Godding (more about this word later) and excellent, state-of-the-art medical care, my "maybe not" became the affirmation that led to victory over the sepsis and a chance to extend my life.

I probably share a common experience with people who have come close to dying, but somehow managed to survive the threat. The experience to which I refer is a certain compulsion to review and reflect on many of the assumed truths by which we have guided our lives. I am not the same person I was before I declared, "Maybe not!" This compulsion, which I find moves through my life in an uneven rhythm, has urged me to come out of my closet. It says to me, "Be a damned heretic out loud for a change!" One interesting definition of heresy is to hold an opinion that is profoundly at odds with what is accepted. If you persevere through this material, I imagine you will agree that I am profoundly at odds with much of establishment thinking.

Here are five themes I chose to use as a way to organize the sermons. Nearly all of these sermons were preached in United Church of Christ (UCC) churches— most them in the UCC church in Midland, MI and all of them are 21st-century documents.

1. Way-walkers creatively celebrate the health of brokenness.
2. Way-walkers dare to be foolish, weird and embrace insecurity
3. Way-walkers heal themselves and transform the world.
4. Way-walkers watch their language and respect the power of the Word.

5. Way-walkers are humble, self-compassionate people who rise above self-interest.

Sermons are a distinctive form of rhetoric. Maya Angelou said: "I've learned that people will forget what you said, people will forget what you did, but people will never forget how you made them feel." Sermons are not essays or research reports; nor are they poems or drama. There are many of these elements embedded in the preaching process. Sermons address themselves to the way we *feel* about life, faith and a plethora of issues. I have endeavored to share honest research, occasional quotations, a bit of poetry and some dramatic fragments. The reader will find brief references which are earmarks of the fact that these were all delivered as part of a worship service. For example, there may be comments about "last Sunday" or references to choral anthems, bulletin covers, etc. The writing style in the sermons also reflects the fact that these were written to be preached. Sometimes the way I write for preaching may be a bit unconventional or unexpected. Often a sermon text is more like a work in progress than other types of writing. This is because the "work in progress" is completed by preaching the sermon.

I deliberately chose to leave in elements of live preaching. Where need be, notes are added in brackets to clarify some inclusions. I am a lectionary preacher, which means that I use the lections (readings) for each Sunday that have been agreed upon by a majority of churches. The Lectionary follows a three-year cycle, which means that we start over at the beginning of the fourth year. The designated lections are noted along with the title of each sermon. The reader may notice that there is more than one sermon tied to certain lections. There are a few sermons in the collection that do not focus on the lectionary. Perhaps noting how I treated these duplicates over time may reveal some of my own processing or what I might call proto-theology—which gets articulated in Part 2.

Readers may certainly read the sermons in Part 1 in sequence but may also choose to pursue a particular theme regardless of where it comes in the book. Part 2 will probably make more sense if it is read in the order written (at least the first time). Finally, readers are invited to share their reactions and comments with me via email to gillettcarl@gmail.com.

Part 1: Story-telling, a Work in Progress

Way-Walkers Creatively Celebrate the Health of Brokenness.

COMPASSION IS NOT CORRECT
July 3, 2011. Psalm 145:8-18; Matthew 11:16-19, 25-30

Jesus and John the Baptist were cousins. Because Elizabeth, John's mother, and Mary, Jesus' mother, seemed to have a more than casual relationship and because families in that time seemed to live rather close together and be involved with one another across the life span, it makes sense for us to suppose that John and Jesus more or less grew up together. However, it is hard to imagine two more different people by the time they got to be adults. John became a Nazarite. He made a vow not to cut his hair—ever; he lived off the land (maybe we should consider him to be an early environmentalist) eating locusts and honey, drinking no alcohol, wearing a loin cloth made of animal skin and probably a shirt made of camel hair. He would not have bathed ever, and it is doubtful that the loin cloth was tanned leather. He would never have shaved his beard. I think if you were with John, you would want to stay upwind. Perhaps that aspect of his appearance would have helped him keep the Nazarite vow to have nothing to do with women. He was an outspoken man: he seemed not to care what the authorities thought of him whether the authorities were Roman or Jewish. He was willing, maybe even eager, to argue with anyone who came along. Eventually, his "in-your-face" style would cost him his life.

By way of contrast consider Jesus: one of the first accounts of Jesus' appearance as an adult is the story of his attendance at a wedding where he increased the wine supply and apparently provided a superior wine in the process. He found women to be important, talked to them (which Rabbis at the time were not supposed to do), and had women for friends. Where John was blunt with the authorities, Jesus was crafty and careful, focused on continuing his ministry and working around the authorities part of the time. Our celebration of the Last Supper, which has become a highly stylized ritual in the Church, obscures the fact that Jesus wanted to have a dinner party with his disciples the last night of his life. John confronted where Jesus taught. John demanded where Jesus invited. John was a social isolate while Jesus was deeply involved with a lot of people. John demanded confession and Jesus offered healing.

In our gospel lesson this morning, Jesus does what the professors asked us to do in college. He says, "Compare and contrast" John and myself. Then he deliberately weaves their work together. He says "We played the flute for you, and you did not dance; we wailed, and you did not mourn. John came neither eating nor drinking, and they say, 'He has a demon;' the son of man came eating and drinking, and they say 'Look, a glutton and a drunkard, a friend of tax collectors and sinners.'"

Jesus is describing the folk who listened to both men preach as emotionally detached people. They are at the game but not in it. We might think of them as people whose favorite response to just about everything is "yes, but." Yes, the outfielder caught the ball, but he fell down and got his uniform dirty. Yes, the doctor fixed my deformed ankle, but he left a scar. Yes, we need to feed the hungry, but I can't afford to pay more taxes. Yes, we need to clean up the environment, but don't regulate my industry.

My grandfather was a great fan of Tiger baseball. Long before there was television, my grandfather would listen to the games on the radio. He was quite involved. The speed of his rocking chair was connected to the action in the game, and he would laugh uproariously whenever there were arguments between managers and umpires. Once in a while, he would manage to go to a Tiger game. Now if you went to the game with him, you had to understand that he would be there when the stadium opened; I never did quite understand why batting practice was so important. No matter what the score, there was no leaving before the last out. I was thinking about him last week as I sat watching a Tiger baseball game. Now mind you, I was working on my laptop, peering over the top of it at the TV screen when there seemed to be a loud enough roar. One of the things that I have that my grandfather did not have is instant replay. I am confident that if I miss some important play in the game, the broadcasters will offer me a replay. In fact, Thursday night I watched a replay of the game the Tigers had played that afternoon. The TV folk cut some of the innings out to fit the game into their time constraints: my grandfather would have been incensed. Some of us have DVR's attached to our TV sets to record all manner of programs so that we can watch them when it is convenient. My grandfather may have been physically separated from the site of the game, but he was involved. I am detached, I can watch, I can analyze some parts of the game endlessly as the TV replays the same play over and over from many different angles. I am certainly not involved like my grandfather was; compared to him, I am detached and distant.

Over and over again throughout the gospels, we find Jesus dealing with the Pharisees. One commentator described the Pharisees as people who ". . . acted the formalisms of their faith above its deep commitment." When the disciples walked through a wheat field on the Sabbath and plucked grain to eat, the Pharisees accused them of breaking the Sabbath by harvesting grain and thus working. The Pharisees were the essence of propriety. They dotted all the "i-s" and crossed all the "t-s." They wanted people to see them doing the correct thing--so they blew horns when placing their offerings into the temple treasury. In order to make sure no one broke the important religious laws, they made extra rules to assure the law didn't get broken. Jesus found them more interested in being correct than being compassionate; more interested in their own salvation than the welfare of others. The Pharisees were very good at saying "yes, but." Yes, you have an interesting point, but we need to discuss it more thoroughly. Yes, some people are hungry, but we can't feed them on the Sabbath. Yes, we enjoy eating meat, but the butcher is ritually unclean and can't come to temple.

Jesus goes on, in our gospel reading today, to thank God for hiding things from the wise and revealing things to the infants. I think he is talking about the contrast between the Pharisees and the common people. He is, in fact, thanking God that the Pharisees don't get it but that ordinary people do. In the process, he seems to endorse the importance of being in the game. Involvement, however messy, is better than detachment; deeply held and expressed emotions are superior to carefully controlled and suppressed feelings. When he talks about how infamously awful places like ancient Sodom or Tyre (which was nearby) would have repented if they had been offered the same experiences as he was offering people, he is pointing out that the detached "yes, but" attitude is ultimately deadly because it cuts us off from each other and from God.

At the close of this reading, Jesus has this to say: "Come to me, all you who are weary and are carrying heavy burdens and I will give you rest. Take my yoke upon you and learn from me; for I am gentle and humble in heart, and you will find rest for your souls. For my yoke is easy and my burden is light." I feel that this statement mirrors the sentiments in the Psalm reading today where we find God described as one who is ". . . good to all and whose compassion is over all that God has made." Certainly, Jesus' description of his way as easy is a sharp contrast to the socially and politically correct Pharisees with their endless rules and constant concern for how they looked to others. Jesus is asking for involvement, not analysis; commitment, not detachment; risking, not "yes-butting." In essence, Jesus is inviting us to get in the game, take some risks, and avoid the safety of detached, uninvolved, replay analysis.

About 25 years later the apostle Paul would have to deal with the difficulties the Corinthian church was having—difficulties that eventually destroyed the effectiveness of that place. Those difficulties could probably all be described as a colossal and complicated argument about who was right, about whose views were correct, and about which teacher was the correct authority. Jesus found that the Pharisee's perspective led them to do preposterous things which he described as their willingness to swallow camels and only strain out a gnat. There is a Buddhist saying that would seem to fit here: "If you cling to an idea as the inalterable truth, then when the truth does come in person and knock at your door, you will not be able to open the door and accept it." That would seem to describe Jesus' concern about the Pharisees, about the politically correct, and the self-righteous right.

Jesus is about compassion and love. Forget the focus on being correct and proper. He certainly implies that being right is much over-rated. He might have said that being right isn't being righteous. Involvement is messy; commitment can't wait until the replay machine wears out. Compassion is not correct. By the time compassion figures out the correct approach, the people in need of the help will be lost or dead. Pain is now; compassion is now. There is no time to be correct. Jesus' way of doing things is easy because it delivers us from the paralysis of analysis, from hundreds of rules, and from endless detached viewing of the replay. Jesus calls us and asks us to make a commitment: dance, mourn, laugh, weep, but whatever you do: get in the game. **Now!**

SACRED WOUNDS

July 31, 2011. Genesis 32:9-31;   Matthew 14:11-21

There is a program on National Public Radio called "Car Talk." It is hosted by two brothers who call themselves "Click and Clack, the Tappet Brothers." I don't know a lot about automobile engines, but I am pretty sure that I don't want to hear the tappets in the engine clicking and clacking. According to the program, these brothers share offices with a legal firm named "Dewey, Cheatum, and Howe." That name popped into my head this week when I began reading the Old Testament lesson for the day. If there ever was a saga about cheating, lying, and conniving, it is the story of Esau and Jacob. Let me set the stage for you (while you keep in mind that we are talking about our spiritual ancestors). Isaac and Rebekah had twins. The pregnancy was difficult, and Rebekah felt like the two babies were fighting with each other in her womb. She delivered Esau first, who is reported to have been all red and very hairy. An older translation of the Old Testament refers to Esau as "an hairy man." However, Jacob, who was the second born, had a smooth complexion. Esau grew up to be a hunter. He may have been the original red-neck. I waited for a traffic light last week behind an old pickup truck with a decal on the rear window that said, "Born to hunt, forced to work" and I just knew it was Esau's truck. Jacob, on the other hand, was a mama's boy, preferring to live in the tents and actually doing part of the cooking—which at that time would probably have been considered woman's work. We are told that Isaac liked Esau, but Rebekah preferred Jacob. One day, when Isaac felt that his own death was near, he asked Esau to go out and bring him some fresh game to eat and told Esau that when he came back Isaac would give him his blessing. Rebekah, ever the solicitous wife, overheard the conversation, conspired with Jacob to delude poor old Isaac who couldn't see well --he probably had cataracts—and steal Esau's blessing. This makes one wonder about the state of Rebekah and Isaac's marriage. They even covered Jacob with the skins of the animals they killed to feed Isaac and put Esau's clothes on Jacob, so Isaac would be fooled by the smell and the hairy feeling. The ruse worked. Jacob got Isaac's blessing. I probably shouldn't tell you in plain English in church how Esau felt when he came back and saw that he had been cheated. I cannot even imagine how Esau must have felt about his mother. Rebekah found herself fearful that Esau and Jacob would kill each other, so she went to Isaac, lied to her husband about her fears, and got permission for Jacob to leave home and find himself a wife. I even wonder if Rebekah feared that the conflict between the brothers could result in one or both of them turning on her. I suspect it was in her best interests to get her co-conspirator son out of town.

Jacob went off to seek a wife from the family of his mother's brother or, as we would put it, from among the daughters of his Uncle Laban, who would, of course, have been his cousins. Eventually, he struck an agreement with Laban to serve him for seven years for his daughter Rachel. When the time was up, they had a wedding and when Jacob woke up the next morning he was in bed with Leah, Rachel's older sister. He had been cheated. Personally, I wonder how much Jacob drank at the reception that allowed Laban to fool him. To make a very long and complicated story short, Jacob put in some more time and was finally able to marry Rachel, the woman that he loved all along. However, Laban accused Jacob of cheating him and tried to prevent Jacob from leaving. Laban kept changing the conditions of the deal, while Jacob manipulated the breeding of the animals to make his flock larger than his father-in-law's. They had a nasty confrontation which we would say ended in a draw. They erected a stone monument to mark the boundary between their two territories and created a phrase that, in one of history's ironies, has become a benediction: "May the Lord watch between you and me while we are absent one from the other." We may use it as a benediction, but I suspect it was originally a reference to God insuring that the two men stayed out of each other's way—it was an appeal for God to maintain the boundary.

That nearly brings us up to date. Jacob is on his way home with wives, children, servants, and livestock. He gets word that Esau is coming. So, Jacob devises a strategy: he sends his flocks, his children and his wives ahead of him so that they would provide the advance guard between himself and Esau--whom he still feared. So here we have Jacob, the spiritual giant--revealed as a lily-livered, chicken-hearted wuss who is willing to let women and children take the heat and protect him from his brother. Jacob spends the night alone. He ends up wrestling all night with a figure he can't identify. When dawn is breaking, the unknown assailant wants to leave, but Jacob demands a blessing first. So, he gets a blessing and is told he will now be named Israel. But in the process, Jacob's hip gets dislocated and, he comes away from the encounter limping.

It is believed that Jacob wrestled with God. It appears to me that Jacob had what subsequent spiritual leaders would call a dark night of the soul. Years of cheating, lying and conniving had caught up with him. He was in fear of his life and dreaded the day to come. He struggles all night with a strange figure and neither seems able to prevail over the other. I believe this story describes Jacob finally admitting that it is time for a moral inventory, for trying to figure things out, trying to understand who he is and what is important. He comes away limping, wounded by the encounter with the divine and marked forever. The story probably seeks to explain why Jacob, now known as Israel, had a limp, but it also tells us that this sort of struggle, this in-depth encounter with the forces within, has a lasting effect. An immediate result of the struggle was that Jacob put himself ahead of all the others and went to greet Esau the next day without the benefit of the buffer which he had used his family to create earlier.

The encounter changes Jacob's identity. It would take him some time to "grow into" this new understanding of who he was, but this single night marked him forever. Jacob's new name, "Israel," means "he who strives" and the Hebrew text tells us that he has striven with divine and human beings and prevailed. I think Jacob struggles with the warring forces within himself. Prevailing in the struggle suggests that he achieves a new level of moral integration and he leaves this situation forever changed—a change symbolized by the limp. His descendants would honor this change by refusing to eat meat from the hip socket and thus remember always the enormous significance of this night.

Our gospel lesson for this morning recounts two critical episodes from Jesus' ministry. As Matthew tells the stories, Jesus has been traveling and teaching and healing. But now he comes to his home town, where he was invited to teach in the synagogue. And how do the home town people respond? They look at each other and say, "Where does he get all this stuff?" When Luke tells this story, he also adds that the people of Nazareth wanted to kill Jesus. Matthew pairs this story with the account of John the Baptist being beheaded by Herod to please a whim of his wife. Jesus reaction to all this, according to Matthew, was to withdraw and go to a deserted place to be alone. Jesus came face to face here with the implications of his teaching and healing. He faces rejection and death. Perhaps his retreat to a deserted place is a reference to his facing the so-called dark night of the soul. Of course, it wasn't long before people found him and came seeking his healing touch. He is called out of his solitude and reflections by the needs of the people.

Jacob had a spiritual encounter which left a physical mark on him. Jesus had a spiritual encounter that certainly made him stop and think and may in fact have left a psychological mark on him from this day forward, for now he knew how costly this journey would eventually be. Both of these men learned that spiritual experiences are not necessarily sweet, inspiring, mountain top times of singing and rejoicing. These spiritual encounters are rough, frightening, demanding and overwhelming. Neither man can easily escape them. Both of them are driven into these experiences by the events around them. Apparently neither of them was looking for or seeking such things. I know that our translations tell us that Jesus "withdrew." However, the Greek text tells he "departed or went away from there." There is no hint that Jesus needed to go meditate. He just needed to get out of town, get away from a very scary situation. Yet the Spirit, in the form of hurting people, pursued him and forced him to resume what we now call his ministry.

I see both of these men as being wounded by their encounters with God. Jacob's wound is obvious: he limps. Jesus' wound is perhaps more subtle, but he is now committed to pursuing a course of action that he knows will get him killed. History has made it easy for us to see Jesus as wearing a halo and being a man above all the stresses and distresses of ordinary life, but we can't see Jacob that way. The story of Jacob and his family could be made into a sit-com titled "Dysfunctional R We." He never made sainthood. We talk about St. Peter and St. Paul, and a seemingly endless number of other pious folk some Christians call saints, but there is no Saint Jacob. Of all the characters in the Bible, Jacob is probably most like us. He goes along with nefarious schemes, he cheats, he lies, he deceives his own father; his relationship with his mother is, to say the least, strange—it smacks of what we call the Oedipus complex. Jacob complains about the way he is treated--and he may even have been drunk on his wedding night (how else do we explain his not realizing he is sleeping with Leah and not Rachel?). Jacob tries to placate his father-in-law and his brother and clearly doesn't trust either Laban or Esau (even when Esau wants to reconcile and get the family back together). Jacob spends a lot of time being scared and does his share of complaining. He doesn't get along well with a lot of people—his father, his brother, his father-in-law and sometimes his wives. He responds to being manipulated by manipulating right back. He and Laban got into a situation of escalating manipulation, sort of a down and dirty game of "can you top this?"

Both Jacob's and Jesus' stories teach us that spiritual experiences are often inflicted upon us in the midst of difficult and even horrific situations. They show us that spiritual encounters will disrupt our own plans and sometimes our needs to make ourselves feel safe. These stories also tell us that spiritually significant events may be forced upon us; they may even imply that the most powerful spiritual events are those that come upon us from outside the familiar borders of our lives.

It is almost second nature for us to complain. When things don't go well, when the wind changes direction, when rains come, or drought prevails, we complain--and of course we complain about politicians and the government (especially this week [during the Presidential campaign] why even John McCain is complaining about tea party folk) and there is always constant complaining about the weather. Perhaps our list of people we struggle with doesn't match Jacob's, but we have our own collection of folk with whom we don't do well. Jacob discovered that one deception led to another and that there were plenty of people around to aid and abet his tendencies. Jacob is a lot closer to everyman (or everywoman) than we think Jesus is. And yet God chooses to invade each man's life and insist that these folks commit themselves to serving in ways that they may not have contemplated. God demands that they "re-vision" their lives and change their priorities.

God fashioned a great people and founded two great spiritual heritages by using Jacob as a way of entering into human life; God founded a ministry of compassion, healing and caring by using Jesus to proclaim the good news that God loves everyone. I suspect that both men would have been incredulous if somehow, they could have been shown what they started would become.

I think we would do well to ask ourselves a very serious question, especially in the midst of difficulties or unwelcome circumstances. The question is: Where is God in this? What is God saying to us? In life's tough times, we tend to get rather selfish and focus on that well-known trio: me, myself, and I. However, God may be asking us to focus on something else. If Jacob didn't find out anything else from the experience we read about this morning, he found out that all his fears about his brother and all his scheming about how to save his own hide were a completely unnecessary waste of his energy. I wonder how many times we have repeated that particular lesson. I think that many times I would have been better served if instead of spending so much energy and time focusing on me, I had used those resources to discover how God was in the situation and perhaps to learn what opportunities were hidden in the circumstances I feared.

There is a rather humorous blessing which goes something like this: "Please, O God, bless this mess." Life is often messy. Jacob and Jesus discovered that. God doesn't always see things the way we see them. Jacob and

Jesus discovered that. God's priorities are not always our priorities. Jacob and Jesus discovered that. Jacob and Jesus invite us to discover that God is in the mess we call our daily lives and that God is challenging us to see things differently, to change our priorities, and to get on with the business of making humankind our business. In the midst of the mess, people are hungry, hurting, scared, and anxious. Spiritual contemplation doesn't just occur in deserted places or alone in the middle of the night (although it certainly can happen there). It also happens in the midst of the mess. We find ourselves often hurting from the things that seem to happen to us. Perhaps if we would focus a bit differently, we would discover, like Jacob, that our hurts are sacred wounds, wounds which God will use to claim our attention and to demand our service and even send us in new directions. Those sacred wounds might leave us limping like Jacob, but if so, then we, like Jacob, will be able to make sense of the wounds. Out of the pain and anxiety Jesus felt, came works of healing and compassion and a host of people were fed and served. Do we have the courage to identify our spiritual wounds? What will we bring to the world out of our own sacred wounds?

BROKEN

July 29, 2012. Psalm 22:1-11; Psalm 23; Romans 8:18-29; 31-39

Let me tell you a story; in fact, let me tell you two stories. The first comes from an incident reported about 200 years ago. Some of you may have heard me tell this story or perhaps read it for yourselves in the UCC Stillspeaking Daily Devotional where it appeared on May 12 this year. The second story comes from about 38 years ago; I am sure this story will be new to you.

Two hundred years ago Lyman Beecher was the pastor of the Congregational Church in Litchfield, Connecticut. During his pastorate, a debate arose in the congregation about whether they would install a wood stove in the meeting house. Before then they had never had any heat at all in the meeting house. If it was cold, people would come to worship thickly bundled. Some folks thought a wood stove would be an improvement; others were dead set against this new technology intruding into their sacred space. The pro-stove contingent prevailed, but apparently by a narrow margin. The first Sunday after the stove was installed some of those who had opposed the installation of the stove complained that the meeting house was too hot for them. The men started taking off their jackets and loosening their collars. Some of the women were furiously fanning themselves, trying to stay cool. Lyman Beecher got into the pulpit and said, "You will notice that this is the first Sunday we have had our new stove. And next week we will put some wood in it and start a fire." We will come back to this story shortly.

The second story is the story of two women. The story is true, but I have changed their names to preserve their privacy. We will call one Sandra and the other Susie. Sandra was 55 years old at the time and Susie was 49. The two women lived in the same neighborhood—it was a short walk from one house to the other. I suppose we could say they came from very similar socio-economic backgrounds. They were both married and had children—and they went to the same church, where I happened to be the pastor. They also shared another attribute: both had been diagnosed with cancer about the same time. Sandra took to her bed and eventually to a hospital bed. She withdrew from the world, didn't have much to say to anyone and sort of grunted at me when I visited her in the hospital—and then she would roll over and turn her back to me, even though the cancer did not involve her brain or voice. Susie had a mission: she had a son who was planning to be married soon and Susie was determined to be at that wedding. When I visited Susie in the hospital, she was usually holding court from her bed with many visitors. Part of Susie's self-imposed physical therapy to recover from her mastectomy was to brush her hair vigorously to exercise the muscles in her arm, chest, and shoulder. As soon as I walked into the room, the hair brush came out, so she could show me how well she could brush her hair. Susie most always had a smile on her face. She walked down the aisle at her son's wedding and was the perfect "mother of the groom" at the church and the reception.

Susie died 4 and a half weeks after the wedding; Sandra's death preceded Susie's by 10 days. I had the good fortune to be with Susie when she died: she never complained, kept trying to smile and kept eye contact with me for as long as possible. Sandra died in silence with her back turned.

These two stories, which seem to be very different, have a common thread: sometimes it is called the placebo effect and sometimes (as with Sandra) the nocebo effect. However, we are learning that these effects are more than just an attitude. Recent research has taught us that acting on what we believe can produce "subliminal conditioning" which can actually control bodily processes—including immune responses, even when we're not consciously choosing to act on the beliefs that created the conditioning. Some of the biology of the placebo response has been demonstrated to involve active processes in the brain. Those folks in Connecticut who were working up a sweat sitting by a stone-cold wood stove were probably being manipulated by their own subliminal conditioning which told them that they were overdressed for a heated room. To take this a step or two further, today's brain imagery techniques do lend support to the theory that thoughts and beliefs not only affect one's psychological state, but also cause the body to undergo actual biological changes.

Susie's attitude toward her disease undoubtedly helped to release natural pain killing opiates within her own body; Sandra's attitude probably suppressed those natural opiates. One researcher on the subject of pain has stated "Pain is unavoidable, but suffering is optional." You may know stories similar to those of Sandra and Susie. You might even know about something like the wood-stove incident. What we can learn and need to learn from these stories is that what we choose to believe is significant. Our belief systems are much more important than just being decorative fluff on the surface of life. However, I am not just talking about what we say we believe, I am talking about the beliefs that we live by.

The story of Sandra and Susie can also remind us of something else and that is the power of community. It has been said by researchers in the positive psychology community that what we all fear is being alone. Being alone does strange things to people. Probably one of the reasons our brains are so much larger than any other creatures is because our brains are built for living in community and for being in touch with about 150 other people. If I am left to my own devices, I can easily convince myself that I am right about everything, that the world is exactly the way I think it is, and that I can safely eat all the ice cream I want. However, when I expose these theories to other people, I get feedback and usually that feedback says, "Well, Carl, some of your ideas are fine, but several are weird, and a few are just plain dumb." Sandra's decision to withdraw increased her suffering; Susie's decision to engage with others throughout her illness decreased her suffering.

David Brooks, the NY Times columnist, commenting on the horror in Aurora, Colorado last weekend [mass shooting killing 12 and injuring 70 in a movie theater] noted a couple of things about people who go on killing sprees: he points out that most of them have an exaggerated sense of their own significance which they feel the world doesn't properly recognize and that most of them live very solitary lives. He goes on to say, "The best way to prevent killing sprees is with relationships—when one person notices that a relative or neighbor is going off the rails and gets that person to treatment before the barbarism takes control." The isolation of these dangerous people feeds their unrealistic self-perspectives. We are created to be in community and when we disregard this aspect of our nature, things don't go well--whether we're talking about a Sandra who suffers excessively and dies miserably or about a maniacal killer who destroys the community he needs.

We heard two Psalms this morning. We listened to part of Psalm 22, and to that very familiar and comforting Psalm 23. We hear two different beliefs here. One of those says, "I am a worm and not human; scorned by others and despised by the people." It is very tempting to notice that this individual feels less than human and abandoned by God because he is out of the community. The other perspective, which says that God is with me always, ends by saying, "I shall dwell in the house of the Lord my whole life long." In other words, this writer feels he is in the community and will continue to be in the community. Out of community or in community; without God or with God; Dead or Alive.

When I look at this component of these readings and when I think about Sandra and Susie, I begin to understand what hope is. In our reading from Paul's letter to the Romans this morning, we hear Paul telling us that hope is something that can be experienced but not seen. Hope is not about believing that we'll get an increase in income next year; hope is not about believing I'll have a bigger house or better health or a longer vacation. Hope is about knowing that we are not alone. It is about knowing that we are part of the kind of community where the Spirit of God is dwelling.

The stove Incident, which makes us smile, can remind us to pay attention to what sort of mental habits we are developing. The beliefs that we practice and by which we live will impact our brains at a non-conscious level and will lead us to react to unexpected events in ways that are sometimes curious and even inappropriate. Holding negative beliefs that set us apart from community, which make us think we are subhuman worms, will at least result in increased personal suffering and perhaps social disasters. Affirming positive beliefs that uphold hope and bind us to community will help us to use more of our own resources to decrease suffering—our own suffering and the suffering of others. Sandra and Susie can remind us that pain is unavoidable, but that suffering is indeed optional. The beliefs to which we commit ourselves will alter our physiology and shape our responses to the circumstances of life.

I titled this sermon "Broken." I invite you to think about ways of being broken that lead to two different results: being broken down and being broken open. If I tell you that my car is broken down, then you'll assume it won't run and is at least temporarily useless. If I allow the pain I experience to break me down, then I will follow Sandra's example and become essentially non-functional, wallowing in my own hurt and misery. But if I allow the pain I experience to break me open, then like Susie, I am likely to find many resources within myself that I didn't even know God had given me. We can apply that same perspective to our society. If we allow ourselves to suppose that events like the catastrophe in Aurora demonstrate that our society is broken down, then we will give up, just like Sandra did.

We will be tempted to pull away from social engagement, skip voting in elections, let somebody else call the shots and turn our backs on each other. But if we realize that this catastrophe can break us open, break apart barriers to community, break destructive habits that isolate us one from another, then we can respond to disaster with a commitment to engage, to build neighborhoods, foster community and celebrate our common life. If I allow pain to break open my defenses—the same defenses that would keep me isolated-- if I allow pain to remind me that, as John Donne put it, no one is an island, then pain, instead of being my enemy will become an instrument of my growth and draw me into the community where I need to be.

You and I have experienced pain and we will continue to experience pain. It is, as the saying goes, the human condition. The ability to feel pain is also critical for our survival: it prevents me from doing any number of foolish and dangerous things. In a rather perverse way, I suppose I should be glad I can feel pain. But since I have this ability, and need to keep it, I also need to develop and apply beliefs that will help me avoid turning my aches and pains into suffering. Pain is a physical reaction; suffering is a conscious decision—Susie and Sandra showed us that.

This morning I am going to let Paul have the last word, for these words give us a hope to live by that will sustain us: "What then are we to say about these things? If God is for us, who is against us? He who did not withhold his own Son, but gave him up for all of us, will God not with him also give us everything else? Who will bring any charge against God's elect? It is God who justifies. Who is to condemn? It is Christ Jesus, who died, yes, who was raised, who is at the right hand of God, who indeed intercedes for us.

"Who will separate us from the love of Christ? Will hardship, or distress, or persecution, or famine, or nakedness, or peril, or sword? No, in all these things we are more than conquerors through God who loved us. For I am convinced that neither death, nor life, nor angels, nor rulers, nor things present, nor things to come, nor powers, nor height, nor depth, nor anything else in all creation, will be able to separate us from the love of God in Christ Jesus our Lord."

THE CHILD INSIDE
December 30, 2012. Isaiah 9:2, 6-7; John 1:2-14

I have an interesting little book titled "Oral Sadism and the Vegetarian Personality." On the front cover is a warning: "Reading these selections from the Journal of Polymorphous Perversity may cause uncontrollable laughter and a rapid elevation in mood." The very first article in the book is one which presents childhood as a syndrome. It suggests that there are five diagnostic markers of the syndrome. People who suffer from childhood will show (1) congenital onset; (2) dwarfism; (3) emotional lability and immaturity; (4) knowledge deficits; and (5) legume anorexia—which means they won't eat their vegetables. However, hidden in the humor of this satirical article is a rather interesting statement: in describing the prevalence of the syndrome, the author suggests that ". . . it has been estimated that over half of all Americans alive have experienced childhood directly." He goes on to suggest that the actual numbers of people who have experienced childhood are probably higher because self-reports are subject to "retrospective distortion."

Our ability to feel empathy for others is based in part on our own experiences. If we have had a broken leg or appendicitis or been unemployed, we find it easier to identify emotionally with others who are suffering those things. We find it more difficult to identify with folks who struggle with issues we have never faced. The humorous article about childhood suggests that many adults have allowed themselves to forget what being a child is like. I imagine that reality was changed on December 14 [The date of the Sandy Hook school shootings which killed 27 people]. Yes, we are horrified when children are victims. Yes, we are troubled when children are mistreated. Yes, we  are disturbed when we hear about child abuse. But the tragedy at Sandy Hook school also touches the child within us all—the part of ourselves we often neglect, discount, or ignore. The assaults on children that have become part of our national community's life are deeply felt by the child inside us all. Jesus told us that if we are going to enter the kingdom of God, we must receive that kingdom like a little child. On the cover of the bulletin this morning is a picture of a sculpture by Giuseppe Penoné. He has carefully removed the rings of growth from a fir tree to reveal its former young shape. What shows up as those beautiful knots in a pine board are actually the branches of the sapling inside. He says: "My artwork shows, with the language of sculpture, the essence of matter and tries to reveal with the work, the hidden life within." It has been suggested that instead of imposing a form on the material, he draws out an existing form. My first encounter with this picture suggested to me that it showed us the child inside of us all. He called this particular work "The Hidden Life Within."

Our gospel reading this morning is probably very familiar to many of you. However, I would like to invite you to look at it with fresh eyes, just as Penoné invites us to look at a tree differently. The Greek manuscripts of the New Testament, in their oldest forms, did not have punctuation marks or even spaces between letters. This practice arose in order to get the most out of the expensive parchment. This means that sometimes it is difficult to determine the exact meaning or structure of a sentence. Verse 9 can be translated as a question: "Was the true light that enlightens everyone coming into the world?" If we read it that way, then verse 10 becomes an answer to this rhetorical question: "The light was in the world and made the world and the world did not know the light." The gospel writer then goes on to tell us that when people accepted the Light that was coming into the world, they were given power to become the children of God. The work of the sculptor that reveals the sapling hidden in the tree is very much like the work of the Word of God which reveals the child of God hidden within every adult. I believe that Jesus' comments about children are not just about young people—I think they are about the child in all of us, the child of God hidden beneath layers and layers of denial, self-criticism and personal rejection; behind all manner of defenses, phony facades, and foolish pretenses. The light that Jesus manifests by coming into the world invites us to realize that we have the Light within us and always have.

We are reminded, as the song Hallelujah says, that there was a time when connections between God and our inner created nature were close, natural, and joyful—a time when we moved in God and with God in the Holy Dark— and every breath was Hallelujah. The song writer asks us to understand that this close relationship was broken by our attempts to use power to manipulate people and control relationships—which both Samson and David did. As these men struggle with their brokenness and wrestle with their temptations to abuse their power, the Spirit wrings out of their mouths the broken Hallelujah. It is not the pristine Hallelujah of naïve childhood; it is not the unsullied Hallelujah of innocent children, but it is the Hallelujah. It is a necessary Hallelujah driven by the desperate need to get back in touch with our Creator, to re-establish a relationship we have often deliberately sabotaged, and to reconnect with our inner child. The idea of a broken Hallelujah might remind us that we adults have to bring our praise for God out of the muck of our indifference, our selfishness, and our mistaken decisions. The song also says that this is a cold Hallelujah. When I think about applying the idea of "cold" to this, I find myself also noting that instead of being an overwhelming, joyful song that it is more likely a badly needed song that we are making an effort to sing even when we don't feel the joy that Hallelujah implies. We sing a cold Hallelujah in the wake of Sandy Hook (and a lot of other places) because we are in desperate need of hope, so we sing it whether we can feel it or not. One commentator has noted that: "Hallelujah is a meditation on the conflict between the human desire for physical union and that of spiritual transcendence, with the final realization of the inability to fully achieve either." The Hallelujah we sing is a broken Hallelujah because it comes out of our pain. If you look at the sapling revealed by Penoné in his sculpture, you will see how fine and delicate some of those branches are and realize how easy it would be to break one of those. Pain can easily be bestowed on these tender, inner parts of us. You will also notice that some of the delicate branches don't reach all the way out to the exterior of the adult tree and that reminds me of dreams unfulfilled, of tasks attempted but never completed, of abilities never developed and used, and of gifts unbestowed. These small parts remind us of times of brokenness experienced earlier in our lives—and how the hurt often lives on inside. The mean words, the bully's threats, the brutal put-downs of the early years walk with us every day. Some of the pain and brokenness has been with us for a long time; some parts of the child within seem really distant.

The song also admits doubt—it says, "Maybe there's a God above" and then it goes on to tell us that God is not manifest in a cry you hear at night nor in someone who has seen the light—God is manifest in the cold and broken Hallelujah. The appearance of God is not about miracles, disruptions in history or world-shaking events: God appears in us and in others. The Christ we see, as the Russian writer Tolstoy tells us, we see in each other's faces. In our mutual brokenness, love shines through and we see the child hiding in the people around us. The broken Hallelujah ". . . suggests that even through loneliness and thwarted desire" we are "still able to create and to give praise for the gift of creation."

[The sermon was interrupted while the people sang together]

I've heard there was a secret chord
That David played, and it pleased the Lord
But you don't really care for music, do you?
It goes like this
The fourth, the fifth
The minor fall, the major lift
The baffled king composing Hallelujah
Hallelujah, Hallelujah

Hallelujah, Hallelujah

Your faith was strong but you needed proof
You saw her bathing on the roof
Her beauty
in the moonlight
overthrew you
She tied you
To a kitchen chair
She broke your throne,
she cut your hair
And from your lips she drew the Hallelujah
Hallelujah, Hallelujah
Hallelujah, Hallelujah

Maybe I've been here before
I know this room, I've walked this floor
I used to live alone before I knew you
I've seen your flag on the marble arch
love is not a victory march
It's a cold and it's a broken Hallelujah
Hallelujah, Hallelujah
Hallelujah, Hallelujah

There was a time you'd let me know
What's real and going on below
But now you never show it to me do you?
Remember when I moved in you?
The holy dark was moving too
And every breath we drew was Hallelujah
Hallelujah, Hallelujah

Hallelujah, Hallelujah

Maybe there's a God above
And all I ever learned from love
Was how to shoot at someone who outdrew you
It's not a cry you can hear at night
It's not somebody who's seen the light
It's a cold and it's a broken Hallelujah
Hallelujah, Hallelujah
Hallelujah, Hallelujah
Hallelujah, Hallelujah
Hallelujah, Hallelujah*

The New York Times columnist, Maureen Dowd, had a long quotation in her Christmas Day column. She quotes the Rev. Kevin O'Neil, a Roman Catholic priest (who sounds markedly like a UCC minister). "For whatever reason, certainly foreign to most of us, God has chosen to enter the world today through others, through us. We have stories of miraculous interventions, lightning-bolt moments, but far more often the God of unconditional love comes to us in human form, just as God did over 2,000 years ago. We are human and mortal. We will suffer and die. But how we are with one another in that suffering and dying makes all the difference as to whether God's presence is felt or not and whether we are comforted or not. One true thing is this: Faith is lived in family and community, and God is experienced in family and community. We need one another to be God's presence."

*Artist: Rufus Wainwright Lyrics Song: Hallelujah Copyright © 1985 Leonard Cohen and Sony/ATV Music Publishing Canada Company.

If we are going to be with one another in sickness and in health, in joy and in sorrow, in plenty and in want, then we must

understand who we are and what gifts we have. In order to know who we are, we must get acquainted with the child inside. Many of us have surrendered the child's innocence and naiveté for the so-called sophisticated cynicism of conventional adulthood. Most of us have given up on wonder and awe and instead prefer to see the world through a plethora of analysis and theories. We prefer boring certainty to promising dreams; we prefer solid facts to colorful imagination. But lurking inside of us, just like the sapling in Penoné's sculpture, is the child who delights in imagination, who believes in everyone, who knows dreams can be real, who is certain that we can do anything to which we set our minds. In order to be present to others, in order to be a vehicle of the manifestation of God in the world, we need to engage and display that child inside. And of course, this child likes to touch, to hug, to engage body, mind and spirit with others. We will need to dare to be different, to dare to touch, to hug and to invent new ways to engage with each other. I am much more likely to engage with someone who offers "to be with me" instead of someone who offers "to do something for me or to me." Most of us, when we are hurting, anxious, scared, depressed, confused, and frustrated simply need someone to keep us company, to be with us so that our negative emotions will not separate us from the community and leave us alone in our turmoil. It certainly is more comforting and reassuring to connect our inner child with the inner child of another person, than it is for two adults to sit together spouting theories and platitudes. It is the child inside that can tell stories and it is the child inside that wants to hear stories--stories that can be used to make sense of things, stories that remind us of promises, dreams, possibilities and gifts. In the process of mutual story-telling, the inner children come out to play together and joy comes alive, Hallelujah, broken or not, gets sung, and wonderful things happen. The Hallelujah song reminds us that "love is not a victory march." Love isn't about doing stuff, it's about being real, being present with each other and sharing the moment, the now, which is the only time we actually have. The poet, Dawna Markova, has a poem that the child within can hear, say and live. She writes:

I will not die an unlived life.
I will not live in fear
of falling or catching fire.
I choose to inhabit my days,
to allow my living to open me,
to make me less afraid,
more accessible,
to loosen my heart
until it becomes a wing,
a torch, a promise.
I choose to risk my significance;
to live so that which came to me as seed
goes to the next as blossom
and that which came to me as blossom,
goes on as fruit.
Fully alive.

Father O'Neil goes on to say at the end of Dowd's column: "A contemporary theologian has described mercy as 'entering into the chaos of another.' Christmas is really a celebration of the mercy of God who entered the chaos of our world in the person of Jesus, mercy incarnate. I have never found it easy to be with people who suffer, to enter into the chaos of others. Yet, every time I have done so, it has been a gift to me, better than the wrapped and ribboned packages. I am pulled out of myself to be love's presence to someone else, even as they are love's presence to me.

"I will never satisfactorily answer the question 'Why?' because no matter what response I give, it will always fall short. What I do know is that an unconditionally loving presence soothes broken hearts, binds up wounds, and renews us in life. This is a gift that we can all give, particularly to the suffering. When this gift is given, God's love is present, and Christmas happens daily."

I would suggest that when we are "pulled out" of ourselves, the child within is manifest. The sculptor had to remove the outer part of the adult tree and much of the accumulated stuff inside to free the inner sapling. Freeing the inner child means dropping the elaborate defenses, fancy justifications and clever distortions that are so much a part of daily adult life. These are the things that hide the light of the child inside and muffle the joy of that child's voice.

People often admire the pure, innocent voices of children; we love to hear choirs of children sing. It's time that we let the inner child sing the broken Hallelujah. It's time that we celebrate like children the power of love and rejoice together that indeed love is not a victory march:

instead it is a pilgrimage that reaches out to others and moves us closer together to become the community in which the Christ of Christmas is made manifest. Let us be determined that the people who walk in darkness will see the light of our inner child and be drawn closer together and closer to God; closer to peace and justice; closer to harmonious living and constant forgiveness.

ARE YOU VIBRATING YET?
August 17, 2014. Matthew 15:10-28; John 7:1-13

I wonder if the local newspaper would publish a column titled "Jesus Lies." I wonder how folks might react to being told that Jesus discriminated against foreigners. There is a considerable theological history about the Christ being unchanging from generation to generation, so what might people make of the notion that Jesus is reported to have changed his mind? You might have noticed that we have such things being reported in our Scripture lessons for this morning. At the end of the gospel according to John, the writer tells us that "there are also many other things that Jesus did; if every one of them were written down, I suppose that the world itself could not contain the books that would be written." In other words, John is telling us that his gospel contains a selection of Jesus' teachings and actions. In the ancient world, scrolls were a rather pricey commodity. They could be obtained in a more or less standard length. The gospels that we have can each be written on one scroll, thus economizing and making the sharing of those scrolls easy. On top of that, early writers did not put spaces between words or use punctuation because such things wasted precious space. When we consider these realities, the selection of materials that writers chose to incorporate in their narratives becomes even more critical. In the light of these realities, why in the world would we find reports of Jesus discriminating against people or of him lying to his brothers? I'll come back to this in a bit.

My intention this morning is to challenge you to think about things from a theological perspective. In order to do that, it might help if I would clarify some terminology. We might start with the word "belief." This word implies certainty about things. When we tell someone that we believe them, we are endorsing their statements. When we say that we believe in God, we are expressing certainty about the reality of God. The word "faith" usually emphasizes people's willingness to trust in the validity of certain concepts (like love or truthfulness or commitment). I find that there is often a lot of confusion about how these words get used. In the hands of many Christians, belief gets equated with certainty. Hence, we have folk investing 27 million dollars in the construction of a creation museum which is designed to demonstrate certain beliefs some people hold with great certainty, leading them to conclude that obviously dinosaurs and humans inhabited this plant simultaneously, even though contemporary science says otherwise. These people are certain that the world is about 8,000 years old. Over 250,000 people visit this monument to certitude every year. There is indeed still an active organization called the Flat Earth Society which believes against all challenges that the earth is a flat disc.

Our desire for certainty in a world that keeps changing at a faster and faster pace can entice us to believe in certainty. Many of us don't like the idea that Jesus might change his mind or that ancient views of cosmology might be wrong. But the quest for certainty can lead to illusions which can easily become delusions or even hallucinations. The Flat Earth Society seems to me to have pushed their beliefs beyond delusions about reality into hallucinations—

in which people see things no one else sees. Less you think I am being silly, I want you to know that the Flat Earth Society is still active and has a new logo promoted last year [2013] which shows the earth as a disc resembling the picture on the UN flag. They believe the North Pole is the center of the world and that the edges are surrounded by a 150-foot-tall wall of ice. They also are telling us that the sun and the moon are each 32 miles in diameter!

We can also see a conflict of belief in the turmoil in Ferguson, Missouri [On August 9, 2014, an 18-year-old African-American man, Michael Brown, was fatally shot by Darren Wilson, a white policeman with the Ferguson Police Department] where both sides in this horrible confrontation are declaring conflicting beliefs and supporting those beliefs with other beliefs that may, in some cases, be totally extraneous to the issues at hand. We may find the beliefs asserted by the Flat Earth people to be amusing, but no one is amused by the powder keg of racial tension in Ferguson.

Faith, on the other hand, as famously defined in the Biblical letter to the Hebrews, is said to be ". . . the assurance of things hoped for, the conviction of things not seen." Faith describes an attitude, a perspective and is not driven, like belief, to demonstrate certainty. Faith is often content to be intuitive about the nature of things without having to create artificial or elaborate truths.

A recent issue of Time magazine (July 24, 2014) featured an article about atheists who have apparently created an atheist church. I find it an interesting commentary on our times that we have the rise of an atheist church in the same century and in the same country as the construction of the Creation Museum. I suspect that the perspectives that drive each of these organizations derive from an effort to resolve doubts that have been raised about many traditional beliefs. One group accepts the questions raised by doubt as issues of certainty while the other group seems to ascribe to the advice once given to a preacher about his sermon—when your point is weak, shout!

Faith engages in a dialog with doubt. It doesn't attack people who raise questions because it understands that the development of a spiritual perspective on life requires a dialog between faith and doubt. Faith understands, as did the German philosopher Hegel, that a developing spiritual perspective is nurtured by a process that incorporates the contradictions often encountered between faith and doubt. If the opposing forces in Ferguson would each step back a bit and admit that there are some doubts about what happened there and some doubts about the hardened positions about race, then dialog could happen. Owning doubt might lead to an integration of concerns and lead to a more constructive approach to the underlying issues. Doubt could even facilitate honest and open grieving about the tragedy.

Back for a moment to the story of Jesus who called the Canaanite woman "a dog." This is a very important, critical story not only because of its outcome but because Jesus engaged in a discussion with a woman, which religious teachers of his time were not supposed to do. She comes to him having heard of his ability to heal people, seeking help for her daughter. At first Jesus ignores her, but his disciples who are getting sick of her persistent demands convince him to talk to her. He then tells her it is not fitting to throw the children's food to the dogs. The woman is very clever. She doesn't argue about being called a dog but says even dogs are entitled to the table scraps. Jesus is astounded at her faith and immediately grants her request. She raised doubts about the faith Jesus was professing and that led to an expansion of his faith as he was able to see that his ministry wasn't just for people in Israel but was indeed for all who were willing to profess faith in his message. Clearly this story shows us one example of Jesus changing his mind in a way that shows us that his own faith and sense of ministry was a growing and changing spiritual perspective.

We see a similar illustration in the story we heard John tell us this morning. Jesus' brothers are taunting him and pushing him to go to Judea for a religious feast which comes in the fall of the year. Jesus is avoiding this trip for fear that he will be killed. His brothers, who apparently have their own doubts about their older brother, seem to be provoking a challenge which would either establish Jesus' truth or make a folly of his pretentions. Lots of younger brothers would like to make trouble for the big brother. So, Jesus lies to them. He says he isn't going because the time isn't right. Then after they go off to the festival, he sneaks in behind them as an anonymous pilgrim and eventually preaches and stirs up a whole host of doubts amongst the folk who heard him. Or perhaps Jesus didn't lie at all. It seems more likely that Jesus changed his mind—again he changed his mind when he was compelled to deal with the doubts his brothers had about his ministry.

Here we have two clear instances of Jesus dealing with the doubts others raised, doubts which the positions of others raised in his own mind about how he understood his ministry.

Hegel, whom I mentioned a moment ago, is famous for his understanding that each thesis generates an antithesis. The contradiction between thesis and antithesis generates a new synthesis. Then of course the synthesis becomes a new thesis, and off we go again from thesis to antithesis to synthesis. Hegel's view of things has suffered because Karl Marx used his ideas to promote communism. However, Hegel is not about communism. Indeed, as he saw what is called the dialectical movement, it became a process which developed into ever more complex and sophisticated perspectives by incorporating the contradictions between both thesis and antithesis into ever more spiritual perspectives. He had faith that this process would lead to a comprehensive, evolving unity.

If we think about an alternation between opposites, images like pendulums and vibrations come to mind. The Latin root for the word "doubt" means to vibrate! The word vibrant, which of course comes from vibrate, means that something is throbbing with energy and life. It is a short step to understand that to be alive is to vibrate. If we are going to profess a vibrant spiritual life, we're going to be vibrating between faith and doubt.

Things that vibrate often produce sounds: music is a collection of vibrations. What vibrates might change—it might be a piano string or a violin string; a harp or the reed in a clarinet; it might be a human voice or the head of a drum or the column of air in an organ pipe, or some partially filled wine glasses. If this community of faith gets involved in sharing the doubts and faiths of many people, there will be vibrations. If my doubt encounters your faith and we allow ourselves to be articulate about it, our vibration will produce a new synthesis. If your doubt pushes against my faith, we may discover a way to vibrate together. In so doing, we will be incorporating into our community the same process Jesus used to nurture his own spiritual life. The confidence he thought he had was challenged by the Canaanite woman who raised doubts and the resultant vibration helped Jesus to revise his vision and her daughter to get the needed healing. The original very limited view Jesus had of the people to whom he was called to prophesy was forced to grow into a more encompassing perspective. The vessel of fear that kept Jesus from challenging Jerusalem got busted by the vibrations of doubt that his brothers expressed and consequently Jesus' own courage grew.

The vibrations of faith and doubt dancing together in this community, in any community, can produce sounds of challenge and joy, acceptance and growth, confidence and connection. We know that we will never be alone even though we are free to wonder, to question and to contribute to the music by expressing our doubts as well as our faith. Indeed, if we understand the critical place doubt plays in spiritual growth, we might well acknowledge that we have a duty to doubt just as we have the privilege of sharing our faith. Any musician can testify to the fact that the full power of music is made possible by the blending of sounds—even dissident sounds—into one harmonious whole. Come into this community to grow your faith and deepen your doubts so that together we may find a song that celebrates life, love, truth and joy and sends waves of nurturing vibrations all over this city and indeed all around this world.

Way-Walkers Dare to Be Foolish, Weird and Embrace Insecurity.

REVISIONS CREATE NEW VISIONS
June 26, 2011. Genesis 22:1-14; Psalm 13

I need to offer a warning. This sermon may be considered to be "R" rated as it contains scenes of violence, references to abhorrent practices, and images that may be distressful to some folk (actually I hope to all of you).

In 1843, the year before our Olivet College [in Olivet, MI] was founded; Soren Kierkegaard wrote a little book entitled *Fear and Trembling*. This book is an essay on the story we read from Genesis this morning about Abraham and Isaac. Kierkegaard, among other things, wanted to lift up the psychological, spiritual, and intellectual turmoil in which Abraham found himself immersed when he dealt with what he believed to be a call from God to sacrifice his son. One way that Kierkegaard highlights the anguish in which Abraham found himself is to suppose that this journey into the wilderness to make the sacrifice was made in silence. No one knew what to say while presumably everyone knew what was really going on.

This story probably is about 3,000 years old. It comes down to us from a time in history when apparently child-sacrifice was practiced. There are indications that a rather large number of primitive cultures all around the world practiced child-sacrifice. While there are some difficulties discovering actually what happened, there are also indications that near neighbors of the early Hebrews had an organized system of child-sacrifice. These people apparently had a large bronze figure with extended arms. A child would be placed in these arms and then the statute would be heated with a fire built at or in its base. The heat caused the statutes arms to extend and the child was then dropped into the fire and cremated. It was also reported that the priests beat drums during this ceremony to drown out the sound of the infants screaming thus preventing the child's parents from hearing the horrible anguish of their child. There are indicators in the prophet Micah, who was also active about nearly 3,000 years ago and also in Jeremiah who was writing about 2500 years ago, that the Hebrew people were aware of these horrifying customs of their neighbors. It is not clear whether or not the ancient Hebrews, before the time of Abraham had similar practices.

It is in this context that Abraham becomes convinced that God is demanding that he sacrifice his first born (and only) son. Before we look more closely at this story, I invite you to consider what some of the roots of this nearly universal practice of child-sacrifice might be. It appears that in most of the societies practicing such things there was a two-part belief: that God is a fierce power who threatens to destroy people because people are wicked, wrong, messed up, and inadequate by nature. The only way for these inherently flawed people to protect themselves from the vicious and somewhat capricious actions of this dangerous God is to make a sacrifice that proves to God that the people are submissive, obedient, compliant, and terribly sorry for their inadequacies. The sacrifice of one of their children seems to be supreme proof of the people's faithfulness. There are even stories from some cultures that families bought or adopted children from poor families and then sacrificed these poor souls as substitutes for their own birth children. This led in at least one case to families feeling forced to "repent" of these wicked ways and sacrifice their birth children when the sacrificing of substitute victims didn't seem to appease God and gain the people the right divine favors. If these people's perspective sounds a bit like the concept of original sin that would pervade centuries of Christian thought, you may be onto something. The doctrine of original sin may have eventually been separated from the practice of child-sacrifice, but the two actually seem to be related.

Back to Abraham: here he is struggling to be a faithful servant of God--who seems to demand child-sacrifice. So, in *Fear and Trembling* (as Kierkegaard put it), he sets out on a three-day journey to some sacred place fully believing that he is going to slaughter Isaac. We get a clue to how far back in history this happened when we note that Abraham not only took wood for the sacrifice but carried the fire. There probably weren't any very good tools for fire starting available yet. I think about the terror this man felt carrying a blazing torch for three days, doing whatever must have been involved to keep the fire going, knowing all the while that he was going to set his son's flesh ablaze with this fire. Abraham gets all the way to the site for the sacrifice and asks the two men who had accompanied them to wait behind while he and Isaac go forth to worship a God who wants a cremated child. Imagine Abraham and Isaac alone on the mountain, Abraham trying to calm Isaac's fears by reassuring Isaac that God will provide the appropriate sacrifice, Isaac tied on the funeral pyre. By now Isaac had probably figured this out. But then, at the last minute—literally—Abraham hears from God who says, in essence, don't do that. The sacrifice of a sheep is almost anticlimactic. I wonder if Isaac watched the animal being burned thinking, "That might have been me." Kierkegaard says this: "Abraham had to choose between the ethical requirements of his surroundings and what he regarded as his absolute duty to God." What Kierkegaard doesn't say is that Abraham, in the midst of his intense anxiety, discovered a different view of God. Abraham was willing to stand against the culture around him.

While Scripture doesn't tell us much more about this, I can imagine what might have happened after Abraham and Isaac came back from the mountain. First the two men who went with them would wonder what happened because even if it wasn't articulated, everybody knew what was supposed to happen. What happened after the guys got home? I'll bet that there was a lot of explaining to do and perhaps a lot of parents who secretly cheered Abraham on and rejoiced that now they would be able to avoid child-sacrifice. The radical revisioning of contemporary religious practice that Abraham accomplished gets lost in the shuffle of history—except that perhaps Micah and Jeremiah both harked back to this story when they opposed child-sacrifice later. Unfortunately, the substitution of animal sacrifice prevented the "revision" from eliminating the concept that people are worse than worms and have to do something to avoid the wrath of a perpetually angry God.

Abraham challenges us to follow his example and to engage in a process of revisioning that will create new visions. We are challenged to complete what Abraham started. Abraham started a process that has gradually over centuries reduced the idea that we have to appease this angry God with a variety of gruesome sacrifices. It took a while but finally by about 70 CE, 40 years or so after Jesus' crucifixion, animal sacrifices were gone. When the Romans destroyed the temple in Jerusalem, animal sacrifices ended. I believe that Pliny the younger, who was governor in Asia Minor in the early years of the church, complained to Rome that the rise of Christianity had reduced the demand for sacrificial animals and made the farmers in his country restless because they had lost a market for their cattle. The Church, of course, has tried to use the death of Jesus as the "final sacrifice" thus justifying the end of sacrifices. However, not much has been done about that abominable doctrine of original sin and its accompanying portrayal of God as a divine being who needs an anger management course.

There are some rather curious but important ramifications of believing in worthless people and a wrathful, vengeful God who is threatening destruction constantly. Most of us don't like to feel badly about ourselves even if the church's theology says we should. So, we engage in some behind the scenes, sometimes subconscious, maneuvers. We look for someone or a group of someones upon whom to project our bad feelings. We seem to think that if we can identify someone as worse than we are, we won't be so bad and maybe that irate old man in the sky will go after them instead. Thus, arises something called discrimination – a process whereby I get to project my fears that I am a worthless pile of biological waste onto someone else. It helps me to do that if I can focus on how different from myself the victims of my projections are. Sometimes that takes the form of focusing on the idea that my victim is younger or older than I am or has a different colored skin or curious hairdos or wears tattoos. Sometimes it takes the form of my deciding that another person's beliefs are not only different from mine but also at odds with the angry Author of Life. We don't seem to even notice the contradiction inherent in the idea that the author of life would be interested in destroying lives and approving of those who do that—especially in his name. People seem to do very well at projecting all their self-hatred upon the different and it doesn't seem to matter what the difference is but only that the difference exists.

There was a very interesting movie that came out in 1948 called "The Boy with Green Hair." It very thoroughly showed how people come to fear and hate someone who is different, especially when they can't figure out why that difference exists. It is not surprising that some of the people involved in making that movie fled the country and went to Europe to live and work after Senator McCarthy convened the infamous congressional Un-American Activities Committee hearings. The movie shows how a World War II orphan woke up one morning in his adoptive family's home with green hair. The difference tore up the community. Some blamed the milk man for delivering tainted milk. The boy was ostracized, beaten up, criticized, and mocked all because he had hair that was a lovely shade of green. Different has often meant deadly.

We have all kinds of theories as to why prejudice develops and gets sustained, but perhaps we have not adequately looked at the theological roots to be found in a theory that makes God into a vengeful, angry, dangerous figure and reduces human beings to worthless piles of waste.

The theologian Matthew Fox, whose theories cost him his standing in the Roman Catholic Church, wrote a book called *Original Blessing* in which he proposed that God created human beings in a state of blessedness not in a state of sin. If we can finally get rid of the irate God who hates people, then we can also restore the image of human beings to original blessedness. If we discover that loving ourselves puts us in synch with the God of love who created us, then what we will be interested in projecting is not fear and hate but love and hope.

Listen to the prophet Micah talking about this (and listen for the reference to chil-sacrifice): "With what shall I come before the Lord and bow myself before God on high? Shall I come before him with burnt offerings with calves a year old? Will the Lord be pleased with thousands of rams, with ten thousands of rivers of oil? Shall I give my firstborn for the sin of my soul? He has told you, O mortal, what is good; and what does the Lord require of you but to do justice, and to love kindness, and to walk humbly with your God?" Micah said this nearly 800 years before Jesus began teaching.

Psalm 13 shows a writer wondering about how the face of God is hidden. I wonder if the face of God is hidden behind primitive images that we have not had the courage to challenge—images of God as an angry man, images of God as resenting human beings, as demanding that people conform to curious and weird rules that seem to have nothing to do with life. The Psalmist ends his Psalm reiterating his trust in God's love and promising to sing to God because God has dealt bountifully with him.

Jesus pointed out that the face of God is the face of love and invites us to discard the primitive imagery that hides God's face. We are invited to challenge so-called authorities who bolster their self-importance by insisting that we believe in the same God those folks who killed their children did. If we are willing to love our children instead of slaughtering them, if we are willing to love ourselves instead of degrading the blessed image in which we were created, then let us be willing to be rid of a Creator who needs anger management and instead embrace the Author of all life as the Being worthy of our worship. We are made in love by the Source of Love: by re-visioning the old images we can create a new vision—a vision that will create hope, promise mercy, provide justice and become a vision to which people will be attracted.

Make no mistake about this challenge: the re-visioning called for here means that we will be advocating a different view of what the crucifixion of Jesus is all about. If we abandon the image of God as an angry, vengeful being who appreciates the slaughter of children, then we can also abandon the idea that Jesus is the first-born child of God who gets slaughtered on God's behalf for our benefit. We will find ourselves at odds with a lot of powerful church people—and you know it is dangerous to mess with church people. Attempting to re-vision this would get us in trouble with a lot of churches. Abraham and Micah and Jeremiah and Jesus are watching: are we willing to re-vision the image of God? The difference between the primitive idea and the new vision are as striking as the difference between using a five-pointed diagram to represent a star and seeing a star as the telescopic picture displayed on the bulletin today [from the Hubble telescope]. May we have the courage of Abraham and the vision of Jesus and see to it that love abounds in our theology and in our lives.

HERE COMES THE DREAMER
August 7, 2011. Genesis 37: 2-28; Matthew 14:22-33

Last Sunday, I talked about Jacob and his family and pointed out some of the dysfunction in this family and suggested these stories could form the basis for a sit-com series titled "Dysfunctional R We." Today we are going to take a look at another story from this family. Jacob had 12 children—but he had them by four different women. He had six children with Leah, the wife he got tricked into marrying and two by her maid; he had two children with Rachel, the woman whom he really loved, and two children with her maid. The two children he had with Rachel were Joseph and Benjamin. Rachel died in childbirth with Benjamin, so we can probably presume that one of the other women in the household became the mother-figure for Benjamin. Thus Joseph, Rachel's first child, was the only one actually mothered by Rachel and Joseph became Jacob's favorite. It has also been suggested that Benjamin wasn't born until after Joseph had been abducted, so at the time of our story today, Joseph would have been the youngest child. By the time he was a teenager his dad had given him a long-sleeved robe—known to history as the coat of many colors and to many of us (thanks to Andrew Lloyd Weber) as the Amazing Technicolor Dream Coat. One of the realities of such a garment was that one could do no manual labor or real hard work wearing it. It has also been suggested that the robe resembled those of royalty. Jacob's blatant favoritism toward Joseph, which apparently included excluding him from the hard work of the household, did not sit well with his brothers. Joseph didn't help his own cause much by sharing his dreams with the family. In one dream, he reports that all the brothers were in the field binding sheaves of grain and suddenly his brothers' sheaves bowed down to his sheaf. That dream probably aggravated the brothers at two levels: first, the youngest is sharing a vision of ruling over his older brothers and secondly, the idea that Joseph would actually be working in the fields seems to be contrary to his brothers' experience. As if that wasn't bad enough, Joseph goes on to tell another dream to the whole family in which not only the brothers bowed down to him but also father and mother. Father was not pleased. The story makes it very clear that the brothers hated Joseph and were also jealous of him. To make matters even worse, while the brothers were some distance from home pasturing the family flock, Dad sent Joseph to check up on them and asked Joseph to bring back a report.

There are a couple of other details that can help us deal with this story. Two brothers are mentioned by name: Reuben, who is the oldest, and Judah. These two brothers both had Leah for their mother. There was a lot of animosity between Leah and Rachel, Joseph's mother, given the fact that Leah was not the woman Jacob had wanted to marry in the first place. The two women competed with each other. They even argued over mandrakes which Reuben had brought home to his mother; mandrakes have narcotic properties, so perhaps it isn't too much of a stretch to think that there were drug issues as well as fertility issues between them. Leah, on this particular occasion, gave Rachel the drugs as part of a bargain that Leah got to have sex with Jacob that night! Much later, after Joseph had become an important figure in Pharaoh's government in

Egypt, Joseph would warn his brothers not to quarrel with each other. The family dysfunction goes on and on and on.

However, let's get back to the young Joseph wandering around the wilderness looking for his brothers. At first, he couldn't find them, but with help from another shepherd in the area, he finally figured out where they were. When the brothers saw him coming they said: "Here comes this dreamer . . . let's kill him, and then we shall see what will become of his dreams." Reuben, remember he is the eldest, intervened and got them to put Joseph in a pit with the idea that he would come back and rescue Joseph. But while Reuben's back was turned, Judah would make a deal to sell Joseph as a slave to a passing band of mercenaries. Apparently, they never did tell Reuben what had happened. The brothers eventually conspired to slaughter a young goat, dip the fancy, long-sleeved robe in the blood, and tell Dad that Joseph had apparently been devoured by a wild animal. Deceit, conspiracy, and treachery seem to be rather prevalent themes in this family.

We also read a report from the Gospel of Matthew this morning about Jesus appearing to walk on the stormy waters of the Sea of Galilee to reach his frightened disciples in their storm-tossed boat. If you read this report carefully, you will see that perhaps it is not to be taken as literally as some folk suppose. Our translation tells us that the disciples thought they were seeing a ghost. However, the Greek text suggests that the disciples were seeing an illusion, a phantasm, and that they were frightened by it. Peter wanted to try walking on the water too, but soon found that the storm was too much for him and he began to drown. Jesus got him back into the boat and they all sailed out of the storm and to shore. Peter reminds me of a saying I encountered several years ago: "It's all right to build dream castles, but don't try to move in."

It seems to me that these two Scripture lessons have a link: dreams are the link--or perhaps we would prefer to call them nightmares. People have been fascinated with dreams and the interpretation of dreams forever. Even Sigmund Freud nearly 100 years ago, made a major production out interpreting dreams. However, there are obviously problems with taking dreams literally, as Peter seemed to find out when he tried walking on the water. Joseph's family members allowed themselves to be provoked by the dreams. While the account of Peter trying to walk on the water seems to involve some sort of demonstration about the power of faith and doubt, it does seem to me that Peter is trying either to get one up on the rest of the disciples or to make himself equal to Jesus.

We try to maintain contradictory ideas about dreams: we reassure our frightened children that the scary dreams aren't real; we have ridiculed far-out proposals for innovation and change as empty dreams. On the other hand, we at least give lip service to the notion that dreams are important. Bottom line: We don't trust the dreamers in our midst.

In 1963—yeah, I know that was a long time ago—I was an associate pastor in a church in suburban Cleveland, Ohio. We held a meeting at the church, attended by a rather large number of church people, to discuss a fair housing ordinance that was being proposed in the town. I tried to articulate the scriptural dream of a just society where everyone was welcome and treated fairly. One member of the church in the back of the room shouted out, "Come on pastor, no one really lives that way." Well, we may not be all the way there yet, but we are closer to living that dream than we were nearly 50 years ago. We have gotten where we are because we have let the dream lead us.

The human eye is a marvelous and curious thing. There are two kinds of receptor cells in our eyes. There are cone cells which see color and are mostly closely clustered near the center of the retina. There are rod cells which see only black and white, which are mostly around the periphery of the visual field. These rod cells are more sensitive to light then the cone cells. The result is a curious phenomenon: in very low light levels, we can see more clearly if we don't look right at what's in front of us but look more to one side or the other. Sometimes those rod cells alert us to danger even when they don't clearly show us what object is out there that threatens to get in our way or to hit us. I think dreams are like those rod cells—they give us a hint at things, they suggest possibilities as yet not clearly seen at all. The truth that is lurking around the edges of our awareness may indeed be the reality that needs to be invited, explored, and discovered. It seems to me that these two kinds of visual cells are like the difference between hard, more or less logical, facts and intuitive hunches.

Both Scripture lessons ask us to move away from simply embracing and endorsing the way things are. They both invite us to consider the possibilities that only dreams can imagine—the prospects beyond logic, the potential beyond what is so obviously real. As a rather young man I went to see a movie titled: "Destination Moon." The story was about an attempt to fly human beings to the moon. It was a fun fantasy sort of thing; it was a dream on the screen and yet it wasn't very long before the dream became a reality. Obviously at this point we have been there, done that. But without the dream it wouldn't have happened. Without the dreams that Joseph had, the family might not have survived the famine that beset them after Joseph got to Egypt. Without the dreams Jesus and his disciples had, there would be no Christian Faith.

Do we dare to dream? Are we willing to risk being dismissed as dreamers? Will we honor our intuition, our hunches and our rather chaotic feelings about how life might actually be lived? Or are we too quick to pronounce "That's ridiculous?" Jesus didn't tell Peter he was being ridiculous—he just invited him to have deeper faith, more confidence in his convictions, more determination to make his dreams real.

You may recall that in one of those congressional budget-cutting frenzies (I think during Abraham Lincoln's presidency) a member of congress proposed closing the patent office because everything had been invented. I don't think this particular legislator did much dreaming. Much of the current turmoil in Washington seems determined to ignore the value and power of dreams. Where are the dreamers who will pay the price of unpopularity, rejection and ridicule to help us move beyond the conviction that we have arrived and need to go backwards, and who will lead us back onto the road so that we may keep moving?

After his rejection, Joseph led his family to the safety of Egypt; after the midnight storm, Jesus led his disciples back onto the journey of healing and helping people. In a few minutes we will gather around the communion table to share a dream of humankind being one, interconnected loving family. Do we have the courage to dream? Do we dare commit ourselves to following those dreams and making them into reality? Will we believe in the power of the truth we only see dimly or are we going to get trapped by our devotion to the hard data of the way we have always done things? There might be a sign on this table in front of us that reads: Dreamers wanted. Will you apply for the position? Will you be a dreamer?

TRANSFORMING NOW
August 21, 2011. Romans 12-1-8; Matthew 16:13-20

Our gospel lesson this morning has Jesus discussing his identity with his disciples. We can approach this text in a couple of different ways: we can assume that this is a test that Jesus gives to his disciples to determine how they're doing at understanding his teaching and whether they have figured him out yet or we can assume that Jesus is engaged in an honest discussion with his disciples about his identity. If we assume this is a test, then we are probably falling prey to the temptation to think that somehow Jesus is not really human and is setting the disciples up to force something from them or to use them as puppets to promote his cause. On the other hand, if we are really comfortable with the idea that Jesus is really human, then we are eavesdropping on a conversation in which Jesus is soliciting the disciples' opinion about who people might think he is. Given the fact that Scripture compresses accounts of events into very brief reports, our reading this morning could very well reflect an extended discussion that Jesus and his disciples had about who he is, what his ministry is or is supposed to be, etc. Various ideas are thrown around including questions about whether Jesus resembles certain important historic figures in the theological history of Israel. Then Peter offers an astounding suggestion: "You are the Christ, the son of the Living God." Jesus pounces on this and declares that Peter could only know this because of some divine inspiration. It wouldn't surprise me that Jesus drew this conclusion because he knew Peter pretty well and figured Peter wouldn't have come up with this all by himself. It makes sense to me to suppose that this discussion would have incorporated a lot of the various disciples' thinking about why they have decided to leave their ordinary lives and tasks behind to go with this itinerant preacher. Jesus also realizes that such a claim would create an even bigger stir with the authorities and he ends this discussion by ordering the disciples to keep quiet about this.

Peter's assertion would be so controversial because it would require a complete rethinking by the religious authorities about the nature of the Messiah and the future of Israel That would have probably undermined the accommodation between the local civil authorities and the occupying Roman army. The political situation was very unstable: Pontius Pilate, the Roman governor for the region who ordered Jesus crucified, would eventually be recalled by Rome for his bungled handling of political affairs. Jerusalem would be destroyed by the Romans within 40 years of Jesus' death. Jesus certainly knew his way around the territory and had a very clear sense of how to deal with the political intrigues and would have realized that Peter's astounding assertion would have raised havoc.

The Apostle Paul probably wrote his letter to the church in Rome about the same time as Matthew penned his gospel. Paul, in today's reading, talks about how proper service to God involves resisting conforming to the present age and allowing one's self to be transformed by the renewing of one's mind. It seems to me that Jesus and Paul are looking at similar realities. Jesus understands that Peter's revelation would make it impossible for people who believed in him to continue to conform themselves to the patterns and practices of the present age. Paul, who outlived Jesus by about 35 years, would have already witnessed the way Christian living turned things upside down. He himself was often the victim of harassment and persecution and came close to being killed for the faith several times before the emperor Nero finally had him executed. Both of these men are concerned about timing: Jesus wants to keep things quiet for a while in order to continue his work and Paul wants to make noise now--and in both cases their concern seems to be how to have maximum effect on the situation.

Paul believes if we allow our minds to be renewed that our perspective will be transformed, and we will be able to discern the will of God. Such discernment, in Paul's thinking, is linked to how people are going to act in the world. He goes on to urge people to realize that everyone has gifts to share, but that we all don't have the same gifts. He seems to urge us to maximize our gifts and abilities—in other words, to make the most of what we have in order to advance the cause of Christ in the world.

Christianity has often been distorted and turned into a religion about "pie in the sky by and by." But Jesus and Paul are very focused on the present moment, on what is happening now. Jesus wants space and time in which to work before the full implications of his teachings catch the attention of the politically powerful; Paul wants Christian people to be living their lives of faith in full view of the world. Neither is concerned about "pie in the sky by and by." Yet both of these men have a perspective that is informed by much more than the values and practices of the present age. I prefer to think that they are focused on bringing the power and the reality of the Beyond into the present moment. Beyond the present age, beyond the present value systems, beyond current political systems, and beyond contemporary worry systems, is a reality that can help us put things --all things--into perspective. There is a story about an astronomy student who was overwhelmed by the enormity of the universe he was trying to observe and got depressed about his life and went to his professor and said: "Professor, astronomically speaking, human beings are insignificant." His professor replied, "Astronomically speaking, human beings are the astronomers." I find the professor's idea to be encouraging, positive, and optimistic; it is certainly not smacking at all of insignificance. What is Beyond, whether it is a theological or an astronomical Beyond, so overwhelms the petty details in which we get stuck that it transforms the situation. It is such a magnificent plentitude that it is like pouring gallons of water into an 8-ounce drinking glass. The reality of all that water overwhelms the little glass; and the reality of the great Beyond overwhelms the reality of our ordinary, rather routine, lives. Christianity is not really about escaping the world; it is about living in this world with power and joy, peace and hope.

If Jesus and Paul are concerned about timing, how might we be concerned about timing? These two men seem to understand what the Now moment needs. What does our Now need?

At the end of the passage from Romans we read today, Paul lists three qualities he wants people to exhibit as they work to make the best use of their gifts. These are openness, eagerness, and cheerfulness. What if we would live in the Now with openness, eagerness, and cheerfulness?

I suspect we would not only find that we are being transformed by such renewing of our minds, but that we would also find ourselves very much out of conformity with the so-called spirit of the age.

We are assaulted on every hand by political rhetoric that often exhibits more heat than light. We dwell in the "oh my god" culture which is horrified by economic change and other scary changes. We are constantly told that we can't do things like provide health care for everyone while we contemplate sending space probes hither, thither and yon and want to put a robotic vehicle on Mars. In all the sound and fury that constitutes the daily TV news, and that fills the print media with dire statements, I find very little openness, eagerness or cheerfulness. I see a lot of closed mindedness, reluctance and despair. Our age seems to require us to be skeptical, cynical, and pessimistic.

Jesus and Paul lived in very unstable times. They were both constantly threatened, not only by political and religious authorities, but also by lots of common, small-minded people who definitely did not want to think outside the box. Yet these men found the courage to persevere, to counsel openness, eagerness, and cheerfulness; to praise the hopeful and the faithful. I think they found this courage by allowing the reality of the Beyond to flow into the present and let the power and joy of the greater reality break down the confining limitations of the present age.

If we believe in a God who is still creating, who is still speaking, and who is still promoting change, then we can open our minds, our hearts and our eyes to behold the wonder of the Beyond flowing into the present moment. The present moment becomes blessed by the infusion of a reality that is greater than our pessimism, our despair, and our fears. The power of the Beyond demands that we keep reminding ourselves that our perceptions are limited and that our knowledge is far from complete about any subject one can imagine.

We are called to transform now. We are invited to link the reality of Now to the resources and potential of the Beyond. I am not talking about what comes next—which we usually call the future. I am talking about allowing ourselves to experience a God and a reality that is Beyond our own perceptions, Beyond our usual thinking, Beyond our familiar concepts. The Beyond might be called the fullness of reality. Perhaps Paul was thinking of such a concept when he wrote to the church in Corinth that "No eye has seen, nor ear heard, nor the human heart conceived what God has prepared for those who love him." In the same passage in which Paul writes this, he speaks of the contrast between the attitude of the present age and the age created by God through the gifts given to people. Paul is clearly not talking about what happens after death or about some magical heaven with gold streets: he is talking about allowing the power, the beauty, the joy and the peace of the Beyond to flow into the present and transform the Now. Now is the kingdom of God. Now is the Peace of God. Now is the gentle, persistent mercy of God. We are invited to live with joy in the Now and let our Now be filled with the beauty and grace of the Beyond so that our Now is not limited by the miserable, short-sighted, self-centered conceptions of the age in which we seem to live. It has been said by those of a philosophical turn of mind that, "Our perception is our reality." If that is really true, and I think it is, then let's make sure we transform our perceptions by the renewal of our minds so that the reality in which we live is not some negative, painful, hopeless place conjured up by a bunch of pessimists, but is instead a Now filled with sunlight, with the fresh air of creative thinking and the sound of joy to be found amongst people who are declaring themselves to be open, eager and cheerful because we are committed to believing in an open, eager, and cheerful God. NOW.

BIRTHING A REBEL
January 1, 2012. Isaiah 61:10-62:4; 10-12 Luke 2:22-40

This first day of the year 2012 is also the eighth day of Christmas, which means we are just a little more than half way through the Christmas season. Christmas actually ends this coming Thursday. There is, of course, a song about the 12 days of Christmas which has been often parodied and for which at least one group of economists estimates the annual cost. This Christmas it would cost you over $100,000 to provide the various gifts for your true love. Today's gift would be 8 maids a milking. I wonder how many people in our society know what a "maid a milking" is? I wonder if hand -milked milk could pass governmental approval and be sold at the supermarket. The song seems to have originated in England in 1780. I imagine that 232 years ago 8 maids a milking would have been a considerable economic asset to a dairy farmer. It is quite likely that by now the 8 maids have been replaced by one machine, made in China and imported through Indonesia.

A couple of weeks ago I got one of those email ads selling me a special external hard drive for my computer on which I am supposed to store my pictures and other treasures to pass on to my family. The advertisement claims that this special little external computer drive will last for 100 years and will keep my treasures safe. Aside from wondering how the company could claim to have tested this device to prove it would last 100 years and also from wondering how I could follow up on the warranty in 100 years, I found myself wondering if there will be computers as we know them, especially with USB ports which this device needs, in 100 years—after all 100 years ago there were no such things. So, with all these tidbits in mind, I decided that there isn't really any future in forecasting the future on the first day of 2012.

Our gospel lesson for this morning, however, contains some forecasting of the future that I feel is important for us to understand. I want to invite us to step away from some of the traditional pageantry of Christmas for a few minutes in order to shift our perspective on our own history. The idea that Jesus was born of a virgin didn't really gain much historical traction until Christianity was over 300 years old. The reality at the time of Jesus' birth was that his mother was pregnant out of wedlock and that Joseph had some concerns about marrying her. The shepherds who came to worship the infant were considered to be unclean and thus excluded from common religious practices. Hanging out with shepherds was clearly not something that socially proper folk would have done. Nazareth had an ugly reputation—it was not a good town. Another reality is that the wise men didn't show up at the stable at all. They arrived at the house of Mary, Joseph and Jesus about two years later. Imagine the harried mother of a two-year-old having three kings descend on her! Today's gospel lesson describes Mary and Joseph as devout Jews who took their baby to the temple for presentation to God. They encountered two prophets there: Simeon, presumably an old man, and Anna who was 84 years old. It is amazing that Anna had lived that long since the median life expectancy for a woman at that time was 38. It is also astounding from our perspective that Anna is identified as a prophet. For centuries, we have been assuming that

82

prophets were men. Luke wants people to be able to identify this woman, so he tells us her father's name and also their tribe. Simeon is delighted to be a witness to this event and says that his life purpose has been fulfilled now that he has seen the infant Jesus. Simeon is said to be "in the spirit"—in other words he might appear to be possessed or in an ecstatic state, most likely an off-putting way of presenting himself. Many would at least raise an eyebrow if we told them that God talks to us. Yet Simeon also sounds a word or two of caution: he says that "This child is destined for the falling and rising of many in Israel, and to be a sign that will be opposed so that the inner thoughts of many will be revealed—and (he says to Mary) a sword will pierce your own soul too." This last remark is sometimes understood to be a reference to the fact that Mary probably outlived her son and may have witnessed his execution. Certainly, the way Jesus' life unfolded would not be every mother's dream for her babies.

The entire Christmas story is a counter-cultural experience. Among the poor is born a king; out of the riff-raff of the underclass comes a revolutionary whose entire life will challenge and upset many powerful people. The unclean and the outcasts will be welcomed. Even the lepers will be loved. This Jesus will stand the value systems of his time on their heads. His behavior was so radical that even his family came on one occasion to take him home because they said, "He is beside himself" --in other words out of his mind. One of my personal problems with the way we celebrate Christmas is that it feels to me like we have succeeded in domesticating Jesus—making him socially acceptable. I doubt that we would find an encounter with

Jesus to be a soothing, pleasant experience. We would be more likely to see him as a ragged non-conformist who seems to be, as the saying goes, "a pickle short of a full jar." We would certainly find him to be a challenging and demanding presence who has no concern with being proper or doing things in good order. Even being socially appropriate might be unimportant to him.

I know that I have quoted George Bernard Shaw to this congregation before, but I still think this quotation of his fits Jesus and helps us to see the challenge before us. Shaw said: "The reasonable man adapts himself to the world; the unreasonable one persists in trying to adapt the world to himself. Therefore, all progress depends on the unreasonable man." Jesus is the unreasonable man. Mary and Joseph, that non-conformist couple from the most unlikely community and background, had, on Christmas Day, an unreasonable son. The two prophets at the temple, Simeon and Anna, celebrate his unreasonableness.

Isaiah's call to prepare the way of the Lord becomes a call to make a highway for the Unreasonable One. Simeon tells us that the Unreasonable One will be opposed by many and his manifestation will cause the fall and rise of many in Israel. It is quite tempting for us to see this as a reference to the fall of those in power and the rise of the powerless—in other words the coming of the kingdom of God will wreak social havoc. However, these prophets stop short of making predictions as to the form that the future will take. They know that the new life associated with the kingdom of God can only happen when the current ways of injustice, discrimination, and violence are out of the way. They witness to the hope but leave the details to be accomplished by those who will follow them by following the Unreasonable One.

On the table before us wait the communion elements. The bread and drink here are symbols of the body and blood—of the life—of the Unreasonable One. When we partake of these elements today we are invited— in fact we are challenged—to incorporate into our own lives the perspective and attitude of the Unreasonable One. In bygone days, the church was sometimes described as Mother Church. I invite us to reclaim that role, to become as Mary—the poor, rejected, unwed mother—and do whatever we need to do to give birth to rebels, to give new life to the Unreasonable One in our midst that from this place and from among this people will go forth a challenge to the whole world to turn its unjust value systems upside down, to welcome everyone, to offer healing and support and care to all regardless of their circumstances. May we find the courage to be counted among the colleagues of the Unreasonable One, dare to go to the Nazareths of our own time, and risk hanging out with the socially unacceptable. Let us have the courage to be found in places, with people, and doing things which no reasonable folk would consider to be proper. Let our New Year's resolution be to become Unreasonable Ones; let our predictions for the coming year focus on refurbishing and changing value systems until all find themselves included in a socially just society. Thanks be to God for the power of the Unreasonable One, our brother, in whose company we will spend the rest of our lives.

UPSIDE DOWN CHRISTMAS
December 29, 2013. Genesis 37:2-24; Matthew 2:13-23

Our opening hymn this morning was "In the Bleak Midwinter" and it sings of the stable that sufficed for Jesus' birth in the dead of winter. The hymn we will sing after the sermon carols about the summer and welcoming the Christ Child "warm in our sunshine and sweetness of air" in a place where the snow isn't falling, and people have beaches on their minds. The first hymn was written by a woman living in England; the second was composed by a woman who lives in New Zealand. The temperature in Bethlehem this morning is 75 degrees. The title for this sermon comes from that second hymn. What we learn from this comparison is an indication of how much of our own environment we have projected onto the celebration of Christmas. Most of us probably can't imagine Christmas without snow. I can remember my own children at an early age protesting one year that it wouldn't really be Christmas without snow.

The actual date of Jesus' birth is completely unknown. The church decided it would celebrate this occasion by trying to take over the Roman holiday of Saturnalia which climaxed on December 25 –which was much closer to the winter solstice at that time. During the celebration of Saturnalia, most civil laws were suspended and partying to the maximum was in vogue. Various lights and candles were also involved, and the Romans went caroling from house to house—demanding treats or threatening nasty tricks (something like we used to do at Halloween). While the church's customs about caroling may be traced to Roman times, we have dropped the

Roman tradition of going caroling naked. (I don't know if this change is based on morality or the cold weather we have this time of year.) Interestingly enough, the Romans elected a victim upon whom to heap the blame for all of the wild and licentious behavior during the holiday and they actually killed their victim at the end of the festivities, sacrificing him to their gods. We have borrowed heavily from those ancient customs and piled many of them onto Christmas.

Over the years the Christian Church has done a similar thing to Joseph, the father of Jesus. The church has focused so much attention on a variety of beliefs about Jesus' mother, that in order to maintain its unscriptural views about Mary, we had to cobble together a bunch of nonsense about Joseph. Even though Scripture tells us that Jesus had at least four brothers and a couple of sisters, church doctrine forced a denial of the plainly stated facts. The result of all this is that Joseph is supposed, in pious imagination, to have been much older than Mary, a widower with several children of his own and then, of course, it makes sense to suppose that he was dead by the time Jesus was into the heart of his ministry. This is frankly, simply rubbish concocted to support doctrines about the perpetual virginity of Mary and sustain the notion that sex is sin. In the process, Joseph just about disappears.

What do we really know about Joseph? He was an artisan, perhaps a carpenter. Most likely he worked by the day. It is not likely that he owned any land. He lived with his family most of his adult life in Nazareth, although they seem to have lived in Bethlehem for a while. Jesus was two years old when the wise men showed up and found Jesus in a house with his mother in Bethlehem. The little town of Nazareth, population about 400 persons, was only four miles from the city of Sepphoris. That city was undergoing extensive and apparently elaborate reconstruction at the time and it may be that Joseph went there to work. Jesus tells a parable about a man coming to the city square and hiring workers from amongst the men hanging out there and it is quite possible that the parable is based on experiences Jesus had going to work with his dad. There are several comments in the New Testament to help us know that Joseph was around for at least a good deal of Jesus' life. We also know one other very important thing about Joseph: he was a dreamer. The Gospel of Matthew records four of his dreams—and we read about three of them this morning.

The first dream we read about today shows us Joseph getting the "word" to get out of town and go to Egypt. He not only does this, but this man took his wife and two-year-old son on a journey of close to 60 miles all the way to Egypt without any evidence of planning or preparation and they left in the middle of the night! We really don't know how long the family stayed in Egypt, but it is quite likely it was at least a year and perhaps a little longer. Then Joseph had another dream—well actually he had two rather close together. In one dream God tells Joseph to go back to Israel. It seems logical to suppose that he would have headed for Bethlehem. But then there is another dream and he moves to Nazareth instead. There were probably two things that Nazareth had going for it: first, it was much farther from Jerusalem then Bethlehem and ruled by a different dictator than Jerusalem and second, because of the building going on in Sepphoris, there was probably work there for Joseph. In his sermon last Sunday, Roger [the resident pastor] talked about Joseph trying to protect his family—all this moving around is part of that endeavor.

Joseph is a dreamer. The Hebrew people were rather suspicious of folk who made claims based on their dreams. The ancient prophets mocked dreamers who used their dreams as the basis for various pronouncements. But Joseph has dreams in which a messenger of God appears. Given the Hebraic reluctance to even write or say the name of God out loud, it is likely that the verbiage about a messenger is a cover. Joseph had dreams in which he encountered God. He made major changes in his behavior based on these dreams. I have a pretty strong hunch that I would not be well received if I got up tomorrow morning and told my wife I had a dream in which I was told to sell our house and move to Switzerland. People are skeptical of such behavior. If I tell people that I talk to God, no one says much about that, but if I start claiming that God is talking to me--well then people get a bit weird. While we can understand some of the historical reasons that Joseph has been discounted and ignored, we probably aren't facing one of the major issues in all of that: Joseph has dreams.

We read another story about a dreamer in our Scriptures this morning. This one is also named Joseph and he had the audacity to share his dreams with his family and they found that irritating. When Joseph was sent on a mission by his father to check up on the welfare of his brothers who were a distance off herding sheep, the brothers saw him, rolled their eyes and said, "Here comes the dreamer." That story then quickly moves through a plot to kill the dreamer and then puts the dreamer in the hands of foreigners who take him out of the country and this dreamer also winds up in Egypt, where he continues to have disturbing dreams.

Dreamers are troublesome people. I imagine that Joseph, the father of Jesus, was not popular with Mary's family who probably ended up not knowing what had happened to their daughter and sister. It was not at all customary, in that era, for common people to move about. They usually stayed close to their birthplace unless they were dislocated by civil or military authorities. But by the time Jesus was six years old he had lived in two different countries and in at least three different political jurisdictions, so perhaps it's not surprising that he was comfortable moving around as an adult. It seems highly probable that Jesus, as a child, heard stories about dad's dreams and all the moving around and being a rebellious, homeless dreamer would have seemed natural to him. When Jesus tells his disciples that he has no place to lay his head, he may have been referring to his own homeless state. In fact, as an adult Jesus seems to have made Capernaum, a town on the shore of the Sea of Galilee his home base— which would have put him 25 or 30 miles from Nazareth, where he had been threatened with murder for daring to interpret Scripture in unconventional terms. At least no one has threatened to kill me over the content of one of my sermons! It seems to me that the two Josephs we read about today and Jesus share a common characteristic: they are dreamers. They see a different world than most people see. They look at the way things are and they ask, "Does it have to be this way?" And having said that, they expand their dream perspective and show us a vision of a world that could be.

We are told that shepherds were the first to learn of Jesus' birth. Shepherds were considered to be unclean. These men were, in many respects, social outcasts. When Jesus himself declares that he is the "good shepherd," he is offering a play on words or perhaps a paradox. He may be describing himself as a "good outcast." Perhaps his life on the margins of society as the son of a wandering dreamer helped him to understand the plight as well as the essential goodness of the outcasts. When Jesus speaks of the time coming when Jerusalem will be destroyed, he may be giving voice to the mutterings of the outcasts among whom he and his family lived. Revolutionaries come from the margins of society. There is no such thing as a mainstream revolutionary. Whatever one needs to be a rebel, one cannot be a rebel without being a dreamer. The person who complains about the way things are but has no dream of a better world is not a rebel or a revolutionary. He or she is simply a sourpuss.

George Bernard Shaw once said: "You see things; and you say, 'Why?' But I dream things that never were; and I say, 'Why not?'" He also said: ""The reasonable man adapts himself to the world; the unreasonable one persists in trying to adapt the world to himself. Therefore, all progress depends on the unreasonable man." Joseph might have been such an unreasonable man. Three wise men had come to see his toddler son and brought expensive gifts. King Herod was aware of that and wanted to use whatever information these mysterious visitors could discover to destroy Joseph's son. But Joseph and company take off in the middle of the night and Herod (who was sometimes called a fox) was out-foxed. Joseph had a dream of a better world and he had a dream that his son would help to make that come to pass. He was so irrational that he thought he could beat Herod--and he did. He was so irrational that he thought he could make a difference by listening to God-- and he did.

I have a story that I have told some of you, but it seems to fit in here, so at the risk of boring some of you, I'll repeat it. I have a sweat shirt that says, "I put the fun in dysfunction" on it. I also have a black T-shirt which says (in scrawled white letters), "I only do what the voices in my head tell me to do." We were on a cruise a number of years ago. One day it was cool, and I wore that sweat shirt and people talked to me, pointed at the shirt, laughed and carried on. A couple of days later it was much warmer, so I wore the T-shirt: no one would talk to me. We seem to be afraid of folk who hear voices in their heads or in their dreams.

We are suspicious of people who base their actions on what God is telling them to do. Irrational dreamers get ostracized and the world church has done exactly that with Joseph. Having an upside-down Christmas involves rehabilitating the irrational dreamer and homeless wanderer who was the father of Jesus of Nazareth who was also a wandering, homeless, irrational dreamer. He turned things upside down. He hung out with the unclean, not only talked to women (which religious teachers were not supposed to do) but he talked to whores and Samaritans— whom he dared call good. He healed lepers—the most outcast folk in his world—and became one of the dreamers whom we kill or try to kill, like Martin Luther King, Jr. and Nelson Mandela. Recently there were celebrations over King's "I have a dream" speech, but I can tell you that on the occasion of that speech there were a lot of people who didn't want to hear the dream and thought this man was surely irrational and perhaps even crazy.

We sang a hymn last Sunday that starts out "Jesus our brother." The sentiment sounds oh, so sweet. Are you willing to have Jesus for a brother? Are you willing to be in the family of an outrageous, irrational dreamer? If Jesus is your brother, then crafty Joseph is your father. On top of that it makes crazy John the Baptist your close relative— you know the one who ate bugs and went around saying, in essence, "The end is near." Are you sure you want to be in this family? If you really do, then perhaps you may want to pay attention to the voices in your head—they're there, you know them—they tell you every day that a lot of stuff sucks and that a whole bunch of business-as-usual practices are unfair, unjust and just plain wrong. We hear those words and we don't say a word.

If you decide to join up, turn Christmas upside down and see it as a radical celebration of the irrational, then the day may come when you will sit down with Joseph, Jesus, Martin, and Nelson and have a conversation that begins: "I have a dream."

Way-Walkers Heal Themselves and Transform the World

A DISCERNING HEART
July 24, 2011. 1 Kings 3:5-28; Romans 8:26-39

My paternal grandfather, who lived into his mid-80's, was a gentle, kind man who went out of his way to be helpful to others. He grew up as an orphan: his mother died in childbirth for a younger sibling and my great-grandfather (who wasn't so great), abandoned the children. Grandpa was essentially a hired hand on local farms when he was very young—probably 8 or so. These difficult circumstances of his childhood made him very sensitive to the needs of people whom life had somehow deprived of basic needs. In the last few years of his working life, he and my grandmother moved into a house out in the country on about 20 acres of land. Most of the land they sharecropped out with a local farmer, but my grandfather, who had always had a garden, now had a major garden and one of his most bountiful crops was strawberries. I used to spend part of my summer there and I learned to harvest stoop crops. I recall one year that toward the end of the strawberry season, Grandpa had more strawberries than Grandmother could freeze or the local folks would buy. So, my Grandpa went door to door in the small town of Eaton Rapids, down near Lansing, with a tub of strawberries and gave them away. I never knew my grandfather to be cross or angry— he was quite patient with me and taught me to use his power mower, which was almost as big as I was then.

Because he had a very large garden, in addition to the lawn mower he had acquired a garden tractor—which in those days was a beast of a machine that you walked behind. It was more than I could manage. On the days when he wasn't working at the post office, we did power gardening. However, there was one requirement imposed by my grandmother on those occasions. We would all have breakfast together and then my grandfather would go out to start the machinery. My grandmother made me stay in the house until she heard both machines running because she said, "I don't want you to hear what he says while he is trying to get those things started." I suppose it was a while before I realized what she was doing. Truth be told, she was probably protecting me from hearing some words I had already heard on the school playground. Grandmother thought if she could protect me from grandfather's street vocabulary that I would be a better person or at least not be put off by my grandfather.

When I was a student in seminary, I knew a man who was a Ph.D. candidate in New Testament studies. He maintained if we translated the New Testament from Greek into English faithfully and rendered the New Testament in a style of English that did justice to the style of the Greek originals, people wouldn't let us read it out loud in church. After all the New Testament was written in koine Greek, which means street Greek and not classical Greek. It does often seem to me l that the translators, like my grandmother, go out of their way to make the language palatable to us. Although I don't really know Hebrew as well as I know Greek, I suspect that the same thing is true for the Old Testament. The newer translations of the New

Testament routinely render the Greek word "brothers" as "brothers and sisters" in English--which probably is an accurate interpretation of the spirit of the original. But sometimes I wonder where expressing the original spirit and conforming to the current culture gets into trouble.

We can see that in the passage we read from 1 Kings this morning. Our translation has Solomon asking God for an understanding mind. However, I do know that in this case the Hebrew behind the phrase "understanding mind" is really "discerning heart." I suppose that "mind" is used for "heart" here because we believe people think with their minds and not with their hearts. Ancient people were more likely to identify the heart as the center of their being whereas we tend to lean toward identifying the brain as the more distinctive part of ourselves and I suspect that most of us equate "mind" with the functioning of the brain. Our emphasis on the brain may set us up to ignore the emotional dimensions of our being, to suppose that we are primarily cerebral, and encourage us to elevate logic over feelings, and information over intuition. In many ways that is the reverse of our spiritual ancestors. Solomon's wisdom was not a cerebral accomplishment.

Let's focus for a moment on King Solomon, his prayer, and the most famous illustration of what is often called "the Wisdom of Solomon." Scholars tell us that Solomon was probably about 20 years old at the time he made the request of God, which I find remarkable because I doubt that I was that mature at age 20—and I have known some 20-year-olds who weren't anywhere near that mature. Solomon thanks God for giving him his father David's throne and acknowledges that he is surrounded by an enormous number of people. He is apparently keenly aware of the challenges he faces in being king over this nation. He asks God for a discerning heart so that he will be able to distinguish between good and evil. He implies that unless he can do that, he will not be a fit king for God's chosen people. God is impressed and pleased with the request and because Solomon did not ask for riches or long life, God agreed to give him a wise and discerning heart.

Then we have the famous story of Solomon rendering a wise decision. You have just heard this story, but I want to call your attention to a few details about it. First, while the women are reported to be prostitutes, Solomon does not take this into consideration. In fact, since it is probably safe to assume that the story was written down quite a while after the event itself, I suspect the label applied to the women betrays the prejudice of the writer. Perhaps we might conclude that a major feature of being wise is not to be distracted by labels.

That is obviously not true of at least one man [aka Trump] trying to get a nomination for the office of president of the United States who recently said that it was right for communities to forbid the construction of Islamic centers of worship in their towns. He is clearly distracted by labels as we all are sometimes. But I digress.

This entire story about Solomon's wisdom turns on the compassion of the heart. He can feel the energy flowing between these two women and himself. We would probably say that he relies on intuition--his own and the intuitive instincts of a mother—to make a ruling that discerns between good and evil. He also introduces one more element into the process. We might say he takes it to a different level; Solomon forces a perceptual shift. Instead of getting into a debate about who said what, he calls for a sword and proposes to cut the baby in half and give them each half a child. Of course, this stirred the compassionate heart of the real mother who prefers to give her baby away rather than see it die. Solomon's strategy here is to force these two women to see what the real issue is here: it is about the life of the child, not about their bickering and blaming.

Wisdom, at least as Solomon displays it, includes ignoring stereotypes, being compassionate, being aware of one's intuition, and getting at the crux of the matter—or the heart of the issue. If we dig a little deeper into the origins of the Hebrew phrase that means discerning heart we find a bit of a surprise: the roots of these words tell us that this phrase means "to have a listening center."

The response of the people was to understand that justice results from making wise decisions--decisions that come out of one's "listening center."

I have done counseling work for years and one of the issues that seems clearly present in almost all the problems that people bring to me is that people don't know how to think about their problems. Much of the time the issues get resolved by changing perspective and by learning to think and talk about them differently. We often get so immersed in a perspective that we can't find a way to see things differently and so we need a detached person to help us see other options. I find that this problem with perspective crops up in the translation of the passage we read this morning from Paul's letter to the church in Rome. We read "We do not know how to pray as we ought." That word "ought" jumps right out at me and smacks of religious rules, of proper procedures, and of doing things right and makes me wonder if the translators are stuck with a perspective of expecting the Scriptures to tell us how to do things. The same phrase can be translated as "We do not know how to pray as we need (to pray)." In other words, we go from being told we don't or can't do it right to being reassured that because we just don't know how to meet our own needs here, we can rely on the spirit which intercedes with sighs too deep for words—which is telling us that when we don't have the words we need, God will still understand. In his own way, when Paul tells us that we can be victorious beyond these limitations, he is inviting us to make a perceptual shift.

We might also listen to see how it feels to re-translate "our weakness" with the phrase "our limitations." It certainly feels different to me. I think this is also important for understanding another comment that Paul makes toward the end of this passage. After listing a whole bunch of difficulties that we might face, Paul says, "In all these things we are more than conquerors." The words "more than conquerors" are an attempt to translate a Greek word that means "being victorious beyond." Of course, Paul tells us that we can be victorious beyond all these limitations because we are loved by God.

Students of human perception tell us that we actually create filters in our brain composed of tightly networked neurons that screen out of our conscious awareness about 99 percent of all the incoming stimuli. They suggest that at the conscious level we are only aware of a tiny slice of what our sensory apparatus detects. Things that don't fit with preconceived patterns get filtered out. Things that don't make sense to us get filtered out. We are apparently physically built to see the familiar and ignore the different. The Solomon wisdom story and Paul's reassurance both challenge us to shift our perception. They are telling us that if we have a listening center and because we are loved by God, we will be able to be victorious over our limitations. If I understand that I can be victorious over my limitations, then suddenly those limitations aren't really limitations. What I have seen as limitations may be habitual restraints on my creativity and freedom, but they are really a matter of perception more than anything else.

One scholar said this: "Reality, in the strictest sense, is a product of our own creation and is maintained by our perception." Most of us have had a variety of difficult experiences. We all know something about the pains and woes of mortal life. But it may help us to be reminded that when we feel stuck in the pain and woe, shifting our perception can bring relief and release. We need to make an effort to challenge the way we see things, to shift the issues to a different level, to empower compassion, not only for others but also for ourselves, and to ignore the stereotypes that would prevent a perceptual shift.

If we allow ourselves to understand that there is really no Right Way to approach God, then we can realize that because of God's love we are empowered to be victorious over limitations. If we would focus on developing a listening center in our lives—a focus on hearing at the deepest level, then we might be able to own our own wisdom, celebrate our victories over pain and woe and show compassion to all with whom we share this life.

We can decide to be experts and accumulate and celebrate quantities of information, but while that may make us smart it won't make us wise. We could also decide to pursue wisdom and seek to blend compassion, blindness to labels, intuition and a willingness to shift perceptions into developing the listening center known as a discerning heart. The discerning heart knows love when it feels it and shares love because that listening center knows that we need love and so does everybody else.

WHO WATCHES THE WITNESSES?

June 16, 2013. 1 Kings 21:1-10, 17-21a; Luke 7:36-8:3

The world of literature, books, plays, and poetry finds a certain fascination with the mystery woman. I would be willing to wager that if I started out my novel declaring that dinner was interrupted by a mystery woman knocking on the door, it would be a much better way to begin than by saying that dinner was interrupted by a mystery man knocking on the door. I suppose many of the women among us would simply feel that while they can easily be mysterious, there is absolutely nothing mysterious about the male of the species. Our gospel lesson today features a mystery woman—a woman whose name is totally unknown to history. Her anonymity is very important, but I'm getting ahead of the story here.

The gospel lesson begins with a dinner party. Jesus has been invited to be the guest at a dinner party thrown by a Pharisee, named Simon, at his house. We are told that Jesus had arrived and taken his place at the table. Understanding the ancient eating arrangements is important here. DaVinci's famous painting of the Last Supper depicts a style of eating familiar to the 15th century but not the fashion of the first century. For meals of this sort, even in Palestine, people reclined at the table. There was a particular arrangement of places around the table. There were three couches on three sides of the table, with the fourth side being open so that the servants could get to the table, which, by the way, would have been a rather small table by our standards. If you were standing in that open space in front of the table, the couch to your left would be occupied by the resident family, the couch across the table from you would be for honored guests and the couch to your right would be for lower status folks. Of course, everyone reclining at table would be male. It appears from Luke's report of the party that Jesus was an honored guest, so he would be directly face-to-face with his host. They would have been much closer that folks are at our dinner tables. Of course, the host could also see anyone who was behind Jesus. He sees a woman come up behind Jesus. He apparently knows some things about this woman; he knows she is a sinner. Tradition has supposed that her sin is the sin of prostitution although that isn't really indicated in the story. The woman washes Jesus' feet with her tears, dries them with her hair, kisses them and anoints them with a perfumed ointment. The Pharisee believes if Jesus was really a prophet, he would know all about this woman. I find myself wondering just how the Pharisee knew about this supposed prostitute, especially since he didn't claim to be a prophet. But I digress, at least a little, The woman has an alabaster jar of ointment, probably some kind of perfume. These jars of perfume seem to have been a part of a woman's dowry and the contents was to be poured on her husband's feet at the time of the consummation of their marriage! Holding or kissing a person's feet is a symbol of submission in many oriental traditions— for example in the Hindu marriage ceremony, the bride kneels at the feet of her new in-laws. There is a lot going on behind the scenes at this dinner party. We are foreign visitors who don't have the cultural background to really appreciate some of the more subtle details.

Without even looking at the woman, Jesus uses her behavior as an instrument to confront the Pharisee about his lack of social graces and in effect telling him that this woman is more considerate than he himself is. Jesus is saying, "Hey, Mr. Pharisee, you blew it tonight. You ought to be glad this woman has provided the customary courtesies shown to guests. You are either clueless or rude since you chose not to wash your guests feet, bestow a welcoming kiss or anoint the visitor's head." Then, having made that point, he pronounces that this woman's many sins are forgiven and then he addresses her, presumably turning around to look at the woman at his feet and says: "Your sins are forgiven, your faith has saved you, go in peace." The Pharisee gets criticized and the woman gets blessed.

The second part of the gospel lesson tells us that soon after that Jesus left on a preaching tour traveling through various cities and villages. His entourage included the twelve disciples and many women who provided for Jesus out of their resources. Mary Magdalene, Joanna and Susanna are mentioned by name. Fast forward to the crucifixion: Mary Magdalene and Joanna are there along with several other women. You can look closely at the reports if you wish, but you won't find Mr. Pharisee in attendance at the close of Jesus' ministry.

The mystery woman who anoints, perfumes, kisses, and weeps over Jesus' feet is a witness: she is proclaiming his importance and significance. She does so without speaking a word. She is a mysterious, validating witness. She was being watched. People wondered about her and Jesus' willingness to forgive her. I think Luke may have had a reason for reporting this story just before describing the preaching tour and noticing the women on that tour. The women were watching they certainly could appreciate the enormity of the mystery woman's testimony— anointing the bridegroom's feet at the consummation of the marriage—doing something for Jesus that women would probably not ordinarily consider doing. They heard the forgiveness. And -- they probably said one thing to themselves that hasn't been reported: they said, "Jesus is safe" even as they noticed how welcoming he was to someone who was clearly not all that welcomed by others. The folks around the table who watched the woman and heard Jesus' response wondered about who was this one who even forgives sins.

The mystery woman's witness emboldens those who witness her testimony. They went on to take a significant role in the beginnings of the Christian church. Mary Magdalene may well have authored the ancient document known as the Gospel of Mary. Early on Joanna was thought of as being one of the apostles. Peter and Andrew got mad at Mary and accused her of making up stories when she told them about her visions of the Christ. Levi, who was the one who saw that happening, criticized Peter for being a hot-head and said that it was understandable that Jesus loved her more than he loved the other disciples—and Levi basically told Peter to get over his anger and get on with the program of preaching the gospel. The bold witnessing of these women may have been part of the background that enabled Lydia, a rather well-to-do business woman, to get involved in supporting Paul's ministry and encouraged Paul to entrust a woman, probably Phoebe who was a minister in the seaport that served the Greek city of Corinth, to carry his letter to the church in Rome. In fact, Paul, at the conclusion of his letter to the church in Rome (which is the last letter of his that we have) commends at least a dozen women for their involvement in the work of the early church.

Our Old Testament lesson today tells part of the story of king Ahab, who ruled in Israel nearly 3000 years ago, and his rocky relationship with the prophet Elijah—whom Ahab described as "my enemy." Ahab and his wife, Jezebel—who was a priestess of Baal—had conspired to murder a man named Nabor so that they could seize the vineyard that Nabor had refused to sell them. After Nabor had been killed, Ahab went to take possession of the vineyard and there he encountered Elijah, whom God had sent to confront Ahab. Elijah says that he has found Ahab to tell him that God would bring disaster upon him for killing Nabor and stealing his vineyard. While Ahab seems to repent, the disaster is passed along so that Ahab's kin lose their inheritance just as Nabor's kin had lost their inheritance. Elijah comes as God's witness to speak truth to power. Elijah doesn't wreak vengeance—he is a witness to proclaim that it is coming. Elijah doesn't get any particular power from doing this and in fact, at several points in his career, he seems to have feared for his life because of his efforts to proclaim the sovereignty of God. Again, there are witnesses watching—perhaps Macaiah the prophet who was involved at the end of Ahab's life—perhaps Elisha who sought to inherit Elijah's spirit and become a prophet after him. These prophets continued the tradition of speaking truth to power even when the authorities opposed them.

Jesus and Elijah spoke truth to power—at considerable personal risk. They did not get a lot of direct results. Jesus didn't convert Mr. Pharisee, and Elijah didn't get Nabor's inheritance reinstated. But there were witnesses. We have the names of a few and are told that there were more. Witnesses have a lot of power to change things. Sometimes that power is affirmed by the state when witness protection programs are made available so that the testimony of important witnesses will not be lost. The mystery woman weeping over Jesus' feet remains anonymous and, because she is, we have to focus on what she did, and not on who she was. We need to remember that all of Scripture was written by witnesses: Jesus never wrote a word that we know of, although we do know that he could read. Those famously non-conformist Old Testament prophets like Elijah didn't write reports of their activities.

The February after we moved to Midland, I came to church one Sunday and found that the fellowship hall had been converted into an exhibit celebrating Black History Month. I was surprised to find it here. Eventually that experience led me to understand the place this church and many of its members had taken in the civil rights movement. It was also a rather startling testimony to the fact that this was the place, perhaps the only place in town, where the exhibit was welcome and safe. A few years ago, I came to church and found the communion table swathed in the rainbow symbols of the Metropolitan Church which was being hosted by this congregation. I came to understand that some people who came here as part of the Metropolitan Church felt that this was a place where they were welcome and safe. As most of you know, this church went on to become an Open and Affirming congregation. Last month, as part of our efforts to "Widen the Welcome," we hosted an exhibit encouraging people to welcome mentally ill individuals (and their families) into the mainstream of our society. The "Widening the Welcome" effort wants to help us say to more marginalized folk: you are safe and welcome here. This morning Al Harrow has provided a witness to you which he has never made publicly anywhere. We put his comments between the Scripture lessons and the sermon to emphasize the witnessing nature of what he had to share with us. [Mr. Harrow announced that he is a gay man.]

Black History Month exhibits are now welcome in more public places, our society is discussing openly the rights of people of all sexual orientations, mental illness is not quite the stigma it once was. All this reminds us that when and while we witness, people are watching. And perhaps we could tell Mary Magdalene, Joanna, Suzanna, Salome, Mary the mother of James, Mary the wife of Clopas, and Mary the mother of Jesus that the church finally is giving credence to their witness by inviting women into ministry and advocating for justice and equal treatment for women. We may not always know who is watching, but we can understand that anonymous, ordinary, little-known folk can make a witness that facilitates change by giving other people the courage to do the things that ultimately make a difference. In the civil rights demonstration in 1968 at the Democratic Party's national convention, the cry was,

"The whole world is watching." The whole world is still watching, even more closely due to the technological capabilities we now have; while they may pay some attention to the powerful and prominent, they are really watching the anonymous witnesses to see what they might proclaim. Many of us use the computer to access the World Wide Web, which our software abbreviates as "www." I invite you to give those three w's another meaning: wonderful witnessing words. To what wonders will we witness? Will we seriously understand that folk are watching? The people who watch the witnesses eventually become witnesses too. Let us offer wonderful witnessing words which proclaim that Jesus and his church are safe and welcoming, which assert that all are loveable, forgiven, and have a place at the table of life. Become the bearer and speaker of wonderful witnessing words wherever you are because your witnessing is being watched—watched by people hungry for safety and welcome, hungry for the chance to change, hungry to be loved. What will the watchers see when they watch our witnessing?

COMPASSIONATE PERCEPTION

August 30, 2015. James 2:1-9; Luke 10:25-37

    We live in an era of constant and exponential change. Many of us can remember the early cell phones: they weighted about 5 pounds and had to be carried in a bag. Now the successor of the bag phone fits in my shirt pocket and combines the phone with a computer that has way more memory than my first computer had. While we try to keep up with all these changes in technology, we sometimes miss some of the more profound changes of our times. I want to call your attention this morning to two of these. It was a little more than 100 years ago that a medical scientist (who won a Nobel Prize for his work) discovered that our brains were composed of neurons. Some of his clinical diagrams are still used in medical texts today. But it was assumed that people were born with a fixed number of these neurons and that as we aged, neurons died. We spent nearly 100 years assuming that the only way our brains could change was for them to shrink. Recent brain research, aided by all these fancy scanning machines we have now, has determined that our brains are very plastic: the neurons change the ways that they connect, and new neurons appear on the scene. We now understand that learning and practicing certain kinds of skills changes the way our brains are configured. Neurons that fire together eventually wire together, so changes in behavior change our cranial wiring. London cab drivers who face enormous challenges in finding their way around the city have larger constellations of neurons in areas of the brain devoted to mapping and knowing where we are. There are more neurons in our brains than there are stars in the sky and a nearly infinite number of connection possibilities, so there is very little limitation to the capability to change and virtually no way any of us are going to max out in this department.

Another tremendous change comes to us from quantum physics. We have discovered that there is an interaction between objects that are perceived and the individual doing the perceiving. This showed up dramatically in some lab demonstrations about the way light expresses itself. Light may be observed as waves or as particles. Scientists studying the way light shifts from one state to another discovered that the light would appear the way they wanted it to. If they looked for waves of light, they found waves of light and if they looked for particles of light, they found particles of light.

These changes are part of a shift in our understanding that is carrying us away from materialism toward an understanding that all of reality is non-material. Some might suggest that reality is Mind or Thought and others might suggest that reality is Spiritual. It appears that mind is more than simply the mechanical operation of the neurons in our skulls. Along with all this we are also learning that our hearts generate an electromagnetic field that interacts with people around us—there are various estimates of how far this field extends but it appears that a range of 3 or 4 feet is a reliable distance. Maybe this has something to do with the fact that the hearts of lovers often beat in a synchronized fashion. Even in this digital age, we are on the verge of a revolution in understanding how we relate to each other. This revolution is giving new meaning to a lot of very old teachings.

Jesus talked about the kingdom of God and said that it is all around us and we don't see it. I think physics might be telling us that we don't see it because we're not looking for it or expecting it—but I'm getting a bit ahead of myself here.

Our Scripture lessons this morning repeat a familiar theme. Jesus is asking us to love our neighbor the way we love ourselves. We have probably all heard that time and time again. But it is easy to blow it off. We counter this with quantities of self-talk that focus on our mistakes, our inadequacies, our errors and yes even our sins. We often act as if we didn't deserve to be loved or as if we know ourselves too well to actually love ourselves. Or we claim it is too egotistical to love ourselves. But in the process, we are actually interfering with the chance to develop a healthy spiritual life.

There is a story that comes from the Cherokee people. The story is that there was a boy who was given a drum as a gift. He really liked this drum, enjoyed playing it and showing it off. One of his friends wanted to have turn with the drum, but the boy refused to share and his friend went away and stayed away. The boy didn't like how he ended up feeling about all this, so one day he talked to his grandfather about it. The grandfather said: "You have two wolves inside of you that fight each other to see who gets to run your life. One of them wants to share with others and the other is very selfish and wants to keep everything. When they fight, you feel bad." The boy asked, "Which one will win?" and grandfather smiled and said, "The one you feed."

The ways we choose to think and talk about ourselves impacts the configuration of our brains. The two wolves in the story correspond to contemporary understanding about the old and new brains that we have. The old brain is a primitive part and includes the fight/flight stuff you've probably heard about; the new brain is evolutionarily more recent, and it is where compassion and insight develop, and it can manage the fearful and angry tendencies of that old brain. (You might wonder to which brain Donald Trump is talking.) Loving ourselves actually impacts our neural wiring and the ways our brains function. This will affect our perception of reality: compassionate people are more likely to see the universe as a positive, life-friendly reality. Self-compassion improves our ability to be compassionate to others. Andrew Newberg has learned, through his brain research efforts, that spiritual practices alter the neurochemistry of our brains and ". . . bestow a sense of peace, happiness, and security, while decreasing symptoms of anxiety, depression and stress."

Jesus seems to have known that people who practiced self-compassion would be able to see the kingdom of God all around them and within them. The Gospel of Thomas, which contains our earliest records of the teachings of Jesus, indicates that Jesus thought that there was a correspondence between who we are inside and who we are outside, so the self-compassionate person will also be the one who offers compassion to others. In that process, we might be engaged in changing more than one brain.

Research is also showing that fear-based religion can be hazardous to one's health, leading to shortening of the life span, increasing of a variety of illnesses, prolonging recovery rates, etc. Fear-based religion focuses on that old, reptilian brain and pushes fear and angry responses. The more we focus on that aspect of our physiology, the more we will configure a brain that is involved with fears constantly and which as a result may even exhibit a fair amount of paranoia. We are discovering that the brain likes a balance and resists anything that will disturb that balance. If we have a fear-filled brain, we will have a brain that specializes in maintaining a fearful balance. That will require us to get better and better at identifying enemies, to be supersensitive to threats, and to use our logical ability to explain all this turmoil. That will leave less and less energy to develop self-compassion as well as enhancing resistance to compassion. This also is related to the fact that every religion known to human kind has sometimes degenerated into violence and promoted religious wars against outsiders to the faith.

Changes in how our brains are configured will change the way we perceive reality. Developing self-compassion will help us see things differently. Jesus made an assumption that people do actually love themselves when he asked us to love others as we love ourselves. To me this means that Jesus is promoting self-compassion and is suggesting that developing self-compassion is the right thing to do. The self-compassionate person will see more good in others and indeed in the universe. Let me invite you—indeed challenge you—to take a leap of faith here. We can start by acknowledging that we like being seen, being perceived, being accepted. Many of you know that I was seriously ill last spring [2015]—and came close to dying from sepsis. Surviving that illness has made me more grateful—not only for all the people that helped me and my family through this crisis—but more grateful for being alive, for seeing a sunrise or a sunset, for the taste of coffee in the morning. Lots of people have had similar experiences and have found that gratitude and self-compassion increase. Now here's the leap: if quantum physics is right and our perceptions effect the reality we perceive, then the gratitude I feel witnessing a sunrise will be returned by the sunrise itself; the gratitude I feel toward others will affect them and be returned by them.

There is another reality I invite you to acknowledge. Each of us is a unique individual. The complicated combinations of DNA, history and experience mean that there has never been and never will be another you or another me. If a collection of totally unique, self-compassionate individuals joins together in a community some amazing possibilities emerge. We can blend the multitude of our unique perceptions together to foster a view of reality that will improve life on this planet. The symphony of self-compassion will increase the gratitude expressed and experienced by the larger community in which our smaller, unique community dwells. We will be carrying out the injunction Jesus offered a couple of thousand years ago—we will be perceiving the kingdom of God within and around us.

It goes without saying that the creation of a negative community is also possible. People could join together in sharing the paranoia and anger the old brain can generate. I get regular mailings from the Southern Poverty Law Center documenting the existence of hate groups in this country. In fact, even though there has been a slight reduction in the number recently, the number of hate groups in this country exploded after Obama was elected president. Many of these groups perpetuate the evils of racism and advocate violence to prevent any positive social change. Amongst these groups are enemies of LGBTQ people. In the long run, we can expect, as research is clearly showing, that participation in these groups will have a detrimental effect on the health of their members. But we can't wait for that to make these groups ineffective. Love without justice is nothing more than a "feel-good" ephemeral illusion.

If we commit ourselves to developing a community of self-compassionate folk, then we will not only behold the kingdom of God around us, but we will turn our perceptions into reality as we offer the world a healthy, love-filled alternative to the self-destruction of the hate mongers.

There are alleged communities of faith that are opposed to homosexuality and in fact to any non-traditional expressions of sexuality. These communities are trying to have it both ways by advocating that we "love the sinner but hate the sin." However, as several thoughtful authors have pointed out recently, this still focuses on defining something as sin and then saying to people "It's okay with me if you want to be a stinky, slimy sinner." I do not believe that a self-compassionate community can endorse that simple jingle because that jingle jars all efforts to proclaim love. Communities attempting to live by the motto of "love the sinner but hate the sin" will find that the two wolves will tear them apart resulting in that frightened, angry wolf dominating and turning the community into an "oh, so nice" hate group. Then we will have to wonder when these newly-minted hate groups will join forces with some of those who are supporting Trump's immigration policy ideas. A member of one of these hate groups has proposed making the Mexican border a vacation zone, charging everyone $25 for a permit to go there (with a gun) and paying them $50 for every confirmed kill. I am not making this up. It was reported in the NY Times 8/22/15.

It seems clear enough to me that if we fail to perceive the Kingdom of God and fail to participate in it, we are consenting to the reign of a kingdom of evil. Those extreme so-called Christians who think that the Kingdom of God will arrive like an apocalyptic military invasion are wrong. As Jesus said, the Kingdom is already here—we have only to perceive it and let ourselves live in it. We enter the Kingdom by becoming self-compassionate and letting our compassionate nature perceive the Kingdom; we build that Kingdom by offering true justice that only love can create to the marginalized folk in our midst—be they gay or lesbian; transgendered or bisexual; homeless or hungry; rich or poor; immigrants or strangers of another color.

Self-compassion is not some sort of feel-good fluff. It takes courage to be self-compassionate. It takes courage to challenge the critics from our past and from our current lives and say to them all "I am loveable; I am the unique creation of an Amazing God; I am sister or brother to Jesus, I can see his Kingdom, and I intend to continue his work to bring that Kingdom to all those marginalized by intended or unintended evil."

It is interesting to note that some current research says the efforts to raise people's self-esteem fails and creates many of the same problems it is trying to resolve, while efforts to increase self-compassion result in more compassionate people and expands the available supply of love. Maybe that's because "self-esteem improvement" efforts feed the wrong wolf.

You have more power available than you usually realize. Maybe our power to change the whole world is limited, but what if self-compassion or better yet, the symphony of a fellowship of the self-compassionate, could drop a rock of change, a rock called the Kingdom of God, into the pool of everyday reality—the ripples would go on and on for more than a lifetime and touch many a shore while rocking a lot of boats. How about joining me in taking a leap of faith that will generate ripples of compassion? Do you dare promise to begin by being more self-compassionate?

STORY-TELLING, TRUTH-DISCLOSING, LOVE-REVEALING

December 27, 2015. 1 Samuel 2:18-20, 26; Luke 2:41-52

When I was a bit younger, my family lived at the top of a hill. School was about a half-mile away. To get to school I had to walk downhill, along a rather flat spot at the bottom of the hill and then up a hill on the other side. This gives me the right to tell my grandchildren. "When I was a kid I had to walk half a mile to school and a half mile to get home—uphill in both directions." I'll leave out icy sidewalks and deep snow in recognition that we have neither at the moment. The joke about walking uphill in both directions is a reminder that we tell stories for particular reasons. In this case, it is about letting young people know how difficult life used to be and how lucky they are not to have to walk uphill in both directions. How many stories and jokes could we start with "so you think that was difficult, well let me tell you . . ..?" I went Saturday before last to the Center for the Arts for the annual Christmas music extravaganza. In the middle of the program, there was a recitation of the poem, "Twas the night before Christmas." The narrator invited members of the audience to fill in the blanks at a couple of places and the entire audience supplied the names of "eight tiny reindeer." We know that poem. There are lots of stories engraved in our memories.

It is the custom in the Church to combine readings from the Old and New Testament into lectionaries for the

Sabbath. We heard this morning about the young man Samuel and his mother along with a story about the young man Jesus and his mother. There probably was a time when most people hearing these stories would be familiar with them and could add all sorts of details. However, I'm not so sure we are that aware of the history. Without intending to insult anyone here, I would be surprised if the story about Samuel brought to mind for us the names of Eli, Hophni and Phinehas—not to mention Ichabod, or recollections about how the Philistines had defeated Israel in a battle near Shiloh and had captured the Ark of the Covenant. I'll tell you in a moment or two why this 3000-year-old story is important. But we're going to fast forward to the time of Jesus. If the Star Wars saga can mix up the chapters in its story, so can I mix up the chapters in this story.

Jesus grew up in a Palestine that was under the control of the Roman Empire. Roman governors had nearly absolute power and could pretty much do what they wanted. It was by order of one of these Roman officials that John the Baptist was beheaded. The clash of Jewish and Roman culture was everywhere. Jesus preached in Bethsaida and pronounced judgment upon the community for not repenting. Recent archeological studies disclose that this Jewish fishing village (home to five of the apostles) had a Roman temple in it. It seems that the ruler of the place, Phillip by name—who was himself Jewish—had built a temple to a Roman goddess to ingratiate himself with the Roman authorities at whose pleasure he got to rule the place. There was probably a lot of anger amongst the common people in this fishing village, where there is evidence the Jews were observant of kosher practices, about the duplicity of a Jewish leader who was placating the Romans and making the citizens pay for it.

We also know that the early church made an effort to distinguish itself from the Jewish faith—presumably to avoid the ire of the Romans who destroyed Jerusalem in 70 CE to squash a rebellion. Life as a Christian was dangerous for the first 300 or so years after the birth of Jesus. The emperor Constantine made Christianity the religion of the empire in 312 CE, but before that Christians were regularly persecuted. One early writer tells us that Christians were blamed for the Tiber river (in Rome) flooding or drying up. That blame led to deadly encounters between Christians and lions to entertain the masses who were presumably bothered by the unexpected changes in the river's water level. The question arises about how to tell the Christian story in meaningful ways under the shadow of persecution and death. This is a particularly critical issue because the Christian faith was and still is subversive. One way to do this is to perfect the art of story-telling—the way of using narrative to say a whole lot more than the casual observer might suppose is being said.

That takes us back to Shiloh, Samuel and those folks I mentioned. The young Samuel served as an assistant to Eli who was the chief priest there. Eli was an old man. He was 98 when he died and apparently had cataracts and may have had some sort of problem that made it impossible for him to turn his head. Hophni and Phinehas were his sons. They were corrupt officials who stole the choice cuts of meat from the sacrifices the populous offered at the temple there and sexually abused women who served there.

Samuel became the prophet who foretold the downfall of the house of Eli. He was a young kid in the midst of a corrupt establishment who felt compelled to announce God's judgment over this mess. The whole thing fell apart when the Philistines defeated Israel in battle, killed Eli's sons and made off with the Ark of the Covenant, which was a premier holy object housed at the temple over which Eli presided. Eli's sons apparently took the Ark of the Covenant, which was a box containing holy relics, into battle believing that they had God in a box and that would save the day. When the news of the defeat in battle reached the people in Shiloh, Eli's daughter-in-law went into labor, gave birth to a son and then died. Before she died she named her son Ichabod which is Hebrew for "the glory has departed." That in itself might serve as a code phrase telling us that the ruling regime is no more. People hearing this story years later would recall the saga and be reminded that people of faith pursue justice and challenge the authorities.

If we link this story to an account of the young Jesus confounding the scholars and rabbis at the temple in Jerusalem, we begin to suggest that Jesus himself is a subversive. The reply that Jesus made to his mother who had been searching for three days for him, may be interpreted as meaning "Didn't you know I must be about God's business?" Are we suggesting by linking these stories that the coming of Jesus means the glory of the establishment has departed? Of course, we know that Jesus did a whole lot of scandalous things even though we aren't as sensitive to how radical he was because of some social changes between then and now. He elevated the status of women. As a religious leader, he shocked the establishment by talking to women and including them in his work. That example continued almost immediately—the apostle Paul sent the Letter to the Romans, his theological *pièce de résistance*, to the church in Rome in the hands of a woman. The apostles consorted with women who under the leadership of Joanna (a savvy business woman who had access to the court of Herod Antipas) financially supported the infant church. His revolutionary attitude toward women probably emboldened Mary of Magdala to write a gospel (in which she reported herself rebuking Peter)—a gospel unfortunately mostly lost because of the male chauvinism of the later church. Jesus thumbed his nose at many details of the application of Jewish laws. Picking a handful of grain on the Sabbath because he and his disciples were hungry was considered harvesting or working on the Sabbath and he wouldn't buy that. He was very critical of people's efforts to show off by the way they practiced their religion. He didn't hesitate to pronounce woes on Bethsaida over their willingness to support building a Roman temple in a Jewish community. He later took a whip to money changers in the temple: these people were making a profit on converting the usual currency –Roman coins most likely—into official temple money. They had a system that benefited them. They had God in a box and Jesus arrived with a vengeance saying, "Guess what guys, the glory has departed."

Linking the stories of Samuel and Jesus is a way of emphasizing the similarity of their missions without coming right out and telling the establishment that it's days are numbered. Because Samuel was considered to be a spokesperson for God, it tells us that Jesus is the same.

However, because we think of these accounts as stories, we are invited to interpret what they might mean for our own time.

We have groups of folks here and there claiming they are the authentic, genuine Christians. They will tell you that God is against birth control, abortion, gay marriage, transgendered love, etc. They have God in a box. If we are to be among the subversive followers of Jesus, we need to say to them "Guess what guys, the glory has departed." We have others who proclaim that they have God, who is about segregation, judgment, exclusion and rejection, in a box. They challenge us to say, "Guess what Mr. Trump, the glory has departed."

The subversive Jesus was homeless; some say he was a refugee. He healed people, fed people, forgave people, blessed the joy of common life events like marriage. He proclaimed a God of love, mercy and peace, and let loose a Spirit in the world that no box can contain.

Many of you know that I have practiced hypnotherapy for a number of years. Hypnosis involves lots of story-telling because that process invites people to interpret familiar realities in different ways. A story about a woman who used to bake cookies according to her mother's recipe but one day had great success with changing the recipe, becomes an invitation for a woman to change some familiar ways of behaving. Our teachers of young children tell all sorts of stories in order to teach concepts important for the children to learn—and we find that often those stories provide more effective lessons than trying to get the children to memorize a list of right and/or wrong choices. Many of the parables of Jesus qualify as stories. These kinds of stories disclose truth and often reveal love.

In the next to the last chapter of the Gospel of John, we find this comment by the writer of the gospel: "Now Jesus did many other signs in the presence of his disciples, which are not written in this book. But these are written so that you may come to believe that Jesus is the Messiah . . .." Here we have the author telling us that he has selected the stories to tell for a purpose and that he is not even trying to provide an exhaustive or comprehensive account of the life, teachings and work of Jesus. The stories about Jesus (just like the story about Samuel and a whole bunch of other Biblical folk) are subversive: they announce an alternative set of values, a creative perspective and a passion for justice. In the telling of these sorts of stories, the love of God gets revealed and the boxes of the narrow-minded, mean spirited and frightened power brokers get busted as the power of God gets loose.

Everyone in this room, no matter how old or young, has a plethora of stories to tell. You have experiences that can be transformed into stories that disclose truth, promote justice and reveal love. What stories do you want to tell? Which stories must you tell? Which ones are you afraid to tell? What truth, passion, and love might your own story-telling disclose? The stories about young Samuel and young Jesus are reminders that you don't need special credentials or achievements to be the owner and teller of valuable stories. What truth do you know that you could reveal in a subversive way? How could you disclose your passions about values and life by telling stories? What stories do you need to tell while you still can? To whom do you need to tell the stories? What boxes will you help to bust with your subversive stories?

Will we tell the stories that we have to tell? Will we join Samuel and Jesus in disturbing systems that perpetuate pain and ignorance, suffering and illness? Will we challenge the folk who claim to have God in a box? Will we have the courage to echo the prophets before us and confront false religion, proclaiming that their practices have made the glory depart? How about pledging to be a disturbing story-teller in the days of the coming year? How about incarnating stories that will bring God's glory back as we promote peace, mercy and healing, as we work to establish justice, feed the hungry and clothe the naked, as we celebrate inclusion and acceptance of all? The choice seems simple: will we be people of the box or subversive, story-telling people?

THE TRAP OF SELF-ESTEEM AND THE POWER OF SELF-COMPASSION
July 17, 2016
[Presented at the Unitarian Universalist Fellowship]
Poem "I will not die an unlived life" Markova

I am relatively sure that most of you are familiar with the long-standing conflicted relationship between theology and science. The controversies about this topic have been with the human family for at least 500 years. Many of us have probably decided that the topic is "old hat" and have let ourselves settle for a position about all this that is comfortable for us. So, it may come as a surprise when some new perspectives or discoveries come along to unsettle the familiar.

In some ways, this is a side-effect of the work of Grant Soosalu and Marvin Oka. These two men, who live and work in Australia, have offered us a fresh constellation of things more or less familiar to us all. They have taken Neuro Linguistic Programing, which is essentially an aspect of psychology, a number of discoveries about the human body and some behavior modeling, put them together with a lot of familiar language and shown us a fresh view of human nature.

I cannot possibly present the whole body of their work in my talk this morning, but I want to tease you with a few main features of what they are telling us. We can start with the reality that there is more than one brain in the human body. I would suppose that if we asked almost anyone to point to the location of their brain, they would point to their head. But Soosalu and Oka are telling us that there are brains in the heart and in the gut. They have assembled a very persuasive body of scientific data that backs this up. On top of that they have reminded us of how much our common, everyday language reflects that reality. We are constantly talking about gut-feelings or heart-feelings. Most of us won't even try to do things if our gut doesn't feel okay with that. I'll bet you wouldn't want to fly with an airline pilot who declared that his heart wasn't really into flying airplanes! Soosalu and Oka have titled their theory "mBraining," which is derived from combining the concept of multiple brains with the notion that a brain in action might be said to be "braining."

The further explication of this perspective demonstrates that each of these three brains has a highest expression of its capabilities. The highest capability of the head-brain is creativity, of the gut-brain is courage and of the heart-brain is compassion. Grant Soosalu is quite clear that this theory reveals that many of the teachings of ancient wisdom figures are supported by contemporary psychology. This means it turns out that many of the essential teachings of Buddha, of Hebrew prophets, of Jesus and others are supported by the discoveries of current, scientifically valid research. Science and theology get connected and might even be friends!

Another aspect of this approach is its emphasis on the Neuro Linguistic Programing concept of denominalization. This concern points out that we have turned many verbs in our common language into nouns. Neuro Linguistic Programing, which is known by its shorthand abbreviation as NLP, likes to ask if we can take something a noun claims to describe and put it in a wheelbarrow. If a noun is linked to an object, then said object has to have physical dimensions which would enable us to pick it up and carry it around. So if I'm talking about one of the rocks in my backyard, it is easy to at least imagine that said rock could be hoisted into a wheelbarrow and moved. However, we have turned a lot of verbs into nouns which leads us to some confusion. The highest expressions of the three brains won't pass the wheelbarrow test if we insist that they are nouns. I can't put creativity or courage or compassion into my wheelbarrow. As we sort out this issue we do run into some of the limits of common language. Creating is a verb but when we try to deal with compassion and courage we have language issues. I would propose that the verbal equivalent of compassion is loving and that courage has to be expressed, in English at least, as acting courageously. There is more to this than just linguistic tricks. It turns out the sophisticated brain scans modern neuroscience uses are telling us that our head-brains process data about objects and data about actions in different ways. If we are trying to process actions as if they were objects, we're not making the best use of our own resources and may be setting up some internal conflicts. I think you might see some of the implications here if you think with me a moment about the word "justice." As a noun, it won't pass the wheelbarrow test—which suggests that it is really a verb. Probably to talk about justice-ing wouldn't be very clear, but things get a lot clearer—fast—when we talk about doing justice or behaving in just ways. Another dimension of this is that the rock in my yard can sit there for years and still be a rock. Justice can't sit in my yard for years and still offer just treatment to anyone.

We'll come back to this in a moment. Many of you have probably heard Garrison Keillor's radio program titled "A Prairie Home Companion" and laughed over the News from Lake Wobegon—that little town where "all the women are strong, all the men are good looking, and all the children are above average." Of course, statistically speaking an entire group cannot be above average. Keillor has touched on a curious phenomenon about our society. We all want to be above average. This has led, especially in recent years, to all manner of techniques and self-help books which claim to help us raise our self-esteem. That seems like an innocent enough concept. However, in reality this is a competitive notion: I want my self-esteem to be higher than yours. Our students (and their parents) don't want to settle for "C" grade in school, because it is just average. The pressure on this has led to grade inflation. We have an epidemic of narcissistic personalities in this country. This creates a host of social problems, the least of which is not Donald Trump. If my self-esteem is threatened by an aspiring group of different folks, I may get frightened and that usually leads to anger. In case you haven't noticed, I'm an Old White Guy and the days of my ilk are numbered. That has fed anger, discrimination, racism, bigotry and violence. Involved in a lot of this is the ugly fascination with building self-esteem and defending ourselves against any threats to that precious self-esteem. This innocent-sounding term has become a trap in which a lot of our citizenry is caught.

Jack Kornfield, an American Buddhist teacher and psychologist, said "Most striking of all the parallels between Jesus and Buddha are those dealing with love." He tells a story about being at a Buddhist monastery on an island in the Mekong Delta in Vietnam during the Vietnam war. On this island is a 50-foot statue of Buddha and right next to it is a 50-foot statue of Jesus—the two figures have their arms around each other and are smiling broadly. That was quite an image against a backdrop of helicopter gunships engaged in battle. This is emblematic of the ancient wisdom that Soosalu and Oka are showing us is supported and validated by current scientific research.

Jesus said, "Do to others as you would have them do to you" while Buddha said, "Consider others as yourself." Both of these wise teachers are telling us that we need to use our self-concept as a key for understanding how to treat other people. We have neglected the essential truth in these statements: we may say that we ought to love others as we love ourselves, but I'm here to tell you that if I actually practiced that I might not always treat you very well because there are days when I am not kind or compassionate or loving toward myself! I have talked to folk about doing this and often I am told that this is a self-centered notion—being kind to one's self seems selfish to many. But now there comes some research that reveals that the people who have high levels of self-compassion treat others with more compassion than do folks who suffer from low levels of self-compassion and also from those who focus on high self-esteem. So it turns out that the way out of the trap of high self-esteem is to develop high self-compassioning. Self-compassionate people are very powerful and will demonstrate that power in very altruistic ways.

I read you a poem this morning written by Dawna

Markova. She is a well-known author, public speaker and an expert in the fields of learning, perception and asset-focus. The poem actually forms the basis for a book by the name *I Will Not Die an Unlived Life*. Hear again these words from the poem:

> *I choose to risk my significance;*
> *to live so that which came to me as seed*
> *goes to the next as blossom*
> *and that which came to me as blossom, goes on as*
>   *fruit.*
> *Fully alive.*

If we are going actually to turn compassion into a verb by relabeling it as love, if we are going to make justice an action instead of a powerless noun, if we are going to overcome the violence that besets this society, then we will have to do exactly what Ms. Markova invites us to do: we will have to risk our significance. Our three brains will not exhibit their highest expressions in the forms of creativity, compassion and courage unless we are willing to risk taking better care of ourselves, unless we are willing to risk all the junk we have acquired trying to demonstrate our high self-esteem.

We have been given life. We need to wonder exactly what would be involved if we acted on the idea that we want to pass on the seeds given to us as blossoms and pass on the blossoms given to us as fruit—for that is how life gets perpetuated, transmitted and ultimately transformed. We cannot live in fear of falling or catching fire. We must choose to allow our living to open us, make us less afraid, more accessible and to loosen our hearts.

Ancient literature talks about the hardening of the

heart as a metaphor for people being selfish, unjust and just plain mean. Having a loosened heart means letting love be at our Center and letting it spill all over the world. Even Old White Guys can learn to do this; I'm working on it. I invite you to join me in becoming a courageous community of people who risk their own significance to do justice, share compassion, welcome the rejected, and celebrate the essential goodness of each and every person on this planet.

Way-Walkers Watch Their Language and Respect the Power of the Word

PLACING NO OBSTACLES

Ash Wednesday, 2002. 2 Corinthians 5:20b-6:10; Matthew 6:1-6, 16-21

There is a magazine called "The Christian Century" which was founded at the beginning of the 20th century. The magazine is and has always been a witness to the liberal voice in the Church. It got its name from the belief its founders had just a little more than 100 years ago that the 20th century would see the ascendancy of liberal Christian ideas – in short that it would be *THE* Christian Century! Little did these optimistic liberals know about the evils that would ambush the forces of good in the 20th century. Almost any other name would probably have better described the 100 years to follow the turn of the last century. This historical incident, which has been much noted by critics and cynics alike, serves as an illustration of how we liberal Christians often seem to feel when approaching such things as Ash Wednesday and Lent and Good Friday. Last Sunday night, at the choral vespers, it was noted in the comments about the hymnody, that one particular hymn would seem pretty bloody to us even though it was standard fare a while back. We seem to want to clean up religion, assume that blood, violent death, betrayal, lying, cheating, etc. are features of primitive religion which tried out of people's fears to placate a hostile God. But in the process, we lose a lot. The so-called primitive faith, which was perhaps not quite so rational as ours, had ways of dealing with evil, knew that much of life was ambiguous, and was not so prone to elevating human beings to divine status.

The Gospel of Mark reports the baptism of Jesus. At the end of the baptism ritual Jesus hears a voice saying, "You are my son, the beloved, with you I am well pleased." But listen to what comes next: "The Spirit immediately threw him out into the wilderness." This was the beginning of a 40-day struggle in which Jesus would hammer out the fundamental teachings he would bring to the world. I very much doubt that any of us have spent nearly six weeks on a solitary retreat to grapple with the meaning of our lives. In tonight's epistle reading, Paul alludes to some of the personal privations he has endured to teach the Christian faith. He mentions hardships, calamities, beatings, imprisonments, riots, labors, sleepless nights, and hunger among the trials his work as an apostle has brought him. Probably none of us can come even close to having suffered such pain on account of our faith.

Has the world become more hospitable to faith in recent years that we do not have these kinds of experiences? I don't think it has. I think we have been content to ignore certain aspects of the struggle between good and evil and preferred a quest for a spirituality that comforts more than anything else. We don't want our spiritual life to take much time or effort. We probably could make money selling instant spirituality kits. We would like our spiritual experiences to be like a drive through car wash – you know where you just sit there and something or someone else cleans things up for us.

To encounter the living God is to be plunged into all the ambiguities of life. As the existentialist thinkers would put it, it is to live between being and nonbeing, to be on the boundary between life and death and to be aware that we are there. It is to refuse all palliatives, all painkillers, and all distractions that would encourage us to deny the reality of the boundary situation in which we really exist. To know the blessings of God's presence is to know the pain of the intense dilemma of having all our assumptions, preferences, and familiar customs challenged. For us liberal folk, it also means having to deal with the reality of the irrational, the power of evil, and the truth in the primitive.

Before Paul begins his list of tribulations he has endured, he states: "We are putting no obstacle in anyone's way, so that no fault may be found with our ministry." One of the challenges that I feel we must face as we reflect on how we describe what we believe is to ask ourselves: does the way we state our faith create obstacles for others? I suppose that Paul was referring, at least in part, to his refusal to make rules for the new Christians – rules to replace the old rules from Judaism that he was declaring invalid. If that is the case, then we must consider that Paul was refusing to do anything that would prevent the new Christians from coming up against the paradoxes and ambiguity of believing in the goodness of God in a world dominated by evil. Being thrown into the desert of struggle and temptation, for many of us, means that we have to ask ourselves if our tendency to prefer a rational, logical, and neat spirituality isn't an attempt on our part to avoid the reality of life on the boundary, to deny that the forces of nothingness intrude into our neatly-ordered lives.

One of the major temptations we face is the temptation to reduce spirituality to knowledge to which we can give consent. Belief is, by definition, about committing to that which we cannot necessarily prove. Knowledge to which we can consent is, no matter how complicated the explanation, a stating of the obvious. It is not without significance that our belief system is called The Christian Faith and not The Christian Facts.

On your behalf, I have been doing some hospital visiting in the last few weeks. I haven't really done that for about 20 years on any regular basis. On the one hand, I am amazed at all the technological innovations and at dramatic advances in drugs and various procedures. On the other hand, I find that the dilemmas have not changed at all. There are still complex choices about treatment, quality of life, when to die, etc. There are still limits to human knowledge and mysteries we cannot explain. There in the intensive care ward, amidst the wiring and tubing and monitors, is that intrusion of nothingness into neatly-ordered lives. There people are forced to deal with the limitations of human life and their inability to control as much as they would like.

Jesus goes into the desert because he must. He is thrown there by his involvement with God. There, he must wrestle with the meaning of his call. Sunday we will read a very distilled account of what happened there – but that is about the outcome, not about the process. The process involves intentionally abiding on the boundary between life and death, between being and nothingness, until one understands who one is and who one is not. The gospel lesson for tonight brings us Jesus' own teaching about living on this boundary. He asks us not to make a big public deal out of our private struggle. It was apparently a pious custom of his time and place to display ones attempts to deepen prayer life, to give alms, to turn away from materialism through fasting. However, Jesus probably recognized that this practice of displaying piety led to false piety – a piety of show and not a piety of substance. Jesus himself experienced the desert of temptation without show. He took no one along. He seems later to have told the results of the experience to his disciples, but the process was his own private struggle.

Keeping the struggle private seems to be part of the process of putting no obstacles in others' paths. Jesus' whole ministry was a time of sharing what he had discovered and was discovering. He did not himself suggest a particular path to follow. He endorsed certain qualities of life (like humility) and certain actions (like forgiveness) as helpful in one's search for a closer relationship with God, but he clearly left it to us to discover what path we each need to walk through the desert. However, when he said, "follow me," he was clearly inviting us to walk the path through the desert, through the sufferings we might have to endure, and on to the victory of a life triumphant over death.

This day is not really about ashes or public displays of piety: it is about making a commitment to follow after Jesus and walk into the deserts in our own world and to struggle in those dry, hard, un-nurturing places with the boundary issues in our time, with the places where love and hate, peace and war, plenty and want, safety and fear, health and disease intersect. Give yourself time during the next 40 days to discover where the threat of nothingness intrudes into your ordered life. Let yourself feel the presence of that boundary and let that boundary help redefine who you are and who you are not and thus discover anew what you must do and what you ought not to do.

TOXIC SPIRITUALITY
July 29, 2007. Genesis 18:16-33; Luke 11:1-13

This is a day of interactive computer games. This is also the day in which the TV news programs keep telling us what's coming up later in the program. This congregation has lots of folk in it who are interested in new data. So, before we get too far into this sermon, we're going to engage in an interactive experience to generate some data which will be referenced later. Maybe this will help us all to feel right at home. I invite all who are able to stand up. Now hold your hands out thusly [extend arms with hands palms up, full arm's length from the body and forming a 90 degree angle] and look up. While maintaining that posture, say out loud "Alleluia." Now, in the same position, say "Woe is me." Thank you. Now please sit down. Please fold your hands in the traditional posture of prayer and bow your heads. You may also close your eyes. Now say "Alleluia." Now say "Woe is me." Thank you. More about this later.

Our first Scripture lesson this morning tells part of the story of Abraham. By comparison with many other Biblical figures, Abraham's story takes up a lot of space— about 14 chapters of Genesis—about one fourth of the book. In my Bible that's 16 pages and the accounts of creation only take up three pages! Abraham, known in the beginning as Abram, gets all over the Middle East—he starts out in Ur of the Chaldees—somewhere near Bagdad, hangs out around Damascus for a while, goes on down to Egypt and then back north. He isn't always truthful—told the king of Egypt that his wife was actually his sister and that led the king of Egypt to add Sarah to his harem for a while until he found out the truth. I often wonder what Sarah thought about that! God kept promising Abraham a son, but that still had not happened when Abraham was almost 30 years older than I am now. Abraham however, didn't just sit around. He tried to force the issue. He protested to God who kept repeating the promise. Finally, at his wife's suggestion he sired a son by their maid. Eventually of course he and Sarah had Isaac. But that takes us beyond today's reading. The cities of Sodom and Gomorrah had a reputation of being really bad places and the story is that they were destroyed. But God and Abraham have a discussion about this. God initiates the conversation and indicates to Abraham that he's going to have to do something about those towns. But Abraham, with great respect, but firm resolution, takes God on and the two of them have this session of Ethics 101—something like a professor and his students at the college coffee shop. Abraham wants to know if God is going to wipe out some good people in order to punish the bad people—and Abraham keeps changing the number. What if there are 50 good people? What if there are 45? Well how about 40? What if there are 30 good folks there? Well how about 20? What will you do if there are 10 good people there? Each time Abraham changes the number, God agrees that the cities will be spared for these good people. When this discussion had run its course, God and Abraham each went their own way.

Abraham is no paragon of virtue. He is a nomadic chieftain who behaves much like every other nomadic chieftain of the time. He is skeptical of this God who keeps playing "deal or no deal" with him. Having a son was a primary goal of men in that time. God promised that son but hadn't yet delivered on the promise when Abraham undertook to discuss ethics with God. This discussion happens right after Sarah had been caught laughing at God for what she thought was a foolish promise—that she could get pregnant at her advanced age. Historians of religion speak of God as a fearful and fascinating mystery—well in this particular period of human history God was experienced and thought of mostly as a fearful mystery—a power that unleashed volcanoes, killed the Egyptians' first born, drowned the Egyptian army in the Red sea—stuff like that. So here is not-so-righteous, sometimes deceitful Abraham teaching ethics to God Almighty—and doing so without showing any fear. And the story ends with the two just going their own ways. I find this to be an interesting model of piety—one that is at odds with more recent history.

Look with me a moment at the gospel lesson. Here we have Jesus offering some teaching about prayer. Luke's version of the Lord's Prayer is quite short. It just starts: "Father, hallowed be your name." No decorations. It asks for bread, forgiveness of sins, and that we be spared the time of trial. This version presumes that we forgive others, it *says* we forgive others. Unlike the version in Matthew, there is no conditional "forgive us as we forgive." There is no fancy ending to this prayer. This clearly seems to be an example of prayer, not necessarily the prayer for all time. Then Jesus moves on to tell a story about how persistence pays off and follows that up by saying: "Ask, and it will be given to you, search and you will find, knock and it will be opened."

Then he tops off this teaching by stating that if human beings know how to give good things to their children, so God will give the Holy Spirit to those who ask. Jesus portrays a style of piety that asks, seeks and knocks. No passivity here—lots of energetic involvement.

But between the days of Abraham and Jesus and now, came a period of time we often call the Middle Ages. It was a time of castles, kings, and knights. And the word "Lord" became an important part of the English language. When the Bible got translated into English, the word "Lord" showed up all over the place. In many Old Testament passages where we find the word "Lord" in our translations, the Hebrew word thus translated is really the name of God—Yahweh. That's with whom Abraham was debating ethics. The medieval king held the power of life and death over his serfs. They bowed low, averting their eyes, when the king came by. They were taught to grovel in the presence of the king—who was their Lord. And all of this bowing, groveling, begging with eyes averted, got moved right into the Church. God became Lord. Even Jesus (who was called Sir by his disciples) became Lord. And the faithful began to grovel. And the idea that we could have an ethical debate with God went right out the window. How dare we be so presumptuous? We could not possibly act like Abraham and say to God: "What are you thinking?"

Now, I promised we would look at the data that I think that little exercise with which we began generated. My hunch is that it was easier to say "Alleluia" when you were on your feet and easier to say "Woe is me" when you had your head bowed. A few years ago someone whose name I can't find wrote a book that warned us that our bodies listen to and react to everything we say. I would suggest that this is also true in the reverse direction—that our minds pay attention to our posture. I have found it important when working with people who have difficulty being assertive, to get them up on their feet, shoulders back, chin up and speaking forcefully. It doesn't matter what they say—they can simply announce their name, but doing so with shoulders back and chin up, improves their feelings of confidence.

The standing position that I asked you to take is actually the posture used by early Christians at prayer. No groveling, no hanging of heads, no averting of the eyes. Yet I suspect that today very few Christians anywhere stand up and spread their arms when the pastor says, "Let us pray." If our piety leads us to physical groveling and averting our eyes, then the attitude that behavior fosters will turn around and affect our theology. I know a Lutheran pastor who at least in private refers to the resulting theology as "worm theology." I have never asked him if he has gone public with that phrase. How dare we ask, seek and knock? Who are we to engage God in ethical debate or question the traditions of the church? Such theology centers on what's wrong with us and condemns the celebration of our gifts as a display of pride (which of course is sinful). That feeds the idea that we are deficient and turns around and sends us to pray to the feudal Lord for the stuff we don't have. If truth be told, I think we pray for a lot of stuff.

But what does Jesus say God will give those who ask, search and knock? He says we will get the Holy Spirit. No stuff. We get the inspiration, the support, the teaching of the Spirit. We get invited into a relationship with God that

144

parallels that enjoyed by Abraham who felt free to debate ethics and a lot of other things with God. We get invited into a relationship in which we are respected, not beaten down, in which our gifts are appreciated, not discounted and we get invited into a relationship that helps us make sense of things.

Scripture actually says very little about the Holy Spirit. Theologians across the centuries, to their credit, have said little about the Holy Spirit. At least we have not dragged this idea down into the gutters of worm theology. What I think we can say about the Holy Spirit and the fact that God has promised this Spirit to those who ask, seek and knock, is that the Holy Spirit is God with us, God present. Here is a profound assurance that we are not alone. We ask, we seek, we knock and because we need, God will be present with us and help us make sense of things.

Bradford Keeney has studied and written a lot about the shaking traditions in religious practices around the world. He has written about Shakers and Quakers, about Native Americans, and the indigenous peoples of the Caribbean. In a recent book, he has focused on the Kalahari Bushmen of Namibia in Africa. Keeney looks at the shaking of the tribal shamans as manifestations of the Spirit. He talks about how the shaking and quaking that once infused the religion of the Shakers and the Quakers as well as others eventually died out. The Shakers have all but died out and there certainly isn't much quaking at a Quaker meeting anymore. Keeney says this: "When a mystery is reduced to convenient explanation, whether religious, psychological or scientific, it loses its ability to evoke spirited expression.

After all, when you think that you understand what is going on, you take out the mystery. More accurately, you lose your relationship with mystery and the feeling of awe that accompanies it. Without mystery, there is less room for inspiration. Things have been explained away, and prediction rather than spontaneity now rules . . . ." (p. 111, Keeney, *Shaking Medicine*).

The imposition of the medieval worm theology on our piety takes the mystery away. When Jesus promises the Holy Spirit, he is not promising predictability. When Jesus is talking about prayer, he is not talking about a monologue between a groveling serf and a capricious Lord. I think Jesus evokes the tradition of Abraham. Calling God "Father" as Jesus did puts people into a familial relationship with God. When Jesus urges his disciples to ask, seek, and knock he is inviting them to take chances, to wonder what might be discovered, to open themselves to being invaded by an unpredictable and uncontrollable spirit that will surprise us, bust up our categories, amaze us, disturb us and show us unexpected ways to make sense of things—all the while assuring us that we are not alone.

Spiritual practices that would have us grovel and worm theology that discounts us, create a Toxic Spirituality that poisons the well-springs of the human spirit. How can people who can't love themselves love anyone else? Abraham takes very seriously the idea that we are made in the image of God. Nowhere in Scripture does it say that God made cheap imitation images of God's self. Nowhere does it say that we are discount versions. We are made in the image of Love—created to love—everyone, including ourselves. We are invited to be co-creators of the kingdom of God, making love alive everywhere. Authentic Christian spiritual practice is not groveling, not bowing before some medieval vision of God as the royal despot, it is not a way of thinking and acting that makes despicable worms of people created in the image of God. Authentic Christian spiritual practice is asking, seeking, knocking on every possible door that we may be engaged with God in making sense of things in ways that help people experience the love of God. The God of Abraham and Jesus invites us to participate in a process of asking, seeking, and knocking that opens doors and allows the Spirit of Love to flourish in our midst. We are invited into a dialog. Let the conversation begin.

MESSING WITH THE METAPHORS THAT MESS WITH US

Nov 25, 2007. Psalm 46; Colossians 1:11-20; Luke 23:33-43.

Metaphors are interesting and important things. We use them all the time to explain things. They are especially important when our experiences are hard to put into words. We look for common experiences to use in the metaphor construction. We might tell someone that the pain we had in an odd place in our body was like a toothache because we suppose that nearly everyone has had a toothache at one time or another. We might tell someone that the concert was as much fun as watching paint dry— because we know that almost no one would like to spend time watching fresh paint dry. I don't like roller coasters, so if I told you that something was as scary as a roller coaster, if you like those things, then we wouldn't communicate very well, because you might be thinking about all the fun you've had doing that. Once we create a metaphor that applies to a certain situation, especially if that metaphor gains wide acceptance, then the metaphor begins to shape our perception. For example, we sometimes use the phrase "a walk in the park" to describe something that is easy. Or we say that something was as easy as "falling off a log" when in fact the number of people in this room who have fallen off a log in the past few days is probably rather small. Obviously, these metaphors break down when experience contradicts the meaning of the metaphor. When I was a graduate student in Chicago many years ago, a walk in the park was anything but safe or easy—I had a classmate who tried it, got assaulted and had his jaw broken. One also has to have some experience with logs in order to really appreciate that metaphor. If one student tells another that the math test was a walk in the park, the other student may decide she doesn't have to study—unless, of course, she had my classmate's perception of parks.

Metaphor is the language of faith. In the reading from Colossians today, we find reference to the invisible God. In order even to talk about this invisible God, we must resort to the language of metaphor. Sometimes the metaphors are one word, a word like "father" packs a whole lot of meaning into a small space, as does "mother." Sometimes the metaphors are more elaborate. Psalm 46 speaks of a city that is the habitation of God—so the city is safe. Today is named in many churches as Christ the King Sunday. Some churches refer to it as the Feast of Christ the King. It invokes an ancient and powerful metaphor: the image of the King. However, there are a whole bunch of problems with this. I wonder how many of you personally know a king or have even met one? For most of us this conjures up either some history that we once studied or perhaps something fantastic—like the Lion King. I imagine there are a lot of children who could identify with that image. As I started thinking about this, I began to imagine changing the language: how about Christ the CEO? Or Christ the Secretary General? Or Christ the president? Somehow that doesn't do it for me. Those titles would make me a whole lot less interested in Christ. My personal perceptions of royalty, based only on what I see on TV or read in the paper about European royalty, is that kings (and also queens) are pretty irrelevant. Even royal wealth begins to pale when one learns that the author of the Harry Potter books has more money than the queen of England. Then of course, if we accept the metaphor, it begins to shape our perception: if I think Kings are irrelevant, then Christ the King must be irrelevant too. If the ruler of the universe is a king, well then that means the ruler is male—and for some of us that is not good news.

So, if we are going to deal with the metaphors of faith and find ways to use contemporary realities and experiences to speak of faith, then we have to do some digging. What is going on in these ancient texts? What is to be found here that speaks to us? What might tie all three of today's readings together and would that help us?

The Christ of whom Colossians speaks is, of course, Jesus. The writer of Colossians tells us that Jesus is the image of the invisible God. If we stay away from imposing the trappings of monarchy on this Jesus, then we start to understand God as a loving, healing, and truth-telling teacher who stands by what he (or she) says. Most of us have an abundance of experiences with teachers and we can readily imagine a perfect teacher—whether we actually had one or not. Also, in this passage is a line about enabling us to share in the inheritance of the saints of light. That seems a bit foreign to us as well. Apparently, the phrase "saints of light" made sense to first century people. When we begin to unpack this, one of the startling things which pops up is that the Greek for "enabling us to share" is actually a word which means that God has "found us to be enough." Now that might catch your attention. How many Americans in one way or another believe that they are not enough—not smart enough, clever enough, powerful enough, attractive enough, political enough—you name it and either you yourself or someone you know well will say, "I'm not enough." I was a bit astounded when my granddaughter over a year ago when she was still in sixth grade, told me how she needed certain things in her resume so she would look good enough to the college admissions folks. That memory came back to me this weekend. I was watching a football game and here came a commercial from the National Football League telling us that we had to teach children to play—apparently, we have instilled so much concern in the kids about being enough that many of them don't even know how to play! Jesus comes saying: "You are enough, just the way you are."

The crucifixion narrative in Luke can be summed up in Jesus' saying to what history has called the penitent thief: "Today you will be with me in paradise." The word "paradise" only shows up three times in the New Testament—that might surprise some people. It seems to mean a place that transcends present reality. No, it is not a park or garden or gold city with pearl gates! It is a term that simply means to be present with God in a way that transcends present reality—and can include a mystical experience resulting from deep meditation. However, we have had an abundance of images of paradise dumped on us—whether you talk about the images of heaven as a city with golden streets or that male paradise of some Eastern religions that is filled with virgins. So as soon as we hear the word "paradise," we are off to the races—and probably coming up with something like a physical place called heaven by some where one can meet and greet old friends and relatives. If our minds are bogged down with such imagery, then we will miss what Jesus is saying to this thief.

Psalm 46: "God is our refuge and strength, a very present help in trouble." Surprisingly this God of refuge is in a *city*. There it is: the common thread amongst these different readings. We will not be alone. God will welcome us into a community of the servants of God, because God has declared that we are enough. The thief who is killed on the cross will not be alone; the folk who seek the God of refuge will not be alone. The issue is not about paradise or kings—it is about the assurance that we shall not be alone. The invisible God who is at the heart of all of reality wants to be in relationship with us.

There is a school in contemporary psychology that goes by the name "positive psychology." The people who are involved with this tell us we have to start to understand the human condition by realizing that the most fundamental fear we all share is the fear of being alone. That is why words like "rejection," "abandonment," "inadequate," "estrangement," and "not enough" can strike terror in the heart of our being. We know that people who live alone do not live as long as do people who live in a relationship with another human being.

Of course, first century people to whom Colossians and Luke were written had had it up to here with kings. Every monarchy they experienced was corrupt, ruthless, uncaring, and more than willing to exploit everyone to get what the king wanted—even to the point of killing people. Perhaps it would be easy for them to imagine a perfect monarchy, a kind and benevolent king, because it would be such a contrast to their experience.

A couple of weeks ago, I heard a Saginaw psychiatrist speak about how sick and crazy our society is. Among the things he talked about was the dearth of men who are interested in teaching boys how to be men. He talked about the ancient Native American rites of passage which helped boys become men. I remembered hearing a Hawaiian man a couple of years ago describe how dads and uncles would get involved in a rite of passage for the boys in Hawaii that enabled the boy to kill a wild pig. The pig's head was left by the roadside as a silent testimony to a young man's maturing. While the Hawaiian government has outlawed that practice, it still goes on because of its importance. What the psychiatrist didn't say was that we have spent so much effort getting the males among us to believe they don't need anyone that we now have boys who can't figure out how to become men--and some of the boys are 40 years old. We have made an idol of the person who needs no one. That shows up in all sorts of odd ways: we have an energy crisis and it would be greatly helped if we had a good, local public transportation system. But since we don't need anyone, we'll all buy cars and drive ourselves and public transportation falls apart from lack of use, and the greenhouse gases build up.

We have this rather strange paradox: we are all afraid of being alone and yet we are all strongly insistent that we don't need anybody. I know people who are afraid to ask for the help they obviously need because it is a sign of weakness. To say, "I need" is, to them, to say "I am not enough, I am defective." To us it might be a very exciting image to see ourselves as being welcomed as we are into a community of people who follow the Teacher from Nazareth.

I titled this sermon "Messing with the Metaphors that Mess with Us." We have been more profoundly shaped by the metaphors thrust upon us than we want to admit. The metaphor of Christ the King, whatever else it says, says we are the serfs. Serfs are people at the bottom of the structure of the society governed by monarchy. They have no rights, they can't speak unless spoken to, everything they have is subject to seizure. So, if we are not careful, the King metaphor promotes worm theology in which people see themselves as worthless—in fact people who see themselves as not enough. If we start changing the metaphors, then we open the door for personal change. Some theologians have really shaken up the faith community by talking about God as Mother. If we mess with the metaphors, then we mess with our self-concepts and actually might discover that there are better ways to see ourselves than we knew. We don't have to be alone: the love of God is about being welcomed into a community of love—and I personally would like to say that community exists both here and hereafter.

I invite you to mess with the metaphors—and to start by rejecting the idea that a metaphor is a concrete reality. Heaven was described as a really splendid place filled with material riches and that may have appealed to an impoverished society, but it doesn't do much for me when I can't imagine that I really want anything for Christmas. Heaven originally seems to have meant "where God lives" and if God lives everywhere, then let's get rid of pearly gates and gold streets. If you mess with the metaphors, then you get to mess with your own theology and to begin to respond to St. Paul's invitation to "work out your own salvation with fear and trembling." Your faith is so important to you that you can't trust anyone else to construct it for you.

The metaphors we use will mess with us. If we use metaphors that belong to another era or another culture, those metaphors will keep us in a state of confusion. However, if we mess with the metaphors, challenge them, rework them, find different ways to construct a language that points to the invisible God in ways that help people answer deep questions about the meaning of life, then we will have metaphors that will influence us in helpful, creative ways and we will discover that we can feel invited to be in relationship with the invisible God who promises us we will not be alone.

WATCH YOUR LANGUAGE
October 30, 2016. 1 John 4:1-21; John 1:1-5

This week is anniversary number 499 of Martin Luther's challenging the church of his time to make changes. He put the challenges into a list of topics for debate that is called his 95 theses and the story has it that he nailed the theses to the castle door in Wittenberg, Germany to get the attention of the Archbishop. The blows of his hammer against that door signaled the beginning of what we know as the Reformation. One of the reasons that Luther's efforts succeeded where others had failed is that he and his followers were soon able to use the recently-developed printing press. While the 95 theses were written in Latin, they were soon translated into German so that they could be read more widely. In terms of the impact on life, the printing press of Luther's day might be compared to the Internet of our day.

One of the first books to be printed on that brand-new printing press was a Bible and that began a process which eventually put the Bible into nearly everyone's hands. In fact, there are Bible societies in many countries that have a goal of widely distributing Scripture. Although a large number of people in our country profess to be biblically literate, many people seem to forget that the Bible as we have it was not originally written in English, not even in King James English. Hebrew Scriptures were written, well, in Hebrew and what we call the New Testament is a collection of early church documents written in Greek. The challenge of translating one language into another is very complex. One simple illustration of the difficulty can be found in the fact that in Greek there are three words (eros, philia, and agape) which are all translated into English by one word and that word is "love." One of the challenges of translating Hebrew Scripture into English is that not only is there more than one word for "God" in the Hebrew, but also the fact that Jewish tradition forbids the pronunciation of words for God so they have often been rendered in English as "Lord," which was originally used as a circumlocution to avoid pronouncing the literal name of God.

Much of the language that we use to state and discuss theological concepts is derived from the struggle to translate material from Hebrew and Greek into English. Of course, there is more than just the linguistic difficulty, there is also a collection of historical problems. One of the criticisms made of the King James Bible is that the language used in that book was already out of date when it was first published. Then of course there is the struggle to express spiritual experiences in words. Some of those experiences, such as Moses' encounter with God, probably predate the use of written language. It is widely believed that there is an oral tradition of spiritual story-telling that precedes the transmogrifying of experience into written format.

One of the lasting consequences of the Protestant reformation was the development of the concept of the priesthood of all believers. Among other things, this is the insistence that everyone can and should do theology—in fact, we all do it all the time. We need and want explanations of things and, so we try hard to develop explanations that will help us deal with the reality. Dr.

Andrew Newberg tells us that his brain research indicates that there is a part of the brain that insists we make sense of things, which is one of the tasks and challenges of theology. Most of the time that works okay—although I've had my problems making sense of one of the candidates currently running for president. However, if we're going to be people of faith who take theologizing seriously, it would be helpful to have some different ways of thinking about things. Perhaps a different vocabulary would be helpful. So, in the spirit of the Reformation, I want to offer you some suggestions and perhaps start a new chapter in spiritual story-telling.

When I was a little boy (I was told by reliable sources that I actually was once—although it was in the last century), there were a few adults around who frequently told me to "watch my language." My grandfather, who was an avid gardener, —he raised a gazillion strawberries every summer and grew mountains of potatoes—had a couple of gasoline-powered machines: one was a cultivator, the operation of which was a physical fitness workout because it was so heavy and a lawn mower, which I was allowed to operate. However, on a summer morning when I was at their house, eager to start mowing the lawn, my grandmother kept me inside until she heard both machines running for fear that during the start-up phase I would learn some language from my grandfather that would bring that sharp "watch your language" directive if I dared repeat it. Fortunately, many of my language-watching elders did not live long enough to see those dreaded, forbidden words enter common, everyday discourse. We all probably share some similar version of this story and those stories all point to how important language is.

With that as background, I want to talk with you about something called Neuro Linguistic programming. Neuro Linguistic Programming is an approach to communication, personal development, and psychotherapy created by Richard Bandler and John Grinder in California in the 1970s. One of the issues which Neuro Linguistic Programming invites us to consider is the tendency we have had to turn verbs into nouns. Thus, living becomes life, loving becomes love, creating becomes creator or creation, and so on. Neuro Linguistic devotees are correct in that when we nominalize something (that is turn a verb into a noun), we start thinking about it and describing it in various objective terms—like length, breadth, depth, height, width, weight, size. Clearly those are concepts that don't fit verbs. There is even some evidence from the modern research phenomenon of brain scanning that nouns and verbs are processed in different parts of the brain. One question this raises is, if the brain processes something naturally in one way, like seeing a motion, and is being forced by changes in language to process it another way by describing the "motion" as if it were an event, what kinds of results might be forthcoming? At the very least this could promote confusion; at a deeper level, it might interfere with the development of a coherent view of reality.

There are a number of accounts in the Bible of people having encounters with God. These descriptions really are about peoples' experience with an energy they could not explain. If we watch the transformation of these stories, we see in many cases that the word "Lord" is used to represent this energy. "Lord" is really a medieval term and is about kings, queens, princes and princesses—about people who have royal power over lots of non-royal (or maybe un-royal) folks. Thus, we are led into a centuries-old tradition of describing God as an object—like a king or a wise old man (if we throw in a bit of sexism). I don't believe God is an object for us to manipulate. So, what happens if we think of God as a verb, as a kind of energy in action? We need a new word and the word I am proposing is to refer to Divine reality as "Godding." I think it has some possibilities because it implies action and gets us away from old pictures of kings and queens and their ilk.

Another component of our thinking is our belief that every "thing" must have a beginning and an ending. If we encounter existing objects, we suppose they are in the middle between beginning and ending. This is probably a projection of our experience. We believe that everything that exists had a beginning and thus will eventually have an end. There seems to be plenty of evidence that this is true. For example, I suppose that I had a beginning, although I don't have any memory of not being or of starting to be. I suppose that I will have an end since I have known people to die. I suppose that I will die someday, although I can't prove this and if I die, I may not know that I did. Thus, I conclude that I am in the middle of my life (or late-middle if you prefer). That seems obvious enough, yet it has some difficulties. All the cells that compose my physical manifestation have died and been replaced many times. I have also added a fat cell or two. I am not physically the same person I was 20 or 30 or 50 years ago. But despite that, my identity or personality seems to endure—people still recognize me and so far, I can still identify my own reflection in the mirror. What if that which makes me a person is non-physical, what if instead of being an object I am an action, a verb? Maybe this physical phenomenon you see standing here is energy "personing"? When someone dies, we say that their body decomposes—why don't we describe being alive as a process of composing? This would make it easier for us to see ourselves as a work in progress and we could lay claim to the sentiment that people shouldn't be disappointed with us because Godding isn't finished with us yet.

Because of our fascination with beginnings and endings, we have tended to describe the universe as having a beginning and an ending. There are lots of theories about the beginning—with both the Biblical accounts of creation and the idea of a Big Bang being well known. But there are people in the quantum physics field who are challenging all that. I can't begin to fathom their mathematics, but I am intrigued by the idea that the universe is always. Maybe it is energy universing.

The picture on the front of the bulletin today is one of a star imploding. Stars apparently come and go in the universing so maybe they are actually energy starring and not just objects in the sky. It is fascinating to me to understand that these imploding stars scatter something called stardust across space and it is estimated that because of this reality, our physical bodies are 93% stardust. We are more intimately a part of the universing than we usually admit.

We church folk have a long history of believing in the essential rottenness of people. Theologically it is called original sin—a concept that goes back to a 4th century man named Augustine, or in the Roman church, St. Augustine. This idea that we were created perfect and screwed it up early on has been quite popular. Original sin is often portrayed as having something to do with sex—which is about the kind of theory you might get from a monk who had at least two concubines and was engaged to an 11-year-old girl before his conversion to Christianity. It has so appealed to people wanting explanations of things that no one seems to have noticed that if we were created perfect, we could not possibly have screwed up. More recently, some theologians have called this belief into question and asked us instead to believe in original goodness that got compromised by a certain selfishness inherent in the drive to survive. My wife and I have just come back from visiting grandchildren and celebrating the sixth birthday of our twin grandsons. As I watched them, laughed with them, played on the floor until my bones protested, I could not imagine that they are essentially rotten.

There are some researchers trying to understand some of the basic realities of human life and they think they are discovering that loving is an essential part of human life—and in some ways of non-human life. That stardust seems to come with some inherent characteristics, characteristics which challenge old Augustine's ideas. These same researchers are talking about the importance of loving and of our allowing ourselves to conform to the inherent reality of our personing in a Godding universing by focusing on being more loving in all our living. Of course, they are acknowledging what the major religions of the world have known this for eons. One of my favorite current cartoons shows Jesus and Buddha each floating on a cloud above a warring, fighting earth and one says to the other "Which one of us needs to go down there again and explain about love?"

What if each of us as a personing is the vortex of a swirling of Godding energy that thereby creates a portal in the universing through which loving flows into the world? The beginning of the gospel lesson this morning talks about Godding as the Word—or perhaps we should say, "the speaking." While it is not exactly an accurate translation, we are on solid ground if we render the opening of this gospel as, "Godding is Loving manifesting." This clump of stardust that we know as ourselves is being enlivened by the Godding energy all around us. Our epistle reading this morning contains this phrase: ". . . love is from God; everyone who loves is born of God and knows God." We are invited to be doorways through which loving flows into the world.

I realize that one of the problems I have as a retired preacher is that when I do get invited to preach, I tend to go a bit overboard and try to put too much into one sermon. I am aware that I may have been doing a bit of that this morning. However, I want very much to challenge all of us to watch our language and ask ourselves if we are guilty of trying to promote a faith trapped in a three-story universe to a culture that lives in a quantum physics world. I decided to offer an opportunity for us to see how it might feel if we modified a common expression of faith and incorporated some different language into a familiar hymn. As I worked on this, I looked up the history of the man who wrote the original words. His name was John Newton and he was an

Anglican clergyman in the late 18th century. Newton was a rebel and got into all kinds of trouble. He was involved in the slave trade for a while but quit that when he was 30. The Anglican church almost didn't ordain him, not because of the slave trade connection, but because he was known to consort with the Methodists! As soon as I became aware of his rebel nature, I decided he probably would be fine with a rewrite of his most famous lyrics. With Jim Hohmeyer's help, we will give you an opportunity shortly to sing "Amazing Grace, the Godding Version." When we do, please notice that there are two rather critical elements in this version. One is the use of the word "Godding" and the other is the deliberate effort to value the person as essentially good. There is implied here a certain coherence between ourselves and Godding.

If we continue to be influenced by the efforts to turn verbs into nouns, we are going to be tempted to see Godding as an object. Since we can also manipulate objects, we will be tempted to manipulate Godding. We see an abundance of that approach to Godding as people insist on asking Godding to help them in specific, objective ways and even worse to give their enemies trouble. I watch professional athletics some and I see players after a successful play look up to the sky and offer gestures of thanksgiving. These people seem to be caught in the nominalizing trap and continuing to think of Godding as the old man just above the sky—which in that scheme of things is the upside-down crystal bowl separating the water above the flat earth from the water below the flat earth. If we objectify something, then it becomes part a classification of assembled things and we will find ourselves comparing one thing with another—like comparing cars or houses or TV sets or computers before we choose the best thing. In doing this, we have denied the transcendence of Godding and in the process suggested that we ourselves may be equal to the highest form of reality. If I had to believe that I am the highest form of reality, that realization would lead me to overwhelming despair and hopelessness, or perhaps to the worst case of narcissism the world has ever seen. Interestingly enough, both reactions would lead to lonely isolation. Objectifying Godding makes Godding inadequate just as J. B. Phillips told us over 60 years ago in his classic book, "Your God is Too Small."

I suspect most of us are familiar with the notion that how we talk to ourselves about ourselves influences our moods. If we tell ourselves we are not okay, we will start to believe we are not and that will lead to acting as if we are not okay. However, if we tell ourselves we are wonderful and amazing, we will start believing that and will soon be doing wonderful and amazing things. There is plenty of evidence that validates this. So, what happens if we develop a new vocabulary about our faith and our spiritual lives? You may not be particularly attracted to my suggestions and that's just fine. You can use my suggestions to stimulate your own thinking and that may very well lead to a deeper, more realistic and more supportive spirituality which you express in your own words. There is an inherent blessing in the dictum to "watch your language" and you will find the effort very worthwhile. If we would all do that, then we'll soon be initiating a fresh round of spiritual story-telling that will draw us closer together and inspire us all.

These words to "Amazing Grace, the Godding Version" were printed in the bulletin for that worship service.

Amazing Grace, how sweet the sound
That saved a prize like me
My self became a gem newfound
Much valued, now I see.
'Twas grace that taught my heart to sing,
And grace my fears relieved.
What profound joy did that grace bring,
When I first felt received.

Through many dangers toils and snares
I have already come
'Tis grace has brought me safe thus far
And grace will lead me home.
Godding has promised good to me
Whose word my hope secures.
Godding will be my shield and joy
As long as life endures.

When we've been home ten thousand years
Bright shining as the sun
We've no less days to Godding praise
Then when we first begun.
Amazing Grace, how sweet the sound
That saved a prize like me
My self became a gem newfound
Much valued, now I see.

166

COMMITTED WITNESSES
July 9, 2017. Revelation 3:14-22; Matthew 11:16-19, 28-30

We Americans are great spectators. We willingly and eagerly fill up stadia all across the country on a regular basis to watch baseball, football, basketball, soccer, hockey, tennis, and more being played. The people trying to revive the city of Detroit have been building stadia all over the place. The Tigers are in a relatively new stadium, the Lions have a fine facility next door, and this fall the Redwings and the Pistons will bring hockey and basketball downtown. Each and every team has a variety of fans. Some try to never miss a game while others watch in rather detached ways. I like to watch the Tigers play baseball—but I will often give up on the game if they're losing and sometimes if they are (rarely) winning by a large margin. While there are certainly some folks who are enthusiastic supporters of sports teams in and out of season, most of us who watch are rather detached. We chat with other people during the games, we walk away to attend to chores, to answer the phone, to attend to our smart-phones, or perhaps to eat a meal or go to a meeting. I notice that the teams offer television advertising during the game urging us to get more involved by actually buying tickets and going to the stadium to see the games. But these ads never appeal to my loyalty or exploit my devotion to the team; instead, they offer special deals often involving food or beer. The people who write these commercials want to exploit my selfish interests but not my commitment. They are content with me being a spectator and just watching the games.

We were in Italy for a conference last month and combined that with some travels about the area. We visited the Coliseum in Rome—actually it was the second time I've seen this ancient stadium. We also saw the Circus Maximus where the ancient Romans held chariot races. There were theaters all over the ancient world where people could be spectators. So, the spectating process seems to have been with us for a long time. Our reading from the book of Revelation this morning talks about a town in Asia Minor (modern-day Turkey) called Laodicea. There are ruins of a huge hillside amphitheater there where it appears the ancient folk held chariot races. This city was an important and prosperous place during the time when Christianity was getting its start in the world. The Jewish citizens of Laodicea sent annual contributions to the temple in Jerusalem that in today's money would be about $500,000. One of the citizens of the place, which had a medical school and a thriving wool trade, built a lot of fancy buildings there and upon his death bequeathed the equivalent of about $110,000,000 to the city. When the place was wrecked in 60 CE by an earthquake, the citizens refused any help from the Roman emperor and rebuilt the city using their own resources. I thought I'd share this with you to help you get a feel for what was going on when the church was getting underway. The writer of Revelation accuses the citizens of this place (or at least the church there) of being lukewarm. He says that they are neither hot nor cold. In fact, we might translate that word "lukewarm" as tepid. We are accustomed to drinking a variety of beverages either hot or cold--we can order tea or coffee either way--but I have never seen a menu offering me tepid tea. Apparently the rather well-off Christians of Laodicea were tepid when it came to making useful and lasting commitments.

In our gospel lesson this morning, Jesus tees off on his audience. He tells them that his cousin John (known as John the Baptist or John the Weird) showed up as a Nazerite and the people thought he was crazy. Nazerites didn't cut their hair, dressed in animal skins, and in John's case lived in the wilderness: they would not drink anything alcoholic or even eat grapes. They refused to even comb their hair less they accidentally pull some out. They probably didn't bathe. I doubt we would enjoy being up-close and personal with this man. So then along comes Jesus: he drinks wine, enjoys sharing meals, and makes friends with social outcasts (even the dreaded tax collectors), and, horror of horrors, talks to women. People accuse him of being a glutton and a drunk. Jesus responded by stating that this generation is like children sitting in the marketplace and calling to each other saying: "We played the flute for you, and you did not dance; we wailed, and you did not mourn." Jesus might as well have said: "You're all a bunch of tepid, uninvolved spectators."

The theologian James Alison tells us that because narrative—the story we tell ourselves about ourselves— changes over time we have to revise our own story as we go along because ". . . if we didn't we would be *less* truthful, not *more* truthful." Personally, I constantly see my own history from differing perspectives. Things that were once very important to me don't seem so much so now and things that seemed superficial once upon a time have become more important.

Many years ago, when I was working as a

psychotherapist, I was asked to evaluate a father's petition for custody of his children in a rather nasty divorce case. I agreed to do this work. I met with the father and separately with each of his three young children and at least once in a rather amusing encounter with all three children at once. Then the day came for the hearing. The father's attorney called me to the witness stand and asked the judge to qualify me as an expert witness. If you've never been through that, I can tell you that the judge interrogated me about my education, my experience, my licenses, my views on certain things and then he declared that I was an expert witness. Next came my testimony, guided by the questions of the father's attorney. Soon after this began, the other party's attorney leaped to his feet shouting "Objection, objection!" The judge inquired as to the reason for the objection. The attorney blasted out "The witness is giving his opinion!" There was a moment of silence and then the judge looked at the objecting attorney and said "Sir, that is what expert witnesses do." We are invited to be expert witnesses about our own lives as we respond to Alison's challenge to re-tell our life story regularly. With that in mind, I offer you a metaphor from my own life.

I was a volunteer firefighter for 16 of the 22 years of my life that I served as a parish pastor. I mention this because it gave me more close encounters with death and disaster than I prefer to remember. That experience is deep in my soul with memories of fatal fires and accidents. First responders are often the first to know about a death and the first people to encounter survivors, and those encounters are etched into the fabric of my being. It has been 34 years since I answered my last alarm, but I can tell you much about those tragedies which come alive in my memory sometimes without conscious bidding on my part. There is a link between many of those deaths and the poverty and the wretched housing that often goes with it that feeds my concern for justice for the marginalized.

Alexander Pope, in 1711, famously said: "Fools rush in where angels fear to tread." Firefighters are perhaps a community of trained fools who run into the buildings everyone else is fleeing. Constant improvement in practices and equipment seek to reduce the risk, but the risk is never eliminated, and every year some trained fools make the ultimate sacrifice. That company of trained fools is a special community of people who know spiritual reality in a different way than most theologians. Calling central dispatch for body bags leaves a mark, and it gets worse if you must say, "We need at least six." I feel I hear sirens differently than most people, and my thoughts about good and evil will always be influenced by memories of extracting the bodies from the wreckage in the aftermath of tragedy. That is where I learned that little children hide under their beds in a fire, because that is where we found their tiny bodies. I am forever changed by my experience dealing with the stark reality of lives suddenly and tragically ended. I knew that I had volunteered to help my community, but I didn't realize that I had volunteered to change my life.

My experiences tell me that an expert witness is someone who makes an effort to understand more about living than a spectator ever would, and that the witnesses' expertise is validated by participatory engagement in the nitty-gritty of life. John, whose words in the book of Revelation we read this morning, and Jesus, who chastises people for being uninvolved spectators, are calling us to deep, meaningful participation in the living faith of the disciples of Jesus.

Listening to the gospel lesson today also allows us to hear again Jesus saying: "Come to me, all you that are weary and are carrying heavy burdens and I will give you rest. Take my yoke upon you and learn from me; for I am gentle and humble in heart, and you will find rest for your souls, for my yoke is easy and my burden is light." This brief paragraph seems full of paradoxes. The heavily burdened are invited to take up Jesus' yoke.

Now wait just a minute—let me be clear about this, Jesus. Are you telling me that if I am staggering under the burdens of life, I should add another one? That is exactly what is being asked and I suspect it is because the yoke also connects me with others and with Jesus' spirit too. Suddenly the burdens are lighter because we are participating in the struggles of living with other people. We aren't going it alone.

Traditional firefighters' boots are white on the bottom. There is a reason for that: a fallen fire fighter's boots, showing that color, will ask his fellow fools to help him. Firefighting is a team effort, a participatory adventure--and so is the Christian life. Jesus asks us to participate in a compassionate, forgiving, and loving community. This community has always done more for the world than any of its members could ever do alone. The early Christians were well aware that the wisdom of God is foolishness to the world and there has been a lot written over the generations about Christians becoming fools for Christ. The apostle Paul asked the people of Corinth to "become fools that you may become wise." If you read the letters of Paul in the New Testament, you will quickly realize that they are addressed to communities, not individuals, because Paul understands that the Christian life is a community undertaking—a mutual sharing of the yoke of compassionate service.

Quantum physics tells us that things are changed by being observed. This is a rather complicated concept, but one of the take-aways for us is simply this: if we pay attention to our participation in life and especially in the Christian life, we will be changed in the process. I discovered, as I said a moment ago, that my decision to join the team of trained fools that fights fires was an effort to help the community—but my participation changed my own life, my value systems, my perspective on a lot of important issues. We might say that committed witnesses derive their power from conscious awareness of their participation. The Epistle of James tells us: "Faith by itself, if it has no works, is dead." James goes on to say that he will show you his faith through his works. Part of what made me an effective witness in that child custody case was the experience of being a father. I didn't articulate it at the time, but in retelling the story I realize that my zeal to get those children a safe home originated not in my training and education but in my own participation as a child growing up in a safe home and as a father determined to provide a safe home for my own children. My determination to help those children was also buttressed by the horror of extricating the bodies of children from unsafe homes.

When the pillar of smoke from the burning cars incinerating their occupants rises a couple hundred feet into the still, humid air of an August Sunday afternoon, lots of spectators will swarm to watch. But when the fire is quenched and what fire fighters call the "overhaul" begins and the air is filled with the stench of burning rubber and flesh and the excitement is gone, the spectators disappear. In all those 16 years, not a single spectator asked about becoming a volunteer firefighter.

It doesn't take commitment to be a spectator. But it takes participation at whatever the personal cost to become a committed witness who will advocate for the disadvantaged, wipe the tears of the sorrowful, hold the hands of the lonely. That kind of participation comes through attending not only to what is going on around us but also at what is going on within us. It takes a willingness to get involved in community, knowing that sometimes the needs of others will require us to be inconvenienced. It takes determination to discover our own internal resources, to learn skills and discover how to use them. It is an exciting challenge to find out how we can combine skills, talents and learning to be effective, committed witnesses who are change agents.

I suppose it's obvious that firefighters need certain skills to take risks effectively, but it is just as true that committed disciples of Jesus need to learn skills and take risks: offering love and forgiveness is a complex and sometimes complicated undertaking. The typical translation of this morning's gospel passage asks us to understand that Jesus' burden is easy. But a careful reading of the Greek text of this passage leads to a somewhat different impression. Jesus is saying my yoke is beneficial and the burden is insignificant. Thus, we find Jesus inviting us to bear a beneficial yoke. The benefits of the yoke make the burden thereof insignificant. We might also look a bit deeper at the use of yoke in this context. The Greek for yoke suggests that it is a device or tool for making bearing a burden easier. Perhaps Jesus' reference to his yoke might be a reference to his teaching and that would probably take us to the Sermon on the Mount as one summary of the details of his teaching. Learning to be meek, merciful, and peace-making while thirsting for righteousness is a complex and challenging undertaking. Many of us might easily say that the benefits of experiencing forgiveness make the task of providing it insignificant. Most of us happily soak up the love of others while ignoring what it might cost someone to offer us that love. Love is the greatest gift and the cost of providing that gift is insignificant compared with the benefits it offers.

We live in an increasingly complicated world. The world needs compassionate, committed witnesses whose personal testimony will facilitate change. As you examine your own heart and mind, what will you discover within yourself that will provide the tools you can use to become a faithful disciple with the power to change the world?

Way-walkers are Humble, Self-Compassionate People Who Rise Above Self-Interest

---

SECRET POWER

January 9, 2011. Isaiah 42:1-9; Matthew 3:13-17

At least some of you know that I do counseling work. Not too long ago I was working with a young woman who was struggling to make a major decision. She seemed to be stuck and felt she needed some additional information although she wasn't at all sure what information she needed. Then one day she walked into my office, said she had gotten the information she needed and had made her decision. When I asked her about how she got the information, she explained that it was totally unexpected and from an unexpected source. Then she said, "It was a God thing." She believed that God had provided that which she needed to move forward. I have to believe her. There was no reason for me to argue with her—although I might have if she had told me God wanted her to become a terrorist. However, since her "revelation" seemed consistent with things I believe about God, I could only congratulate her on being able to make the critical decision with which she was faced.

John the Baptist was, at least from our perspective, a truly weird man. He followed the tradition of the ancient Nazerites. These people lived off the land, called no place home, did not bathe or cut their hair or shave their beards. They dressed in the skins of wild animals which I suspect were not all that carefully prepared for use. It wouldn't surprise me if one's nose would announce the approach of someone like John before one actually saw him or heard him. In other words, he was bound to attract attention. He was not a man to mince words. When the Pharisees and Sadducees came out to hear him preach, he greeted them by calling them a "brood of vipers" or as we might say, "a bunch of snakes." Then he went on to tell them that their claims to be privileged with God were bogus and that God was taking an axe to the trees to cut away all the non-productive trees which did not bear good fruit and that those trees would then be thrown into the fire! The political realities of this particular time required that the religious authorities maintain a certain degree of cooperation with the Roman army which essentially was calling the shots, because Palestine was occupied territory. The Pharisees and Sadducees could curry favor with the Romans by keeping the people in a cooperative mood. Now here is this offensive, stinky, noisy man threatening to rock the boat. In fact, John would eventually be arrested and executed because he managed to offend Herod. People like Herod and Pontius Pilate kept their jobs by making sure that the population didn't cause any ruckus. Rome was not at all reluctant to replace officials whose behavior caused difficulties. There are indications that Pontius Pilate was replaced not too long after the crucifixion of Jesus because some of his policies and practices offended the religious establishment and threatened to upset the delicate political balance. Eventually things did fall apart in Palestine and Jerusalem and Rome went to war. The Jews lost, and the Romans destroyed Jerusalem in 70 CE—about 40 years after Jesus was crucified. It is easy to imagine that the seeds of this conflict were already sown when John and Jesus were preaching. It seems obvious that Jesus knew exactly what the score was. But still Jesus comes to hear John preach and seeks John's baptism. John resisted Jesus' request, claiming that Jesus should baptize John instead, but Jesus insisted that this would be consistent with John's teaching and thus complete righteousness or justice.

Following his baptism Jesus experienced a "God thing." He is coming up out of the water and he sees the heavens opened, God's spirit descending like a dove and he hears God say, "This is my son, the Beloved, with whom I am well pleased." Pious imagination has tried to make this into a supernatural event that was witnessed by others. However, the gospel lesson we read this morning makes it quite clear that this is a private spiritual experience which Jesus had which validated his decision to begin his ministry. I would suggest that we know about this because Jesus told his personal story to his disciples somewhere along the way. Perhaps he did that after John was arrested. There are reports of Jesus being very upset when John was arrested and also of having some discussion with his disciples about that. Nevertheless, we are not dealing with some sort of magic here or some disruption of the natural order: we are dealing with a personal spiritual experience that Jesus had and eventually shared with others.

This experience authenticated his call to ministry and convinced him that he should continue the work that John had begun. We might say that Jesus is sustained by this very personal, private experience. This is clearly a life-changing event for him. He will not hesitate to brave the power structure whether Jewish or Roman. He will not mince words. His early preaching will echo some of John's call to repentance and yet he will gradually manifest a gentle nature that is sensitive to the pains and problems of ordinary people.

The Old Testament reading for today is from Isaiah and describes God's chosen servant. The early church connected this passage with the person and work of Jesus. Here we see the tension between working for justice and caring for individuals. The servant is going to bring forth justice for the nations--which certainly is not a timid task. However. this same servant is not going to break a bruised reed or quench a dimly burning wick: in other words, the servant's work will not injure the weak and those already hurting. In some ways, the work of the servant here contradicts our usual understanding of power. Here is power being used to help the blind to see, to release prisoners from both prisons and from darkness. Here is also persisting power that will not grow faint or be crushed. Perhaps the author of these verses understands that working for justice will be a long, drawn-out process and that those seeking to do this work will need energy and commitment for the long haul.

We believe that the public ministry of Jesus continued for at least three years. We also know that according to all accounts, he was strong, committed and brave not only in the beginning but also at the end. The power of his original call to ministry bound him closely to God and gave him a Secret Power that enabled him to persevere against forces and odds that could easily have sabotaged his intent. It seems to me that sharing his story, telling others about his Secret Power, helped him to sustain his commitment. Tradition has it that Jesus went from his baptism into the wilderness of temptation. We observe that event with the season of Lent. Lent follows the season of Epiphany, which begins after the 12th day of Christmas and continues until Lent. Epiphany means appearing or showing. The season of Epiphany traditionally focuses on making the gospel known to the world. It is about taking our understanding, our truth, and our belief out into the world. It is about daring to share.

I suspect that amongst us there are lots of people in this room right now who can say that they have at one time or another dealt with a "God thing." I am also quite sure that most of us are reluctant to mention such things in public. It seems perfectly fine for us to say to each other that we talk to God; but it is another thing to say, out loud, God talks to me. I wonder if we found the courage to speak up and share our "God things" with each other, that might not increase the power of such experiences and help them to become for us a sustaining Secret Power that would carry us not only through rough times but right out into the world where we could say: "Hello world, let me tell you what I believe, to whom I am committed, and how much I love justice and peace-making."

Of course, there are certain risks in doing that sort of thing. Part of this risk is revealed in a story that allegedly comes from the time when our only treatment for severe mental illness was to lock people up. In those days chaplains were among the few who could visit freely in these so-called asylums. The story is that a chaplain was talking to a patient who was quite excited about telling his story which began "Last night God spoke to me . . .." But before he could say another word he was interrupted by another patient who loudly protested, saying "I did not." If we started sharing our "God things" then we would have to contend with the possibility that we don't all hear or experience the same things. This could draw us into conflict, as it did the church in Corinth, or it could draw us into shared discernment in the Quaker tradition and involve us in sorting through the various perspectives and experiences to discover how our individual "God things" impact the community.

Matthew tells us that John tried to "prevent" Jesus from being baptized. Given what we know about John's character and personality we can be sure that this wasn't simply a polite "no thanks." Matthew could have reported that John declined the invitation or something like that. I think this is more in the order of some sturdy conflicted disagreement between two powerful, deeply spiritual men. The conflict was resolved with the baptism of Jesus which facilitated the "God thing." This might help us to understand that sharing our Secret Power, describing our own "God things" to one another could produce the sort of fertile disagreement which would lead to creative engagement amongst us. But conflict between us is probably a lot less likely in this area then conflict within our own minds. Part of me might say that a certain experience is a "God thing" and another part of me might say "Oh yeah? Maybe it's just indigestion or a headache" --or something like Scrooge in Dickens's Christmas Carol, who describes his encounter with the ghost of Marley, his dead partner, as the result of having eaten a ". . . bit of underdone potato."

When we are confronted with things we can't explain, we are likely to suppose that we just haven't figured it out yet or that it isn't real. In other words, we are tempted to think in terms of one kind of reality and all events must fit into that perspective. I suspect that some of you have, like me, indulged in watching some football games on TV in the past couple of weeks. For me, at least, most of my favorite teams did not win and so I felt disappointed. However, it did not occur to me that my reactions were to watching a little dot of light fly around the TV screen really, really fast. My brain made the comings and goings of the little dot into a picture. We chuckle over the fact that the first time our younger granddaughter saw someone's image on the computer screen via the Skype program she looked behind the laptop screen expecting to see the rest of the person whose face was on the screen. What we are really laughing at is that she had not yet learned what we know. If we can trust our brains to assemble images from a computer or TV screen into a meaningful picture, might we not be able to trust our intuitive sense that some things are "God things?"

It might be very exciting for us to share our Secret Power. It might be very helpful for us to know what sustains each other's passions and commitments; what drives our dreams; what personal values are of paramount importance. Rather than get into a conflict either with ourselves or with others about the reality of these experiences, why not just test them out: do they empower us to be more loving; more persistent about justice; more compassionate about forgiving; more sensitive to the needs of those around us? The Secret Power of our own "God things" can make us and this church stronger; that same power can sustain us so that we will not grow weary or faint in the struggle for justice and the quest for peace. Take time to "own" your own "God things" and to let yourselves set doubt aside and praise the God who continues to be a Word in our minds, a song in our hearts, and good deeds in our hands.

HOT PURSUIT

January 30, 2011. Micah 6:1-8; 1 Corinthians 1:18-31;
Matthew 5:1-12

Our gospel reading this morning is a part of the Sermon on the Mount. This is a favorite passage for many people, it has been adapted for various musical versions, it has been inscribed on plaques, published in countless ways, and has become very familiar. Hollywood re-creations of this scene usually have Jesus preaching to huge crowds. One of the problems we have with passages of Scripture that become favorites is that we may miss some of the message enclosed in the plastic wrap of familiarity. We cloak these images with ideas from our own culture and times. But if we allow ourselves to take a fresh look, we might see something that we are missing. I want to call your attention to a couple of details: the gospel actually says that when Jesus saw the crowds, he went up the mountain and then his disciples came to him. This is not a stadium-type preaching event: it is special instruction for Jesus' close disciples. We let the word "blessed" fall easily from our lips without really stopping to think about what it means. The Greek word that is translated as "blessed" also means "fortunate." It is also suggested that the word might mean "advantageous." Sometime try reading the passage out loud and substituting "fortunate" for "blessed." It gets even more interesting if we say "Advantaged are the poor, advantaged are the mourning, advantaged are the meek," etc. Shifting the translation away from the word "blessed" seems to me to move us away from having some sort of status to having special power or opportunities.

Then we come to verses 11 and 12: these are the ones with the stuff about persecution in them and represent a shift in the focus of the sermon from a general concern for people who are meek, who mourn, etc., to Jesus speaking directly to his disciples. The usual idea of persecution here may actually take us to a time after the first Easter when Christians were being persecuted by the Roman government. However, again there is an interesting alternate translation of that word available to us: the word translated as "persecute" also means "to pursue" or "to set in motion." Let's read these two verses a bit differently than the usual tradition and see what Jesus might be saying to us.

"You have an advantage when people revile you and pursue you and say all kinds of evil against you because of me. Rejoice and be glad for your reward is great in heaven for thusly they set the prophets in motion before you."

On the face of it, I find it puzzling to think that I have an advantage if people are coming after me. My first impression is that the concept of Hot Pursuit seems more appropriate to a TV drama or a movie than it does to my efforts to live a Christian life. From another perspective, however, it occurs to me that being set in motion by critics could very well help me clarify my thinking, strengthen my resolve, and deepen my commitment. If folks are concerned enough to pursue me for my witness, then it appears that perhaps I am hitting a nerve.

As I was thinking about this and looking at the reading from Micah today, I was struck by the prophet's declaring that ". . . the Lord has a controversy with his people." What if I am being pursued by God who utilizes the voices of my critics to urge me on and put me in motion? That wondering led me to the thought of a very ancient colleague of mine—I say colleague because we share the same profession—his name, which is probably familiar to many of you, is John Donne. John Donne's life bridged the 16th and 17th centuries. Some of his writings are fairly well-known—he is the source of phrases like "Death be not proud" and "Do not ask for whom the bell tolls, the bell tolls for you." But less well-known is a particular writing of his which I have excerpted and modernized a bit—it comes from an essay "To the Earle of Carlile and his company at Sion." Donne writes: "God, who has often looked upon me in my foulest uncleanness, when I had shut out the eye of the day, the Sun, and the eye of the night, the Candle, and the eyes of all the world with curtains and windows and doors, did yet see me and see me in mercy by making me see that he saw me. . .. God, who when he could not get into me, by standing, and knocking, by his ordinary means of entering, by his Word, his mercies, has applied his judgments, and thus shaked the house, this body, with fevers and trembling, and set this house on fire, with chills and delirium, and frightened the Master of the house, my soul, with horrors and heavy apprehensions, and so made an entrance into me."

So, what is this about? Donne is talking about how God has forced Donne to become aware of God's presence even when Donne is so depressed that he has shut everything and everyone out. In offering us this rather graphic and dramatic account of God's intruding into his life, Donne is reminding us that we are dealing with substantial power when we deal with God. This is not just some pleasant, feel-good, walk in the park on a sunny day sort of experience; God is not simply a giant teddy bear to help us feel good on bad days.

As I think about these things, I find myself asking, does God have a "lover's quarrel" with us? The prophet Micah takes pains to say that the people have forgotten the mighty deeds of God which have sustained them across the years, but even as he castigates people for having short memories, he comes around to what God expects: Micah says, "What does the Lord require of you but to do justice and to love kindness and to walk humbly with your God?" Just as Micah is critical of people who would apparently brag about having the resources to present lavish offerings to God while forgetting how they got to such favored status, so Paul insists that the haughty, arrogant, contentious people of Corinth recognize that the power of God is not revealed in the wisdom of the world.

Jesus focused major parts of his ministry on empowering people whom contemporary society had decided were unclean. Many of the sections of the gospel reading which talk about people being blessed or fortunate or advantaged seem focused on telling the unclean that there is nothing wrong with their status, with being ritually unclean. On the other hand, Paul needs to convince the faction-oriented Corinthians that they are among the unclean—what are you foolish folks bragging about, asks Paul. Paul confronts these folks with a paradox: in order for them to see themselves as recipients of the grace of God, they must first acknowledge that they are not wise, powerful, privileged, or superior in any way. In some ways, the anthem for today ["Turn back, O Man" from Godspell] points us toward the mistakes of the folks in Corinth. The verses speak of our foolish ways that lead us to build tragic empires in our sorrowful dreams. If we would but wake from our haunted sleep, then we could hear the proclamations of our inner God. Paul seems frustrated that the divisive people of Corinth are so wrapped up in their own selfish agendas that they are not able to hear what God is really proclaiming. They are insensitive to the idea that God is pursuing them, much less to the notion that God's pursuit might propel them into a whole different realm of living.

I like Donne's phrase about God who is ". . . making me see that he saw me." If God is indeed pursuing me, then God is making me realize that God is paying attention to me. That feeling cuts two ways for me: it lets me feel fortunate that God pays attention to me and it makes me wonder how I am doing with regard to living the way God invites me to live. So, while I can celebrate the gifts—the advantages—that God bestows upon me, I must wonder what it means for me, in the here and now, (In the words of Psalm 15) to walk blamelessly, and do what is right; to be one who does not slander with my tongue and who does no evil to my friends and who does not take up a reproach against my neighbors.

The Wednesday morning Bible study group [which studies the weekly lectionary with the pastor] wondered if I might want to get caught by the God who pursues me. Perhaps I might, but that presumes that God pursues me in order to catch me. I think it is more likely that God pursues me to get me moving, to push me out of my moral and spiritual lethargy and laziness. If I am honest, I have to say that I have not done all the good that I can do, I have not fought all the battles for justice that need to be fought. The Micah passage puts God's requirements in the present tense: to do justice now, to love kindness now, to walk humbly with God now. It does not suggest that there is a certain amount of stuff I need to do or accomplish, it does not impose a quota nor does it tell me I haven't done enough. Its focus is on what I am doing now. The same approach is taken by Psalm 15: this is how you are to live now. Again, there is no quota and no criticism about not doing enough—instead there is an expectation about my attitude. I am invited to be humble, foolish in the eyes of the world.

God is pursuing us and pushing us. God is ahead of us pulling us forward with invitations. And God is present with us so that we might, as Paul put it, feel the power of God who is the source of our life.

While there is much to be said for the life of spiritual contemplation and for taking time to meditate, it is also clear enough to me that Jesus and Paul are proposing an active spirituality, one that never decides we have arrived. God would give us the advantage of being pursued so that we might, in Donne's words, be comforted and empowered by the awareness that God is making us see that God sees us. What might that mean to us?

EXCESSIVE LOVE
February 20, 2011. Leviticus 19:1-2, 9-18; Matthew 5:38-48

I suppose that most of us have some treasured stories from our college days. I went to college at a time when professors were referred to by their academic titles and when professors addressed the students by their surnames. Classroom speech in that bygone era was very polite and proper. I had a fraternity brother whose name was Harland Blood. Harland was an energetic, rather boisterous person who did well enough in school, although it came less easy to him that it did for some of us. However, his energy often got the better of him and he was known to laugh the loudest and longest, to chatter more than most of us and easily to become the center of attention. One day, when one of his professors was distracted by Harland's antics, the professor addressed him and said, "Mr. Blood, please curb your enthusiasm." The frat brothers saw to it that Harland never escaped that comment. At odd and unexpected times one of us would look at him and say, "Mr. Blood, please curb your enthusiasm." I am glad to say that Harland never really curbed his enthusiasm. I have no idea where his life has led him, but I am pretty sure he never curbed his enthusiasm.

The word "enthusiasm" originally referred to someone who was "god-possessed." Over the years the appropriateness of enthusiastic expression has waxed and waned. People have at different times been the focus of popular displeasure for being too enthusiastic about most anything. Enthusiastic people have been accused of not understanding the situation or not acting appropriately—meaning that they weren't serious enough. I was reminded of this not only by our gospel lesson today but also by one of the Dream Keeper suggestions we received from recent survey of the congregation. One of us dreams that we might ". . . be comfortable dancing in the aisles of the church . . .. and not to be afraid to respond to our emotions, to those feelings in others: to weep openly, to embrace eagerly, to laugh heartily, . . . and to gently show our compassion." I wondered what Harland's professor would have thought of such displays of exuberance.

Our gospel lesson this morning is a continuation of our recent readings from the Sermon on the Mount. Today we find Jesus taking issue with the limitations of the law. The concept of an eye for an eye or a tooth for a tooth might be described as a case of distributive justice. It focuses on the fairness of the exchange, even though none of us wants to lose an eye or take out someone else's eye. James Fowler, who has written extensively about the stages of faith and what we might call moral development, describes a stage in which children argue, often incessantly, about fairness. We have all been witnesses to the lengthy discussions amongst elementary school children about fairness. We have heard the childhood cry of "It's not fair—she has a bigger piece that I do." In some ways, when Jesus takes on these ancient laws, he is suggesting that the concept of fairness applies to an earlier time, when people's moral sensibilities were less developed. He goes on to advocate what we might call a morality of excess. By a morality of excess, I don't mean debauchery—I mean an approach to morality that doesn't keep score. Jesus starts out talking about this stuff in terms of simple demands and offered examples with which his audience was familiar. When he talked about being asked for a coat and giving not only the coat but also your cloak or when one was asked to go a mile to go two instead, he was making reference to the rules by which the occupying Roman army operated. A Roman soldier could, by law, require someone to carry his gear for a mile. That same logic probably applied to asking someone for a coat as well. Jesus asks people to ignore the rules by deliberately refusing to keep score and to respond to the demand with enthusiastic excess.

Jesus then goes on to talk about loving one's enemies and tells us that God is a God of excessive love—God makes it rain on everyone and bathes everyone with sunlight. Sun and rain are requisites of life. No one knows that better than those who farm—whether in the first century or in the twenty-first century. Here Jesus is offering a picture of God as an equal opportunity God: everybody gets an equal chance and that opportunity is not compromised or conditioned by their attitudes or behavior.

Probably by now most of you have figured out that I find fresh ideas when I look back at the Greek text in which our New Testament was originally written. Today is no exception. Jesus says (according the New Revised Version), "If you greet only your brothers and sisters, what more are you doing than others?" However, the Greek behind this has a rather different sense to it: "If you only greet brothers and sisters, what excess are you making?" Jesus seems to imply that we should be excessive in our greeting of others, in our loving of others, and in our serving of others. The Greek word that means "excess" is the same word that gets translated as "abundant" when Jesus, in the Gospel of John, speaks of his coming so that we might have life and have life abundantly. I still want to stick with the literal term "excess" because, at least in my mind, that means having more than is needed or required. There are lots of ways in which we use the term "excess" in negative ways. If I have excess baggage when I fly somewhere, the airline will charge me extra. We think of "excess" so much in physical terms, but Jesus is talking about attitudes, forgiveness, love, compassion and mercy.

At the end of this particular passage, Jesus urges us to ". . . be perfect, therefore, as your heavenly Father is perfect." I have always had some difficulty understanding a phrase that seems to say I can be perfect like God is perfect. This week I went digging into the Greek again and found something that surprised me. The word translated as "perfect" actually means "complete." We are told that God completes God's self by loving excessively without reservation. Now we are told that we can complete ourselves by loving excessively without reservation. It seems obvious to me that what happens when God loves excessively and what happens when I love excessively are not exactly the same thing. But there is a kind of similarity here, just as there would be if two people of unequal resources were to each spend all their resources bestowing excessive love on others.

I think that there is a suggestion here that we are denying our own nature or fighting against our true selves if we are parceling out our love, if we are insisting on a fair and just distribution of compassion, mercy and acceptance. I have no idea how much compassion anyone else can offer.

I don't know how loving you can be or how forgiving you can be. However, I am well acquainted with my own capacities and, unfortunately, very familiar with my tendency to function far short of those capabilities. I know I could love more excessively, more lavishly, and more freely. I could be more exuberant and enthusiastic and if I was—in the old definition of that word—I would thereby be more God-filled. We might make a bit of a leap here and say if we allow ourselves to be complete as God is complete that we will be much more bonded to the God of life and love.

One of the professor's concerns about Mr. Blood is that his enthusiasm would distract him from his work and he would not finish things adequately. There is an important demand that God makes of people recorded in today's reading from Leviticus. The text says: "When you reap the harvest of your land, you shall not reap to the very edges of your field or gather the gleanings of your harvest. You shall not strip your vineyard bare or gather the fallen grapes from your vineyard; you shall leave them for the poor." This text might as well say, "Don't be compulsive or obsessive about getting all you can get, or the poor will suffer." It seems to me that obsession is the enemy of enthusiasm. We won't be dancing in the aisles if we are fussing about getting the steps right. Love is excessive but not obsessive. Love is exuberant but not compulsive. Compassion is joyful but not calculating.

Jesus invites us to complete ourselves, to manifest our created nature by loving excessively. Jesus calls us to dance with him and to meet our Dancing Creator who would indeed dance with us in the aisles. We are called to develop an uninhibited spirituality that drives us to lavish our gifts abundantly on all who need them. Let us be bold enough to realize that there is a big difference between being nice to the neighbor and being loving to the neighbor. Such enthusiasm will also lead us to join Jesus in continually rewriting the definition of who our neighbor is. I think we will make better decisions about who the neighbor is out of our enthusiasm than out of our calculating. We might meet some interesting people if we would just dance in the aisles or even the streets!

The author of the UCC Still Speaking Daily Devotional yesterday wrote about our God-created self dancing through life and then he said: "God is still asking, 'May I have this dance?'" If we will let ourselves love excessively, then I think we might very well discover that we are living completely. It feels to me like it is better to dance through life than to calculate our compassion or obsessively to curb our enthusiasm.

PLANTING GROWTH
July 10, 2011. Romans 8:1-11; Matthew 13:1-23

Those of us who use computers, which I imagine is most of us, have a bunch of symbols on our keyboards. We might not even know the names of them; for example, I wonder how many people know the word "ampersand"? That is, of course, the name of the symbol that signifies "and"; it shares a key with the number 7. Many of the keyboard symbols have more than one meaning. There is the symbol that we can use to signify that candy cost 12 cents apiece which also shows up in our email addresses to say that this particular person is at a particular email service. This symbol shares a key with 2. Then there is the asterisk which sometimes refers to a footnote and sometimes means one number multiplied by another and shares a key with 8. We give symbolic power to all kinds of things. The color red often signifies emergencies or fire alarms or stop. Frequently we need to know the context of a symbol in order to understand its meaning. For example, a flashing red light on a traffic light means something quite different than a flashing red light on a fire truck. Our emotions sometimes tell us the difference here; for example, I probably won't have much emotional response to the flashing red traffic light but I certainly will have one to the flashing red light on the fire truck parked in front of my house when I come home from work.

Our gospel lesson this morning shows us Jesus teaching with the use of parables. He offers a parable, has some discussion about people who understand and people who don't and then he explains the parable. We are so used to the idea of Jesus teaching through the use of parables that we may easily overlook the significance of the parable as a teaching tool. The Greek word for parable and its roots tell us some interesting things. First, the word itself means "parallel story." That makes me wonder about what the story parallels. Second, the roots of the Greek word tell us that this word means "thrown beyond"; in other words, this is a story that pushes us beyond where we are. The "thrown" part of the word implies that the throwing is done intensely. It seems quite in order to think that a parable is a story that parallels something in my life yet at the same time pushes me to go beyond where I am and that is also intense enough to disturb me.

Then there are some questions about who understands and who doesn't understand the parables. Jesus talks about those who apparently see but actually don't see. The people he is talking about are the scribes and Pharisees who had asked him a bit earlier to show them a sign that they could see. Again, we need to pay attention to what the Greek is telling us because throughout this part of the gospel there is interplay between two words which mean "see." One of these words also means "to discern" as well as to see, while the other term means "to see" or "to perceive." The Pharisees asked for a discerning sign, but Jesus tells the disciples that the Pharisees will look but not see, will listen but not hear. In other words, the Pharisees simply don't get it. However, when Jesus talks about the people who do get it, he speaks of them seeing and discerning—the kind of discernment that comes from staring with eyes wide open. The people who get it will understand in abundance; in other words, their discernment will enable them to be "thrown beyond" where they are into a new life.

Now let's look at the parable itself and see what the interpretation might symbolize for us--keeping in mind that symbols often have several layers of meaning. Jesus talks about someone going out to sow seed. The throwing is done extravagantly: the sower flings the seed everywhere. This sort of planting is not a careful sprinkling of a handful of seeds on selected places. The sower pays little attention to where the seed goes. I think part of the reason is that the sower really doesn't know for sure where the seeds will grow and won't grow—he takes a chance that if he spreads the seed widely he will get a better crop. The sower is also a symbol for God, who flings seed everywhere in extravagant abundance—this God is a God of abundance in lots and lots of ways.

Some of the seed falls on the path—and that word might better be translated as "road." The road is a place where people are accustomed to coming and going without paying a lot of attention to the road itself. How many times have we cruised down a highway losing track of exactly where we were; how many times have we driven across town without remembering which traffic lights were red or green? Jesus explains that the birds come and eat this seed and nothing comes of it. He later tells the disciples that this represents evil destroying the seed. (By the way, forget the translation "evil one"; the Greek just says "evil.") Coupling evil with road could be a reference to immoral ways of routinely doing business. In such a context, the seed might just get ignored. We are so focused on continuing to do things the way we have always done them that we don't even notice the opportunity to change. That reminds me that sometimes I tend to keep doing what I have been doing even if my way is not exactly wonderful. The parable also reminds me that by pairing evil with the road, a lot of the ways we routinely do business (at the personal, corporate and governmental levels) are immoral. They take advantage of people; they focus on achieving a particular goal while ignoring the significance of the means that are used to get to that goal. Many, many times we make decisions without ever stopping to ask, "Is this right?"

Then there is seed that falls on rocky ground. Yes, it grows, but it springs up quickly without developing any depth of roots and so can't handle the heat of the sun and withers in the hot weather. Jesus interprets this as representing a person who initially is very enthusiastic and joyful, but then gives up when faced with affliction or persecution. The Greek has an interesting verb here. It tells us that this person is "offended" by the difficulties. It is almost like saying that when bad things happen to me, I cry out, "How dare you?" I might even do that if I don't know to whom to address my complaint. This also invites me to think about the times when I have given up on something because things just weren't fair—or at least they didn't seem fair to me. After all, I was making a good faith effort and when it went sour, I decided to quit because it just wasn't fair. We are tempted to think if we simply believe the right things, that everything will go well, and when it doesn't, we are "offended" and decide to give up on the effort. In such instances, I betray my failure to really develop roots. Perhaps we might say, in current parlance, that I am not adequately grounded.

When Jesus turns to discuss the seed that lands amongst the thorns, he is talking about how the thorns choke the seed and overwhelm it so it can't grow. Again, it is helpful to look at the Greek behind our English translation: Jesus says that anxiety and deception <u>together</u> choke the seed. The deception about material things and anxiety about worldly affairs spoil our growth.   The appearance of the word "deception" in this text is a reminder that we get deceived when we think that material possessions (whether money or other assets) can bring us peace or joy or healing or hope. There is a company with a rather large office complex on US 10 about half-way between Midland and Bay City. This company provides various services and they have a list of them on the side of the building facing the highway. The list includes several things that would be helpful to other businesses (like warehousing) but the last item on the list seems a bit over the top—the last service they promise to offer is "fulfillment." If I could run a business that could sell fulfillment at any price, people would beat a path to my door, but as Jesus indicates, the idea that material reality offers fulfillment is a deception. The anxiety Jesus is talking about is anxiety about the cares of the world. He talks about that elsewhere when he suggests that people get anxious about what to eat or wear or whether they are too tall or too short. The thorny weeds that choke out growth here are very familiar to most of us, for we are often distracted by our anxiety and deceived about how to cope with it.

When Jesus finally gets to the end of the story and tells us what happens to the seed that fell on good soil and grew, he throws in another interesting twist. He says that some seed yields 100-fold, some 60-fold and some 30-fold. Putting it this way forces us to understand that this whole thing is not about how productive we might be but is a simpler, starker question. The issue, to paraphrase Shakespeare, is "To grow or not to grow, that is the question."

Ultimately this parable is about the seeds. It isn't really about the environment. The seeds that don't do well are distracted. We all know that there are seeds which flourish in harsh environments. At my house, we call them weeds and notice that they grow up between cracks in the sidewalk and amongst stones. Someone once told me that a weed is simply a plant growing where someone doesn't want it. Weeds remind me that seeds can grow anywhere with enough determination. Determined seeds have lots of ways to develop roots. Sometimes they extend their roots deep in search of water, but some send out a web of roots near the surface which serves the same purpose. There are seeds which will intertwine amongst the weeds and manage to avoid being choked out. When Jesus explains why the seeds in certain places don't grow, he puts the emphasis on the seeds.

It seems to me that there is another way of looking at this parable, if we are looking at it from the perspective of the seeds. The seeds which fall on the road and get neglected until evil overtakes them might represent our apathy. Sometimes it is indeed easier to be apathetic than to engage difficult issues. The seeds that fall on the hard ground and are "offended" by the difficulties there could represent our tendency to get resentful: we easily resent it when things don't seem fair, or when we don't get our way, or when we are feeling ignored. The seeds that fall amongst the thorns and get choked by the concern about the cares of the world and the deceptive promises of materialism symbolize our innate anxiety. In other words, the three categories of seeds that fail to thrive represent our failure to manage stress effectively. It has been known for a long time that some stress is good for us. For example, really being hungry creates some stress which sends us looking for food. Of course, some of us also learned from that reality that food can comfort us when it reduces natural hunger, so we end up eating to reduce stress when we are not hungry at all. The challenge is not to eliminate stress but to manage it. When we look at this through Jesus' eyes and the lens of this parable, then we might understand that effective stress management is not just a clever thing: it is a sacred duty because our stress either inhibits or promotes our ability to bear fruit. When we bear healthy fruit as a result of spiritually-sensitive stress management, then we find ourselves on the list of folks Jesus described in the Beatitudes: "Then [Jesus] began to speak, and taught them, saying: Fortunate are the poor in spirit, for theirs is the kingdom of heaven. Fortunate are those who mourn, for they will be comforted. Fortunate are the meek, for they will inherit the earth. Fortunate are those who hunger and thirst for righteousness, for they will be filled. Fortunate are the merciful, for they will receive mercy. Fortunate are the pure in heart, for they will see God. Fortunate are the peacemakers, for they will be called children of God.

Fortunate are those who are persecuted for righteousness' sake, for theirs is the kingdom of heaven. Fortunate are you when people revile you and persecute you and utter all kinds of evil against you falsely on my account. Rejoice and be glad, for your reward is great in heaven, for in the same way they persecuted the prophets who were before you."

Perhaps it will seem a bit odd to you, but I think we can make a case for Jesus telling us that effective stress management which takes the spiritual issues seriously will have fortunate results for us.

We are the seeds which an extravagant God has flung out across creation to bear fruit. Some of these fruits are peace, mercy, grace, love, justice, forgiveness and healing. Will we surrender our potential to immoral, but popular, practices that flourish on the road of our lives and abandon those who want and need to challenge the way business is done and life is lived? Will we fail to develop the support systems we need to nourish our growth? Will we be offended by the unfairness and inequity that abounds in our world and thus starves those who are hungry for the fruit? Will we allow anxiety and materialism to deceive us into believing that there can never be the fruit Jesus asks us to bear and let cynicism and skepticism rule the day? Or will we allow our potential to shrivel because we think we can't do as well as someone else?

The Apostle Paul said in this morning's reading: "Those who live according to the Spirit set their minds on things of the Spirit." We have been planted and invited to grow; we have been nurtured and challenged to bear the fruit a hurting humanity needs. Our question is: to grow or not to grow? Will we choose healthy stress management? Will we give love the resources it needs to change the world, or will we just shrivel up and let the emotionally and physically hungry people starve because we can't find the courage to grow or make the effort to manage our stress?

THE MYTH OF INADEQUACY
December 28, 2014. Genesis 1:1-2:3; John 1:1-18

When my wife and I had young children at home, there was nothing quite so paralyzing or foreboding on Christmas morning as the gifts for the children which came with a sheet of paper entitled "Some assembly required." Our bulletin cover is a reminder of that and points to something that often followed closely on the heels of reading those dreaded words. As those who know me best realize, I am not the handiest man in the world. With the correct tool in my hand, I can be downright menacing. Of course, many of the instructions for "some assembly required" often seemed to be written in English by someone for whom my native tongue was perhaps a third or a fifth language. Sometimes the first part of some assembly required was assembling the language of the instructions into something I could comprehend. The reality of these situations is that I often simply either did not know how to do what was asked of me or I didn't understand what was asked of me. My emotional response was more likely to be "I am inadequate—my lack of talent reveals that I lack certain characteristics of the male of the species." It wasn't too hard to slide from there into a more global assessment of myself as being inadequate as a human being. Once I got there, then I was a sitting duck for any criticism about anything from anyone. If you believe you're inadequate, then it is a short hop to believing someone else has to be in charge. However, the man-code requires that I never admit this to anyone, so if you ask me about this later, I'll probably deny that I said it.

Some recent experiences got me to thinking about this business of people being inadequate. I worked for about 25 years (give or take a couple) as a pastoral psychotherapist. As I reflected on this stuff about inadequacy and about the history of my own work, I realized that it was always or nearly always that women coming for help were the people who claimed that they were inadequate or weren't enough. I simply don't recall any male clients offering this complaint about their situation. While I certainly didn't do properly-designed research into my own experience, I would guess that if we were to do such a study today with some active therapists, we would get results that would match my own experience. I remember very clearly one particular case. This was a young couple who had one pre-school daughter at home. He worked as an engineer; she was an at-home mom who had, like her husband, graduated from college. She was an attractive woman, neither obese nor anorexic in appearance who seemed to have a good sense of how to dress and always presented for sessions looking very nice and put together. She was feeling emotionally neglected by her husband and seemed unable to stop thinking it was because she wasn't enough. He got involved in the counseling sometime after she had begun. I remember the first time I met him: he strode into my office, extended his hand, announced his name, and said "What am I supposed to do?" Then there was the day when she said she had to make some schedule changes because she was seeing a dermatologist to have a chemical peel of her face done. I was stunned. I couldn't imagine why because I could see no reason for it. I even wondered about the ethics of the dermatologist (whose name I never knew). She had the peel. Her face healed; her ego did not. Whatever her husband did differently, it didn't touch the issue. She was still not enough and still filled with a sense of inadequacy.

As some of you may know, there are electronic devices available for us to use to control pets. Some of them work by sending an electronic signal to a dog's collar which creates an uncomfortable feeling; these can be used to create a conditioned response. The animal learns to associate discomfort with certain places or objects in the house. Once the conditioned response is established, the electronic device is not needed. We teach the dog to avoid the kitchen counter or the computer room and then the device could be used in some other place. The key here is that the animal's conditioned response gives power to the owner and, in some sense, tells the animal it is inadequate to access certain areas. This conditioned response has been used for generations by people in power to keep populations in subjugation by reinforcing the concept that certain people are inadequate.

At the beginning of Jesus' public ministry, Phillip, an early disciple, approached a man named Nathaniel and told him they had met the Messiah. Phillip said, "He is Jesus, son of Joseph, and is from Nazareth." Nathaniel's immediate response was a conditioned response "Can anything good come out of Nazareth?" The Nazareth of Jesus' youth was a nothing place. It apparently had no synagogue, the population was small—probably about 200 people--and the economy was abysmal. People, like Joseph,

207

had to go out of town to earn a living. Joseph probably worked at construction jobs in nearby Sepphoris which was Herod's capital and a five-mile walk from home. Nazareth was apparently a beautiful rural community that was home to a bunch of inadequate folk. If you were called a "Nazarene" you were being insulted, because a Nazarene was someone with an evil reputation. In ancient Israel, young women who got pregnant without being married were subject to being stoned. When Joseph discovered his fiancé was pregnant, he decided to put her away quietly, probably to prevent her being murdered by folk who were apparently willing to see people like her as woefully inadequate. As a brief aside, I wonder if, when people brought a woman who was subject to being stoned for adultery to Jesus, he might have recalled family stories about his own origins. It seems clear enough to me that God brought forth the Messiah from the midst of folk known to be inadequate.

We read the first creation story from Genesis this morning. In this account of creation, the earth and all that is on and in it was created in six days. Things were called into being by the Word of God. As the story takes us through those six days, at several intervals, God observes the results of the creative effort and declares them to be good. At the end of the story, after human beings have been created, God saw everything that had been created and indeed it was very good. There are two things noticeably absent from this version of creation: one is that there is no determination about the source of evil and no rejection of human beings for being inadequate. The other is that God is satisfied with things being very good. It is not said that things are wonderful or spectacular or fabulous or perfect. Good is just fine with God. The story declares that human beings are, by nature, good. I think we're on safe ground if we add a word to that and just say that we are by nature good enough.

The second creation story is the one where we get Adam and Eve, gardens, sneaky snakes, tempting fruit, shame over nakedness and rejection from paradise. This story by far seems to have been the favorite of generations of religious folk, both Jewish and Christian. I wonder why. Of course, this second story has lots of drama in it and a tragic ending. The first story isn't very exciting. Not much drama, no sex, no shame, no angels with flaming swords. But more importantly, the second story gives power to the authorities, who capitalize on the inference that we are inadequate, to offer us all sorts of palliatives and cure-alls to save us and control us. A spiritual perspective becomes a religious mandate and off we go with religions manifesting power over people. That has been so for thousands of years. I read last Tuesday that the current Roman pope is trying to change that within his church.

In our gospel reading this morning, we find John declaring that Jesus, the Word of God, has come into the world and ". . . to all that received him, that believed in his name, he gave power to become the children of God." In other words, to those who believe they are inadequate, Jesus gives power—power to become adequate—power to be God's children—power to be good enough. Just looking at that by itself explains why the authorities had to get rid of this man. He was subverting the conditioned response of the populace—the belief that they were inadequate, couldn't think for themselves and thus needed to be submissive to authority.

If we look at the history of subjugated folks, we find over and over again some sort of teaching provided by the power structure that these people need to be submissive because they are inadequate. We see it in the long, dismal story of African-Americans, we see it in similar stories about people of Central America and Native Americans, we see it in stories about women and we see it in stories about LGBTQ people. We can see it in the rising disparity in financial resources between the very wealthy 1% of the population and the rest of us. The theories of inadequacy, which are clearly at odds with that teaching in Genesis about all people being very good, are handy because they free the power establishment from having to determine what makes them adequate. The recent rising of subjugated peoples all over the world challenges the establishments' definition of themselves as adequate. Lots of assumptions are getting challenged now just as they were when Jesus was born to inadequate parents in an inadequate village and whose birth was first announced to inadequate shepherds (who were excluded from much of religious life because their occupation made them unclean).

One of the curious questions that therapists often ask people who claim that they are not enough is "What is enough?" Most people don't know how to answer that question. A similar question might be asked of establishment power: "How do you know you're enough?" I suspect the people's inability to answer that question is what provokes establishment rejection and violence against those described as inadequate. It almost comes down to a shouted declaration: "You're inadequate because I said so or you're not enough because I said so." There is no logic in that emotional outburst. The rise of people who have been described as inadequate challenges the establishment's assumption that they know what adequate is. Or even worse, threatens to make us face the fact that we are all the same. In places like Ferguson, MO and New York City it appears that the establishment has gone to lethal lengths to prove either that certain people are truly inadequate or that the establishment alone can determine who is adequate, when and where.

There has been in this country, for some time, a variety of protests about the commercialization of Christmas. We are told that the Spirit of the Holiday is lost in shopping and spending. It is suggested that all the hearty-party stuff with high calorie foods and too much booze detracts from the True Christmas. But the True Christmas has also been buried in a bunch of crazy stories about oxen and donkeys, about flying, singing angels who are totally unbiblical, in piles of tinsel and inflated yard ornaments—and yes even in a romantic Santa House [a local institution in Midland, MI]. Turning the Greek word for "messenger" into the English word "angels" who do all sorts of unnatural things subtly shifts the focus from the message to the messenger. The Birth of Jesus is the original Power to the People event. It has always been a threat to established power because it says persistently, "You are all good enough because God made you that way," and because it says, "You'll be accepted if you simply accept the good news Jesus announces about you becoming a child of God." This means that it has always been in the interests of established power, even established religious power, to distract us from the real Christmas truth.

We currently ask people presenting papers at conferences or writing research reports to disclose any conflicts of interest. So, I have to disclose a conflict of interest here: I am, in case you hadn't noticed, an old, white guy. I am establishment. I am part of a system that is on the way out, part of a system that has told women they're not enough, that has told LBGTQ people that they're not okay and that has told African-American people that they're defective. While my parents did not have money, my racial identity and gender have given me certain privileges. Of course, I had to be educated (and this has happened several times over). I had to learn about civil rights, women's rights, the rights of other minorities, etc. Each time I "went to school" over one of these issues, I had to revise my own understanding of who I am. That hasn't always been easy. Sometimes it has been scary. While I am at a place in my own life where I can appreciate and celebrate the changes in my personal perspective I have needed to make, I am well aware that a number of my kind in the establishment resist such disturbances of their presumed identity. Unfortunately, as the Southern Poverty Law Center has clearly established, we are witnessing a rapid rise of white power groups. Hate groups are making use of the latest technologies to spread the virulent attacks on those they want to define as inadequate. The old, dying system and the terrorists among us have a conspiracy—and they don't even realize it—one just like that of Jesus' time. Our world right now sorely needs the Christmas Message that the power of God is in the midst of the people, that the power of God endorses the innate goodness of everyone and that the idea that some folk are inadequate isn't true.

Our world is confronted by enormous change forces; the situation parallels in many ways the forces threatening the established world at the time of Jesus' birth. Within 75 years of Jesus' arrival, Jerusalem had been destroyed by the Roman armies—the establishment of his day was no more. In a very real way that establishment made its last stand at Masada, that hilltop fortress in southern Palestine where the terrorist remnants of the system of the old order finally committed suicide instead of surrendering to the Romans who spent a lot of time building a ramp to access the fortress and breached the fortress wall in 73 CE.

Contemporary disciples of Jesus need to address the fact that some reassembly is required in our world. That's the inside story about the bulletin cover: the failure of the myth of inadequacy will leave parts and pieces all over the place. We need to use those valuable remains of the old way of doing things along with the abundant gifts we have been given to transform the world, to announce the good news that everyone is enough, that all are adequate, that the God that has created us finds us to be good enough. We need to reassure those who feel threatened that we don't want to reverse the way things are, we don't want to make the poor wealthy and the wealthy poor. We are not interested in retribution. We are interested in justice, fairness, acceptance for everyone--all based on repeating God's affirmation at the time of creation—that it is all very good.

Whenever we tell ourselves we are not enough or inadequate, we do two things at once: we deny ourselves the power that comes with owning the goodness of our creation (thereby wasting our own power) and we offer power over us to those who prefer to define themselves by what others are not and avoid knowing their own essential goodness. You see people in power, who won't recognize their own essential goodness, get trapped trying to prove that they're okay at other peoples' expense.

All of us carry the burden of self-descriptions, obvious or subtle, which have been foisted on us by others—including those powerful folks who would rather keep us in submission. This Christmas let us facilitate a New Birth of self-concept that declares we are enough, good enough in the eyes and mind of God, and go forth to join Jesus in becoming living, breathing challenges to corrupt, obscene and dangerous power. Releasing ourselves from the myth of not being enough will release a lot of energy, energy that currently gets wasted in self-deprecation. Let us use this energy to incarnate the Power of Peace in all that we think and do; let us join the always new-born Christ to refresh the systems that would entrap us, deny people their common humanity and subvert the principles of peace, justice and love.

The people who thought they were not enough and were simply inadequate have discovered God is in their midst, that God in Christ declares all things new and makes a wreck of self-deprecation. Hark! the Herald Angels Shout: watch out world, the Power for Peace is let loose among you!

Part 2: Heresy Out Loud

A Perspective on Doing Theology

There was a time when people who engaged in theological reflection wrote systematic theology and the effort often produced voluminous documents intended to detail the essence of the Christian faith. Thomas Aquinas comes to mind as well the more recent Paul Tillich or Karl Barth. Aquinas called his work *Summa Theologica,* "the complete theology." Tillich's three-volume work is titled *Systematic Theology.* Barth wrote a 14-volume treatise called *Church Dogmatics* (it was bound with white covers which led some to refer to it as the Great White Whale). But what if the day of systematic theology has come and gone? Perhaps the passing of systematic theology is a reflection of the contemporary realization that there is no "one truth" theory about theology (or perhaps about anything). If, as has been said, ". . . all theology is anthropology," (Feuerbach, circa 1841) then the current existential realities of human life suggest that theology today cannot be systematic. We are more than ever aware of the diversity, variety, and complexity of what we could once call the "human family." I am not even sure we can legitimately apply the term "family" to human reality right now unless we are taking that term as the strictly technical term useful to anthropologists. Systematically doing theology is far from my cup of tea. I am keenly aware of the truth in an old saying: the larger the diameter of our knowledge, the greater the circumference of our ignorance.

It seems irresponsible to throw up our hands in the face of complexity and exponential rates of change and refuse to make any serious attempts at doing theology or perhaps we might say "theologizing." Theology has always been a way for faith communities of whatever religious persuasion to address ontological issues. Ontology, the study of being, asks questions about what it means to be. In many ways, ontology is the summation and essence of philosophy which seeks to apply its understandings about the meaning of life to ethics, politics, science, education, wellness, and more. One of my early ventures into the realm of theology was a small collection of brief essays under the title *Theology on the Fly* and was simply an effort to answer a series of questions posed by a former client of mine. In those essays, I demonstrated my understanding that theologizing is always a work in progress which is heavily influenced by the current environment in which theologizing is being done. The present work is a bit different because it is an unsystematic effort to address some questions which various people have raised. Some of these questions come to the surface for me now as a member of a liberal Christian church gathered in a community soaked in modern science. Within this same community, several mega churches affirm a fundamentalist approach to faith. These churches seem to flourish by celebrating a compartmentalization which keeps 21st-century science segregated from dogmatic affirmations which seem more medieval than anything else. I see the process of theologizing as impressionistic art. It is free to focus on issues currently on the heart of a would-be theologian without the ancient burden of having to construct a complete system. Insofar as impressionistic theology is intentionally incomplete, the theologizing process would invite and indeed expect further explication and re-visioning as the growth of human knowledge challenges prior assumptions of the best of thinkers.

This presentation of Way-Walking will involve a great deal of demythologizing as we work to free ourselves from ancient metaphors. The process of demythologizing will also need to de-literalize many of the old metaphors which are embraced as objective facts. Much of the conflict between science and religion involves the tendencies of many religious advocates to take metaphors literally and then conclude that they are scientific facts. This is illustrated by the strange contemporary phenomenon of a Creation Museum which demonstrates that dinosaurs and human beings inhabited the Earth simultaneously, that theories of evolution are not true, and that the Earth is really nowhere near as old as science maintains. The Museum is also an example of what Bishop Spong has called a Gentile heresy: the literalizing of the Biblical story and then claiming that the results of this process are demonstrable scientific truths. This sort of thinking also affirms the Flat Earth theory and claims the Grand Canyon was caused by the flood which Noah escaped in the ark!

Since theology intends to make sense of things and give us some answers to the question, "What does life mean?", some remythologizing will also be involved because we are dealing with aspects of reality that can only be described and discussed using metaphors. Richard Rohr says about metaphors: "The Greek root of the word metaphor means 'to carry across' meaning— to get it from one place to another. The paradox is that, all metaphors by necessity walk with a limp which betrays the inadequacy that hides in the truths they tell us. And yet, metaphors carry a substantial— and needed— load. I value the wisdom of the Canadian writer Donald Braun, who says at the beginning of his book *The Journey from Ennuied*, 'That which is belittled in plain speech finds the respect it warrants in the subtleties of metaphor.'" (quoted by Rohr, Richard. *The Divine Dance: The Trinity and Your Transformation*, Kindle Locations 752-756.)

Andrew Newberg, who has written extensively about the workings of the human brain, has hypothesized a theory of a biological drive, expressed by specialized areas of the brain, which is devoted to making sense of things. Recent research suggests that this specialized area may be the insula. Human beings seem to need to know what life means. This drive may indeed be behind the unending parade of religions and philosophies marching across and through the history of civilization, both Eastern and Western. There are a couple of obvious problems with this suggestion. First, most efforts to explain the meaning of life don't necessarily produce any scientific evidence proving the truth of our explanation; second, if we find an explanation to be adequate for our use, we tend to be done with the question even if no one agrees with us. If I tell you that the meaning of life is joyful and celebratory and someone else tells you that the meaning of life is depressing and bleak, how is one to decide if either of us or neither of us or both of us are right. The criteria for ascertaining what constitutes an adequate statement about the meaning of life is a challenging and perhaps unattainable goal. It may indeed be enough for most of us to engage in answering the question, "What is the meaning of *my* life?"

I include here some things about myself and my history because I believe it is important for readers to know who is doing the theologizing. Theology is in many ways a form of personal story-telling. In order to understand the story clearly, we need to know at least some things about the story-teller. It is also true that we hear stories differently from the way we hear theories or rational essays, so I hope you'll remember the stories I tell even if you don't remember my theories and explanations of things.

There are some other major components of my theologizing: one of these is the insights about language derived from Neuro-Linguistic Programming (NLP for short). Another piece is my effort to appeal to certain ancient languages (particularly Greek and Latin) for what they can reveal about the story behind the story told by familiar metaphors. The mysterious world of modern physics offers useful linkages there to both quantum theory and chaos theory. Full disclosure: Since I am not a physicist, behind some of the theories I will be discussing is a level of mathematics that totally eludes me. But I can still use my cell phone even though I don't understand the physics of the semiconductors that make it work. Perhaps my thoughts will tease or inspire some physicists to bring their expertise to the discussions. In the meantime, I propose that some modern theories of physics invite the creation of new metaphors that can be used to describe matters spiritual and even holy. Finally, my readers might find an awareness of the major influences that have shaped me to be helpful in discovering some of the sources of my thinking.

You will also find me using some of the insights offered to the world by the work of Grant Soosalu and Marvin Oka in their book *mBraining: Using Your Multiple Brains to do Cool Stuff* (2012). These Australian life coaches propose that humans have more than one brain in their bodies. In addition to the well-known brain in the head (the head-brain), Soosalu and Oka show us that there are brains in the heart and the gut, which they label as "heart or cardiac brain" and "gut or enteric brain." There is additional evidence that there may be an equivalent "brain" in the pelvis and that the autonomic nervous system (ANS) also functions at times like a brain. The mBraining system thus proposed has lots of similarities to the chakra system of Eastern thought and that reality will also lead me to incorporate some further reflections.

Heresy

The history of heresy, at least regarding the Christian church, is interesting. The first 300 years that people identified themselves as followers of Jesus, there were many perspectives on the teaching of Jesus, and on the significance of his life. Along with these different perspectives went a substantial body of literature, much of which never got included in the so-called "holy" Scriptures. When the Roman Emperor Constantine made Christianity the official religion of the Empire, all that began to change. He saw that the minority opinion prevailed and the Council of Nicaea (325 CE) produced what is known to history as the Nicene Creed. While this was early in Church history, it was almost 300 years after Jesus of Nazareth was crucified. It wasn't long after that Council that the church acquired certain powers associated with civil authority which led to the custom of executing heretics. Apparently, the first heretic to be executed was Priscillan who was killed in 386 CE; the last heretic to be executed was a Spaniard schoolmaster named Ripoll who was executed in 1826 CE. The Spanish Inquisition is infamous for its horrid enforcement of church doctrine. The tradition of the church's executing of heretics endured for over 1400 years. Unfortunately, the execution of heretics became an ecumenical custom; the Eastern Orthodox church, the Protestant church, and the Roman Catholic church were all involved in executing heretics. When the churches were reluctant to execute people with whom they disagreed, they often resorted to social ostracism, usually called excommunication. The process of defining and eliminating heretics has been part of other religions as well, as the current controversies within Islam might remind us. Quite often people's need for community along with their commitment to unconventional ideas led the excommunicated believers to create new faith communities. Within the Roman Catholic church, as recently as during the reign of Pope Benedict the 16th (2005 -2013 CE), there emerged some confusion about exactly what heresy might be or who might be the heretics. Given the fact that it is currently difficult to define heresy, I thought I might save my readers the effort and simply say upfront that I'm a heretic. I may get rejected or ignored for that reason, but hopefully not killed!

Some Ways to Approach Detailing My Heresy

Because of my deep involvement with and commitment to the Christian faith, many of the details to be found in the fleshing out of my heresies are rooted in Christianity. However, much of what I have to say also involves other religions and how we all need to come to terms with ontological reality. Anything with ontological implications would have de facto theological implications for those professing or following any particular religion. There are certain issues which need to be addressed in this process. One of these issues is language. Whether we are talking about Buddhism, Judaism, Hinduism, Islam, Christianity or traditional teachings (like the works of Plato and Aristotle), we are talking about concepts that were originally expressed in languages other than English. Very few of us could manage to be experts in Hebrew, Greek, Sanskrit, Coptic, Arabic, and the multitude of cultures with which these languages are connected. When we deal with issues of translation, we deal not only with the details of grammar, etiology, and spelling, but we also deal with complex cultural issues which may include different understandings of basic morals and assumptions about the purpose of human life. Although ideally, scholarly translations of ancient languages will avoid distortions arising from the translators' culture and beliefs, this has not always been the case. My familiarity with the Christian

Bible in a variety of translations suggests that certain words, which may be part of our common language, would not be used in the translations. I recall a comment by a student colleague of mine many years ago, a Ph.D. candidate in the field of New Testament studies. He said that if the Greek New Testament were to be translated into contemporary English, church people would be unwilling to read it out loud in worship. For example, there is a passage in Revelation that talks about God spitting out the lukewarm people of Laodicea. The Greek word for "spit out" is the equivalent of the English word "vomit."

Another aspect of the language issue is the tendency, especially in Indo-European languages, to use nouns more frequently than verbs and indeed to use nouns when verbs might be more appropriate. In a New York Times article dated December 27, 2016, David Brooks reports on Perry Link's comparisons of Chinese and English. He noted in a couple of 18th-century writings. the Chinese used 130 nouns and 166 verbs, while the English used 96 nouns and 38 verbs. Brooks pondered, "How much [of] our thinking is muddled because we describe actions as things."

This same reality has been noted by people working with Neuro-Linguistic Programming (NLP). Neuro-Linguistic Programming is an approach to communication, personal development, and psychotherapy created by Richard Bandler and John Grinder in California in the 1970s. One of the issues which Neuro-Linguistic Programming invites us to consider is the tendency to turn verbs into nouns. Thus, living becomes life, loving becomes love, creating becomes creator or creation, and so on. Neuro-Linguistic devotees are correct in that when we nominalize something, turning a verb into a noun, we start thinking about it and describing it in various objective terms. This reality leads NLP to engage in a process called denominalizing, which involves converting nouns into the verbs which seem to underlie those nouns. At least part of the logic behind this concept was echoed by Brooks in his article when he suggested that we are often using nouns to describe activities which are not objects. The denominalizing process can involve the creation of gerunds which in English are often words ending with the letters "ing." Finding gerunds in unexpected places or used in unusual ways can facilitate opening our minds to curious, unusual and unexpected understanding. The significance of this issue is seen by remembering that verbs refer to active processes and nouns refer to static objects.

When we manage to develop a metaphor to describe an unusual or unique experience, that metaphor seems to stick around indefinitely. For example, we still talk about dialing a telephone, but the old rotary dial has long since been replaced with a touchpad. However, the idea of padding or touching a phone doesn't seem to be much used. In certain religious circles, we still talk about the three-story universe even though science has left that image behind for a long time now. One of my concerns is that metaphors transmogrify into literal facts and then become limiting factors when we try to discuss the reality to which the original metaphor pointed. The fact that there are major issues with relating modern scientific concepts to the ancient foundations of religious belief is reflective of the problems generated when metaphors originally designed to overcome the limits of speech get treated as if they were objective facts.

Perhaps 4000 years ago, there appeared *The Epic of Gilgamesh*. Among other things, this ancient document discussed the doings of a god named Marduk. This god killed Timiat, a creature of the feminine persuasion. The story tells us that Marduk divided up the remains of Timiat and used the parts to create the known world. Embedded in that marvelous ancient epic are bits and pieces of stories that seem to have made their way into the Hebrew Bible, including stories about a garden of Eden and a flood featuring a fellow named Noah.

We can chuckle at some of the details of that epic, but we inherited the concept of the three-story universe from those ancient ruminations about nature. We like to think we are much more sophisticated with our theologizing and our philosophizing since, for the most part, we have gotten rid of the notion that there is a multiplicity of divine beings called gods and we like to suppose that we no longer believe in the three-story universe. However, the three-story universe keeps showing up when we talk about things like heaven and hell. We project our own experience, wishes, and discoveries onto the things we study. Insofar as physics attempts to explain everything, I consider that physics often shifts into a secular form of theology. So, for example, because human experience says that life has a beginning and an end, physics has assumed that the universe has a beginning and an end. That assumption has been made without any proof. Has the propensity for such thinking inhibited the development of, *inter alia*, modern physics?

Any survey of world history that regards the comings and goings of religions will reveal that we got from the Epic of Gilgamesh to quantum physics through an elaborate process of demythologizing and re-mythologizing. Often the process of demythologizing has been painful and, in some instances, even deadly to participants in the process. GB Shaw said: "All great truths begin as blasphemies." Whether we talk about Socrates or Galileo or Copernicus or Moses or even Jesus, we are talking about heretics, people who were punished, ostracized and even killed because they called the conventional explanations of things into question. I suspect a careful study of the history of science would reveal that one of the consequences of difficult demythologizing was a leap forward in human understanding, whether such change was confined to science itself or whether it expanded to other dimensions of life. Of course, each episode of de-mythologizing is followed by re-mythologizing because human beings seem to need a working explanation of everything to make sense of their lives. One case in point would be making changes in the way the universe is described. We went from a flat world sitting beneath a blue dome across which the sun was dragged every day by a team of horses to the Ptolemaic geocentric universe where the earth was the center of everything. Then Copernicus, at considerable risk, taught us that the sun was the center of the universe. In this heliocentric universe, everything was supposed to revolve around the sun. Because Copernicus published his work near the time of his death, it fell to Galileo to defend and promulgate the theory for which Galileo suffered. Newton, with his understanding of gravity, helped to create another vision of the universe. This has been followed by other theories which we might say led us to the concept of the Big Bang. Now there are physicists challenging the Big Bang theory, and some of them are even suggesting that the universe is eternal. It seems as if the notion of the Big Bang is not an adequate account of the beginning of the universe. The Big Bang begins with a singularity (which is defined as everything being contained in a single infinitely-dense point), but no one has any real idea what preceded the singularity. Quantum physics is challenging the concept of a singularity along with insisting that the universe is finite and that the concept of infinity is not scientifically defensible. In this perspective, the universe has no beginning (and perhaps no end). The universe is thus described as being eternal (*Physics Letters B.* Volume 714, 4 February 2015). Carlo Rovelli, in a book titled *Reality is Not What It Seems*, suggests that instead of a Big Bang there was a Big Bounce and this imagery suggests a universe expanding and contracting over enormous expanses of time. His suggestion focused my attention on human breathing and wondering if breathing is a metaphor for a universe which expands and contracts and thus has a Big Bounce (or perhaps a series of Big Bounces).

My writing is an effort to re-mythologize contemporary religious faith, especially contemporary Christian faith. Along the way, we will do some de-mythologizing which will have at least two different aspects to it. One aspect will be a process of writing down or saying out loud what many people have only admitted privately to themselves. Another aspect will be a more direct challenge to certain common assumptions. I'm inviting my readers to join me in the process of re-examination of many of the things we have simply assumed to be true. I would count my efforts as successful, not if I persuade you of my opinions, but if I succeed in disturbing your usual way of thinking. I am a great believer that some useful and creative results can come from processes that break up normal patterns of thought and perception.

It is easy to disagree with other people's ideas. It's easy to say, "I don't believe that." Sometimes we may even be able to explain why we disagree. Most of the time most of us, however, find it more difficult to propose an alternative perspective. In other words, it is easier to say "nay" than it is to say "aye." That may be one of the factors that makes it easier for us to slide into a negative perspective about life than it is for us to be positive and affirming about life. I am attempting in this work to offer some positive and affirming ideas to encourage my readers to say "aye" more often than "nay."

One of the early creation narratives in the Jewish-Christian Bible tells us that God created "things" and brought them to the man (who had already been created) and asked the man to name them. There is tremendous power in giving names to things. Name-giving goes along with identifying. Of course, such a process is limiting: if we say that a piece of fruit is an apple, then it cannot, by that definition, be an orange, a lemon or a muffin. The naming process also leads us to try to be precise about our definition of the names we use. So, we add to the labels and apples become Fuji, Gala, Macintosh, etc. With the efforts at precision come narrower and narrower descriptions of the recipients of a name and perhaps more and more denial of unusual or unexpected features of the object or person we're naming.

The process of naming leads to creating metaphors and similes. If we have created the name "king" and used it to describe the head of some unit of government, then we might say that other leaders are like kings. In the process, we attribute certain characteristics to the individual thus described, and this adds to the process of narrowing and restricting the definition. As we rule in certain attributes, we obviously rule out others. However, names have a way of enduring across time, perhaps because they are simply convenient. When I encounter the word "king" as a description of anything, I am transported to the world of childhood stories wherein I see thrones, crowns, knights-in-armor, lots of horses and castles. A couple of years ago, I cruised down the Rhine River in Germany and saw a lot of castles alongside the water. Most of them have fallen into disrepair. I visited King Ludwig's famous castle (which inspired the Disney World imitation). I concluded that castles were interesting, but I wouldn't want to live there, and the whole experience reminded me that the word "king" is not useful for describing any political realities in the 21st century. For us to use the word "king" to describe God, for example, does not help people in this century understand what we're discussing. We could easily be described as people who don't know what we're saying. In doing this, we have made an already difficult and complex process unnecessarily complicated.

We must find ways to deal with the fact that all of reality is interrelated and intertwined and no aspect, perspective or point of view can be disconnected and allowed to flourish on its own. One case in point here is that the reality of nuclear power, sometimes manifesting as weapons, and sometimes as a fuel for generating electricity, requires an ethical perspective on political decisions. Similarly, all sorts of scientific discoveries invite us to ethical reflection: it might be the appropriate use of pesticides, the allocation of limited resources, birth control, or how medical practice deals with untreatable and potentially fatal diseases.

This very complexity tempts us to be less than honest and less than thorough in our ontological reflections. It is tempting when contemplating the enormity of the subject to throw up our hands and run and hide. Politicians, unfortunately, have taken advantage of this, assured us that they can tell us what to think, and thus save us from developing a severe case of ontological trauma. No one can do your ontological contemplation for you any more than someone else can live your life for you. The complexity of the subject also leads me to offer a couple of observations: my ontological reflections are incomplete (I expect them to continue until I die), and the limits of my knowledge and understanding will require that I give inadequate attention to many aspects of the whole ontological enterprise. However, I also believe that we can make a difference. If my reflections stimulate your reflections, then we might very well begin a process of reciprocal ontological affirmation that may help our world to make more effective and appropriate use of its resources. Thus, I will offer you my thoughts about a collection of elements that are important components of ontological understanding. I encourage you to reflect on my reflections, to propose your take on these things and to see where your experiences and expertise will help you supplement my offerings.

Coherence or Incoherence?
(Revisiting "To be or not to be?")

I suggested a few pages back that the denominalizing process proposed by NLP might help us maintain coherence in our thinking about ontology. It will be helpful to keep that in mind as I take us through some ideas about the process of understanding ontology or, from a faith perspective, doing theology or in keeping with the NLP insight, theologizing.

Bob Berman and Robert Lanza have written the book: *Biocentrism: How Life and Consciousness are the Keys to Understanding the True Nature of the Universe.* They make an impressive case for the idea that consciousness is eternal. Part of their argument depends on the concept from physics that energy can neither be created nor destroyed. It may change forms of expression, but it always is. If we apply this to the concept of a human life-ing, we can see Being-in-action. I am getting ahead of the story here, but I mention this to whet your interest in what is significant about not seeing ourselves as objects.

What if the universe is not an object? What if it is a process? Can we still justify our assumption that it had a beginning and will have an end? What if "universing" is a constant process? If we stop thinking of the universe as an object and stop talking about it in terms of nouns, then it becomes a verb, an action, a process, a doing. The universe only needs a beginning and an end in the minds of folks who insist that it is an object, even if it is the ultimately spectacular object. It occurs to me to wonder if human assumptions about our life cycle have led us to project that process onto the universing. Perhaps the logic is like "Well, if we must die, then so does all else." It is a well-established understanding that human beings need to make meaning of events. The objectification of the universing is part of our need to make meaning. Some have described the universe as "our universe;" perhaps they want to think of the universe as their personal property. Such thinking will reduce the immensity of the universe into a simplistic concept which we can mentally manipulate and, so we can avoid feeling overwhelmed. Even if we agree that the universe is unimaginably vast, if we see it as an object with a beginning and an end, then it becomes a manipulative in the various schemes that offer explanations that help us find meaning in events.

Some scientists believe the universe is expanding. They seem to ignore Zeno's paradox. Zeno was a Greek philosopher who lived about 500 years before the birth of Jesus. He maintained that if you took a spear and went to the edge of the universe and threw the spear, one of two things would happen: either it would go somewhere beyond you or it would hit something and bounce back. In either case, you would have proved that you had not come to the edge of the universe. The notion of an expanding universe implies space (or something) into which the universe could expand, and that idea takes us back to Zeno and his idea about the edge of the universe.

If we stop seeing the universing as an object, then the notion of a universing that changes and rearranges itself or looks different from different perspectives doesn't seem to be nearly the problem we have with the universing as an expanding object. Even the notion of expanding seems to imply a beginning. Once we have agreed that there is a beginning, then we seem to need to have an end. There are physicists working with quantum equations saying that the universe has no beginning, that there never was a Big Bang. The physicist Sir James Jeans wrote: ". . . the universe begins to look more like a great thought than a great machine. Mind no longer appears to be an accidental intruder into the realm of matter; we ought, rather, to hail it as the creator and governor of the realm of matter." (Quoted in R. C. Henry, "The Mental Universe"; Nature 436:29, 2005.) It is quite possible that the universe (or universing) has no beginning and no end. If we tell stories to make sense of things and to explain things, then we need to be aware that how we put those stories together may be a major factor in developing the story. Our assumptions about everything having a beginning and thus an end are major influences on the theories we develop about objects and events. We need to be aware of the difficulties in this formula: assumptions = projections = objective reality. The human tendency to see what we are looking for has repeatedly been documented in scientific research. My favorite was the assignment given to a group of researchers to calculate the number of daisies in a field. When the volunteers came back with their results, they were thanked for the efforts and then asked, "How many sunflowers did you see?" No one saw any sunflowers in spite of the fact that there was an abundance of them in the field.

Human beings objectify all sorts of events. We have collections of pictures taken at weddings, graduations, baptisms, reunions and holiday feasts. When people graduate, they often get a diploma which "proves" that they completed a certain curriculum. However, when I review my memories of all these events, I find myself caught up in a sea of feelings about the relating with folks that went on at these events. I very seldom recall the menu of the feast, but I can have warm, comforting memories of the feasting and who was there to join in the festivities. These "events" are markers, way-stations in a process.

My nearly fatal encounter with sepsis happened at the most inconvenient time although I don't know that there is a convenient time for such things. The inconvenience was compounded because we were in the process at the time of moving from a house where we had lived for more than 20 years to a condominium. We hosted our family at Thanksgiving and Christmas some seven months after the sepsis was defeated and the moving was done. The feasting was a welcoming of the family to our new home and a celebration that I was indeed still an active participant in that family. I don't remember the menus in any detail or what kind of wine I drank, but the warm feeling of feasting with family is in my heart. It would be better for me to remember such events as a process during which certain dynamics and experiences were integrated into my living (life-ing) instead of thinking of these events as things.

This objectification of ultimate reality has caused some peculiar manifestations in religious thinking (aka theologizing). When the universe is treated as an object, then Divinity (God) must be beyond that, and we end up with all sorts of imagined answers that might be summed up in the widely-purported existence of heaven and therefore hell, the afterlife and all sorts of poetic fictions. These speculative concepts often end up being treated as basic truth. For example, the concept of hell is a pagan theory often imported into Christian theologizing even though the word "hell" does not appear in the Judaic or Christian Scriptures. The word "Gehenna" is sometimes translated as hell, but it was the name of the place outside Jerusalem where the garbage was burned. "The concept of 'eternal punishment in hell' is an unbiblical pagan doctrine which was embraced and Christianized by the Roman Catholic Church in the early centuries of Christianity and made official when Jerome translated the Bible into Latin in the Latin Vulgate (circa 400 CE). The doctrine of 'everlasting punishment in hell' is founded upon a combination of mistranslations and misinterpretations." (from *God's Plan for All*, a free, online book). To that observation we might add things like Dante's *Inferno*, which offers an extensive portrayal of hell.

If God is not an object (noun), then we might wonder if the appropriate verbal expression would be "Godding"? It would be relatively easy to imagine that Godding is creating in the universing always and unendingly since we got rid of the need for an end when we got rid of the objectification. Christian and Jewish Scriptures, with which I am the most familiar, do all sorts of linguistic machinations to qualify the objective language, so we find lots of use of words like "eternal" and "everlasting." These things might be seen as efforts to get outside the limitations imposed by nouns; however, this creates a variety of problems because we end up talking about eternal objects and both our experience and our consciousness tell us there are no such things. I suppose that efforts to get around this problem helped to create the poetry about heaven and streets of gold and gates of pearl. The manifestations of Godding as recorded in Hebrew Scriptures most often are portrayed as manifestations of enormous and dangerous energy. Moses is not allowed to see God because it was believed that no one could see God and survive, so Moses is allowed only to see God passing by. It appears that ancient people understood God was not an object and could not be seen or encountered as one. God appears as energy—sound and perhaps flashing lights like thunder and lightning or the eruption of a volcano. It could be argued that Christianity's description of God as a Trinity (Father, Son, and Holy Spirit) points to the difficulty of giving even a single metaphoric name to Divinity; that reality gets underscored by the way the Church has avoided getting very specific about the Holy Spirit. It seems to make sense to portray Godding as displays of creating energy. The views from the Hubble telescope of the ever-changing universing would seem to be a contemporary version of Godding on display.

Most ancient wisdom as enshrined in the teachings of figures like Buddha and Jesus is about a process called life-ing. These teachers offered us values to manifest in our life-ing. With the NLP folk, I want to say we should refer to "living" as "life-ing" just because it gets us away from the nominalization trap. Denominalizing our life-ing would help us to be aware that we are all process—constantly changing at every level from the cellular to the total personality—instead of objects. Richard Rohr, in his book, *The Divine Dance,* says that it is time to "re-verb!" Denominalizing is one way we are participating in universing. One of the truly exciting and amazing things about the research going on in the Positive Psychology arena is that time and time again the values of life-ing according to the teachings of the Ancient Ones are getting validated. We are finding that loving, compassioning, forgiving, trusting, inviting and creating are pro-life and help to generate an experience often called "flow." We have the potential to do our life-ing in a way that is coherent with the flow of Godding's creating of/in the universing. We can say we are in the universing at a macro level and the universing is in us at a micro level. The energy of Godding interpenetrates the life-ing process of everyone. We get to choose whether to embrace this reality or deny it and insist on objectifying life.

Here is another reflection spurred on by my last birthday and my near-miss at dying. I know some stories my family told me about my beginning (birth), but I have no memory of the experience. I know that there are a variety of folks in the world who purport to help people remember their births and I won't get into an argument with them about that. I'll just say that I have no direct memory/knowledge of mine. I would suppose that probably those who claim memories of birthing don't have memories of their conception. All of us have no memory of our beginning; we only have the stories we have been told and which we tell ourselves. Every night I go to sleep by some mysterious process, but I am mostly unaware of that happening. Sure, I sometimes remember dreams and even know that when I am dreaming, I am asleep. Sleep is probably the closest analogy we have to death. When I became aware that my disease could kill me and, in fact, that on one particular night I might die, I still didn't have a true death experience. All this is about saying that our knowledge of our own beginning and ending is theoretical. We use this theoretical knowledge to construct our life story, and we project it everywhere and assert that everything has a beginning and an end. We often use this story-telling to keep us in a humble frame of mind. But what if: I am eternal and what I call my current life-ing is just one manifestation of the fundamental reality of my life-ing in the Godding universing? Jesus seems to speak of the kingdom of God as an always and forever reality. Might he be implying that we always live in the Godding flow?

I am aware that some might interpret what I'm saying here as implying that God = Universe. That seems to be a problem for some because it doesn't agree with their preconceptions. It also may seem to be a problem if they insist on continuing the nominalizations. I feel that "verbal-izing" (or "re-verbing") the terminology frees us from a lot of historical, philosophical and theological limitations.

I propose that we use the word "Totality" to be inclusive and as a term, we might use it to encompass all of reality—both what we know or think we know and that which we don't know or think we don't know. At the heart of Totality is Godding. Godding is Loving and Loving is Creating. Godding forever creates in universing out of the loving nature of the Godding-Self. Godding is Energizing. Energy is infinite. It appears in a variety of forms—some spectacular and some ordinary. Sometimes the ordinary is spectacular like a flower blossom or a rainbow, and sometimes the spectacular is ordinary like sunlight or distant thunder. Loving, creating Godding energy is everywhere and nowhere.

Godding creates by birthing loving manifestations of the Godding-Self. Events like black holes and supernovae are components of that birthing. The appearance of individual people who exhibit inordinate excesses of compassion are also components of that birthing. These manifestations may be unique and unprecedented or they may be variations on a familiar theme, but all are epiphanies of the ever-emerging and creating Godding. It is humanly impossible to list all the facets of Godding or all the components of the loving manifestations of the Godding-Self.

The laws of thermodynamics tell us that the universing is running down, dissipating more and more energy until it reaches stasis, has no more energy and thus will be dead. This theory encountered a puzzle: if everything is running down, how do we account for the appearance of new realities? The answer to that is known as the theory of dissipative structures which tells us that a new structure elaborates itself, thus contradicting the "running-down" theory, but it uses a lot of energy in elaborating itself and thus actually conforms to the "running-down" theory because it uses so much energy.

Then we come to a question: will the new structure eventually become so elaborate that it must collapse, as it were, of its own weight? Aha, there is a theoretical exception which says that either the new structure must collapse of its own weight and come to an end, or it can escape to a new order of being where it uses less energy. The concept of something that gets so elaborate and consumes so much energy that it has to either collapse or escape to a new order of being offers us a metaphor for what happens to individuals as their identity (or self-explanation) gets increasingly complex, internally contradictory, unwieldy, and ineffective. First, we notice that as individuals approach the crisis point, their personal systems become more and more complicated and consume energy in the form of attention. These individuals may feel like they are falling apart, and they feel forced to focus on their own "issues," sometimes to a more or less compulsive or obsessive level. It appears that various stress-coping mechanisms move into "hyperdrive" (which of course leads to using more energy) and may often lead to a pattern of "overdoing" these mechanisms without any real change in the results. On the other hand, the option of escaping to a new order of being, gives us the chance to completely shift perspectives and come at life and its issues from a very different way. The new order uses less energy and makes "old things new." Jesus says: "Behold, I make all things new." This means that the new order will incorporate new understandings of life issues and will construct a new identity or self-understanding.

The Chinese pictogram for "crisis" is a combination of the pictograms for "danger" and "opportunity." When an airplane is taking off, it reaches a point where it must either leave the ground or crash. The plane on the ground is the old order of things which elaborates itself and burns more and more energy as it rushes to the point of no return, where it must certainly self-destruct or fly. When the plane actually leaves the ground to soar into the sky, it has become something very different from a rather clumsy, inefficient, and uncomfortable way to travel on the ground.

The new order of being might be a radical transformation of the individual into an avatar, or it might also refer to what happens when the physical person dies and the Godding energy moves on beyond this particular manifestation. It could also be both!

I suggest that the manifestations of the Godding-Self are dissipative structures and that eventually, they will indeed escape to a new order of being—which is what Godding in the universing is all about, constantly moving toward a new order of being. "Behold I make all things new."

Denominalizing While Theologizing
(or Godding, Universing, and Coherence)

NLP has made a serious issue out of our tendency, at least in English, to turn verbs into nouns. Thus, living becomes life, loving becomes love, creating becomes creator or creation, and so on. As previously mentioned, the brain processes objects and motions in different areas and confusion about nouns and verbs can create more confusion. I ask you to keep this perspective in mind while I talk a bit about the process of doing theology or theologizing.

A great deal of thinking—mythic, theological, philosophical and scientific—has gone into speculating about time and eternity. There have been endless controversies and battles over it. My tendency to think this way leads me to assume that many things are true when they may not be. I get hungry, so I decide to fix some food and have a meal. This process gets started at the beginning. If I am eating and get interrupted by a phone call, I may tell my caller I am in the middle of my meal and, eventually, I will finish the meal, put the remains away and clean up my mess, and thus there is an end. There are enough of these things in my life to encourage me to think that anything that exists has a beginning and will, therefore, have a middle and an end. I observe that people die; for example, my parents have died. I can't prove my parents had a beginning, but I can date the day their lives ended. It seems like I came into their lives in the middle, but that's a hypothesis since I cannot prove they had a beginning. I know, however, that they had an end. It is a matter of belief that they had a beginning. As I observe the process of people dying, I assume that is the "way of all flesh" and that I will also die. I can't prove that, and if I do die, I don't imagine that I'll be able to prove that I did! My perception of myself tells me that I have always been alive. My first-person evidence could establish the belief that I have lived forever since I have no awareness of not existing.

Churches, mortuaries, insurance companies, family, and colleagues all urge me to believe that I will die and so I should make preparations for same by drafting a will, buying life insurance, planning some sort of funeral service, etc. If I tell them I don't share their belief, they will all agree that I am in denial about the basic realities of life. I might get referred to a psychotherapist to help me deal with my denial which will be described as unrealistic, illogical or, perhaps, even stupid. These folks all urge me to join them in thinking about my existence as an object. In this fashion, my life-ing becomes an object (life), and I am encouraged not to think about it as a process. That also makes my life an object amongst other objects, and this has a huge impact on what sort of value I attach to this object: is it better than a car or a house? Is it a notch more or less significant than other human objects of different colors, genders, and sizes? If, however, I insist that my life-ing is a process, an ongoing series of actions, then I escape the object trap and suddenly become comparable to all other humans who are busy life-ing. I prefer the term "life-ing" because living has been turned into an object as seen in the question, "What do you do for a living?" If I answer that question with a noun—I am a clergyperson—then I have joined others in converting me to an object. I come to speak of my existence as "my life" and I do it in a way that implies it is an object. I don't ordinarily talk about my living unless I'm using that word as a synonym for my occupation. It might make a lot of difference to talk about how I do my life-ing instead of talking about how I live my life because it moves me from regarding my life as an object to experiencing it as a process.

Much of the research in the Positive Psychology field, as well as the research behind mBraining, seems to offer a much more positive view of human nature than many dominant world religions have offered. To those who wish to focus on how awful, sinful and dreadful human beings are by nature, I pose a simple question: why has this dark, derogatory, depressing perspective not resulted in love abounding more, in violence decreasing and in the arrival of what some would call the kingdom of God? We've tried it this way since St. Augustine back in the fourth century of the common era. It's time for a different perspective. The solid, scientific grounding of much of the Positive Psychology research would commend the validity of that perspective.

We are used to the word "sin." Usually, that word links us to tables of behavioral classifications and a lot of other words that purport to describe sin. We are encouraged to avoid doing sin and priest-craft has reaped a ton of power from this word. There are catalogs of sins that would enlighten us as to the seriousness of various behaviors. You might recall the seven deadly sins list. There are prescriptions about how to obtain forgiveness of sin, all of which benefit the established power of ecclesiastical institutions and their minions. The existence of sin-lists encourages people to be judgmental. These lists require people whose behavior makes these "things" manifest in the world. Our tendency to fear the Other encourages us to project these dreadful aspects upon the Other and that is counter-productive. But the word "sin" originates in Greek with an archery term which means "to miss the mark." Apparently, sin began as a verb and has been nominalized, thus giving a whole class of people power over us and tempting us to judge other people. Let's denominalize it and start using it as a verb. Thus sin = missing the mark about keeping my behavior consistent with my value system. The mBraining perspective suggests that sin is incoherence. Thinking of it along these lines opens the door to the reminder that there is no failure, only feedback and an opportunity to learn, change behavior and move toward coherence, which in mBraining terms would be an integration of head, heart, gut, and pelvic-brains.

In Western societies, there has been a major disconnect between religion and science. We currently confront an amazing anomaly. We have societies which make use of a plethora of high-tech gadgets to the point where we have instant global communication. Obviously, these gadgets have come to us as a result of amazing scientific developments over the last half-century. At the same time, we have a rather substantial number of people often using the high-tech gadgets to communicate who, in the name of religion, deny the realities revealed by science. This kind of blatant disregarding of science has encouraged many folks in the scientific field to disregard religion. There are a plethora of risks to life as we know it as a result of this disconnect. We run the risk of science becoming an amoral enterprise, a risk probably most clearly displayed by the development of Artificial Intelligence (check out the movie Ex Machina). We also run the risk of ignorant religionists acting out immoral desecrations, very clearly seen in the carryings-on of the so-called Islamic State with its beheading of infidels, burning of nonconformists and destruction of cultural and historical artifacts.

Onto this stage steps mBraining. Here are research-based, scientifically-validated concepts that are consistent with and supportive of the spiritual teaching of the Ancient Ones exemplified by Buddha and Jesus. (I would recommend a little book by Marcus Borg, with an introduction by Jack Kornfield. It is titled *Jesus and Buddha* and consists of the parallel sayings of these two Teachers.) The mBraining perspective invites a dialogue with religion and the spiritual traditions of the world. This rather new development, which integrates the discoveries of Positive Psychology with ancient wisdom, offers the world a faith-friendly and scientifically-verifiable approach to living. When I say "dialogue," I am talking about a genuine sharing of and exchanging of ideas in a way that would be mutually beneficial. I see religious and spiritual traditions benefiting from the validation of their central concepts by scientific research; mBraining can enhance the ability of these traditions to address modern people's life involvement. I see mBraining benefitting from the endorsement of its work by representatives of the spiritual/religious traditions. At the same time, the dialogue will challenge the way some religions portray human nature. One of the most obvious examples of how this will happen is that those religions that have tended to portray human nature as inherently corrupt, decadent and worthless will find their concepts challenged. I am thinking here especially, although not exclusively, of the Christian concept of original sin. Another area where this challenge is seen is the opposition of mBraining to the notion that certain people, because of their beliefs, are worthy of destruction/execution. mBraining gets into looking at human characteristics which will be apparent in any culture or faith tradition. The notion that there is no such thing as failure, but only feedback, will be difficult for some faith traditions to embrace. mBraining is challenged to examine more of the concepts of the faith traditions. I say this because the research to date has supported the secular reality of an enormous portion of common spiritual perspectives including values like love, forgiveness, compassion, generosity, and creativity. mBraining needs to look more deeply into the theories and stories offered by religion. mBraining talks about the importance of making meaning, which is also something every religion on the planet tries to do. Some deeper research into that process might help everyone. We might explore questions about what components are involved in making meaning, what common elements are found in various explanatory theories and what are the apparent limitations and accomplishments of various theories. I am aware that there are some commonalities in creation stories. We might wonder what that is about, to what it points and whether it helps to develop concepts about what a theory of meaning needs to contain or address. As I try to construct a meaningful theory about my own life, it would be helpful to know what the main ingredients usually are in such efforts.

I find it interesting that mBraining has rather gradually evolved into including consideration of the sex-brain aspect of human life. The fact that mBraining has found other aspects of human life to be primary got us into head, heart, and gut before considering the genital brain and that seems to be contrary to the teachings of Freud and his followers as well as contrary to the fascination by many religions with sexual behavior. I suspect that this unique way of getting to such important dynamics may give mBraining theories the power to help religions be more realistic and helpful in dealing with questions about human sexuality.

If we review Jewish-Christian Scriptures as a series of recitations of the mighty acts of God, then we discover that God is actually Godding—active, creative, doing. Consider the Christian doctrine of the Trinity from an mBraining perspective and see Father = Creating; Son = Compassionate Loving; and Spirit = Intuitive Acting (mBraining sees taking action as a function of the gut, where courage resides). Is this a way of saying that compassioning, creating and couraging are essential components of fundamental reality? In other words, is the Humaning experience a mirror of Godding?

A "story" has these two components: the value proclaimed and the details of construction. The details are less important than the value. That's easy to see in things like the birth narratives about Jesus or even in the creation stories. Understanding the issue of value and details makes it possible for Judaism, for example. to embrace the creation stories in their Scriptures and the modern theories of evolution.

The well-known Bishop Spong wrote a lengthy narrative about the birth of Jesus and in the process showed us how certain components of the "story," which are usually ignored, are hidden in plain sight. Here is what he wrote about the Matthean birth narrative of Jesus:

"Hidden in this boring genealogy, however, is, I believe, the clue that unlocks the meaning of the story of the virgin birth, so we turn to these verses in search of that vital clue. Matthew includes in the line that produced Jesus, four ancestral mothers. It was quite unusual in that day to place women into any genealogical line, for women were thought of more as incubators than as co-creators of the life of the unborn child. In addition to that, each of the women named was well known to Jewish readers, for their stories were told in the Scriptures with which Matthew's Jewish readers would have been quite familiar. The first of these women was named Tamar. Her story is found in Genesis 38. She is the daughter-in-law of Judah, one of the twelve sons of Jacob. Tamar was pregnant by Judah, which would have been called incest in Jewish society. She bears twins, Perez and Zerah. The line that produced Jesus flowed through Perez, a product of incest, Matthew asserts. The second ancestral mother was Rahab, and her story is told in the book of Joshua (see chapters 2 and 6). She is a prostitute, who runs a brothel located inside the walls of the city of Jericho. She entertains and protects Joshua's spies and apparently later marries one of them. The third ancestral mother mentioned is Ruth. Her story is told in the book that bears her name. After her husband has died, she seduces his kinsman, a man named Boaz, as he was sleeping on the floor after drinking too much wine and she forces him to marry and thus to protect her. The final ancestral mother in the genealogy is 'the wife of Uriah.' We know from other sources that her name is Bathsheba. Her story is told in chapter 11 of II Samuel. She is the woman whose adulterous affair with King David led not only to her pregnancy but also to the calculated murder of her husband, Uriah, while he served in King David's army. Does it not strike you as strange that Matthew, who was the first to relate the narrative of the virgin birth, chose to introduce that narrative by saying that the line that produced Jesus flowed through the incest of Tamar, the prostitution of Rahab, the seduction of Ruth and the adultery of Bathsheba? Is this not an unusual way to defend your founder against the charge of illegitimacy? Was Matthew saying that if a convicted felon, executed in a public place, can be the life in which God is best seen in human history, would it also not be possible to proclaim that a child called 'illegitimate,' could also be the life in whom God was met in a new way? These possibilities need to be taken seriously. In the virgin birth story Matthew will claim a holy origin for Jesus, but then he seems to say that no matter what his origins, God can raise up a holy life even through incest, prostitution, seduction, and adultery. I submit that this is a powerful witness!" (e-Newsletter, "Charting the New Reformation," April 7, 2016)

What else about human nature is hidden in plain sight? mBraining is getting at this question. In common terms, we have gut feelings about things, both positive and negative; we all want to get to the heart of the matter; and there are things we have trouble getting through our heads. For a very long time (at least 100 years) in Western science, we have ignored the heart and gut-brains, yet their reality and truth are hiding in plain sight.

The website www.physicscentral.com tells us, in a more speculative vein, ". . . the exploded remains of a supernova [or imploded star] travel throughout the universe only to clump together with other stardust and give birth to a new star"; and "We can conclude that 93% of the mass in our body is stardust." Carl Sagan also is reported to have said: "The nitrogen in our DNA, the calcium in our teeth, the iron in our blood, the carbon in our apple pies were made in the interiors of collapsing stars. We are made of star-stuff."

Jeremy England is a physicist who has derived a mathematical formula which he claims demonstrates how inanimate matter under certain conditions becomes life. His work could show us how Godding universing links to us at the micro level. The apparently inanimate collections of stardust, under certain conditions, would, according to Mr. England, give rise to life and start an evolving life-chain. If we discover that elements like loving, compassioning and forgiving are inherent aspects of human nature which emerge as life evolves and which we ignore to our detriment, and that human nature is mostly stardust, does it seem too much to wonder if Godding universing is indeed loving in essence? Ancient Ones have taught that Godding is loving and we are discovering that we are at our best when we love in altruistic ways. Is compassion part of the basic nature of reality? Is love inherent in ultimate reality?

mBraining shows us how coherence amongst our component brains is desirable, important and indeed essential. I have raised the question as to whether sin is incoherence or a form of incoherence. Does the reality of stardust, which is one of the ways we are demonstrably part of the universing, suggest that coherence of all reality is desirable and possible?

Of People and Portals

Again, it's about the words. The word "human" is a noun in English, and that implies an object, thing, category, etc., all of which focus on essence, which invites us to consider the unchanging aspects of this object. Philosophical arguments about essence and existence have been around a long time, most recently in the energy put into discussing, defining and celebrating existentialism's protest against essentialism. The idea that there is no such thing as an essential human was a major theme in proclaiming existentialism. (I'll avoid discussing the strange paradox of the essence of existentialism.) With that and the NLP concern about denominalizing in the background, I propose that in discussing issues regarding people in the Godding universing, we use the word "Humaning" to capture both the existential realities of present life-ing and the obvious fact that Humanings are living, breathing creatures. When a Humaning dies, we don't discuss this by referring to a dead Humaning. We turn the dead into an object, call it a body or corpse and go about being done with it. Humaning is an ongoing process. This process has common elements which we might consider together as Humaning physiology, but it also has unique realities most obvious because there is no such thing as two identical Humanings. Each of us is unique, has never appeared before, and will not be replicated ever.

Humanings *are* portals through which the Godding energy flows into the ordinary or materialistic world from the realm beyond. These portals are fractals of the Divine, which means people embody the same dynamics as does the Divine. We repeat the elements which Godding reality manifests.

"A fractal is a never-ending pattern that repeats itself at different scales. This property is called 'Self-Similarity.' Although fractals are very complex, they are made by repeating a simple process." "A fractal is a never-ending pattern. Fractals are infinitely complex patterns that are self-similar across different scales. They are created by repeating a simple process over and over in an ongoing feedback loop. Driven by recursion, fractals are images of dynamic systems – the pictures of Chaos. Geometrically, they exist in between our familiar dimensions. Fractal patterns are extremely familiar since nature is full of fractals. For instance: trees, rivers, coastlines, mountains, clouds, seashells, hurricanes, etc. Abstract fractals – such as the Mandelbrot Set – can be generated by a computer calculating a simple equation over and over." These two definitions come from the "Fractal Foundation" website.

A dictionary definition says a fractal is a

". . . geometrical or physical structure having an irregular or fragmented shape at all scales of measurement between a greatest and smallest scale such that certain mathematical or physical properties of the structure, as the perimeter of a curve or the flow rate in a porous medium, behave as if the dimensions of the structure (fractal dimensions) are greater than the spatial dimensions." The mathematician who coined the term said: "Many important spatial patterns of Nature are either irregular or fragmented to such an extreme degree that ... classical geometry is hardly of any help in describing their form. ... I hope to show that it is possible in many cases to remedy this absence of geometric representation by using a family of shapes I propose to call fractals – or fractal sets." (Mandelbrot, *Fractals*, 1977)

Insofar as we can understand fractals as pictures of chaos, they show us that chaos has an orderly foundation we would not ordinarily see. The mathematical formula can be applied on many different scales. Fractals are not necessarily fixed objects because a hurricane, for example, can be seen to have a fractal nature even though it is a moving, energized system. If the fractal-forming formula is applied to two different systems, one very large and one very small, close analysis will reveal that the pattern inherent in the systems will be the same. Godding can be described as a very large fractal system and Humaning as a rather small fractal system. However, the properties inherent in the two systems will be identical. If we combine the fractal perspective with the quantum physics concept of entanglement, then we can see that both the Godding and the Humaning systems are mutually influential. If love, creativity, generosity, forgiveness, grace, etc. are properties of Godding, then they are also inherent in Humaning. However, just as it might take a microscope to see the fractal nature of a small system, it may take special sensitivity to comprehend the fractal nature of Humaning.

Chaos theory tells us that in large systems, replication is impossible to predict or guarantee. The so-called butterfly effect describes how particular actions somewhere in a system generate unexpected and unpredictable events, which may occur at some time distant from the original action. (That butterfly effect describes a major storm–like a tornado or a hurricane—happening as an unknown consequence of a butterfly flapping its wings. The butterfly and the storm are substantial distances, both physically and temporally, apart.) Chaos theory leads me to believe that human fractals of the divine will not necessarily behave in perfect or divine ways.

There are lots of terms used in both theological and psychological circles about what to call a realm of existence, if there is one, beyond what is ordinarily called common human existence. I will refer to what we ordinarily experience as present reality as the Predominant. I will refer to the transcendent or the beyond as the Alternate. Huxley, in his work *The Doors of Perception* (Huxley, Aldous. *The Doors of Perception and Heaven and Hell* (Kindle Locations 722-724). HarperCollins. Kindle Edition), prefers to think of human beings as having a portal or door between themselves and the Alternate. He describes it as a door in the wall. I prefer to refer to *people* as being portals. Humanings are portals through which the Godding energy flows and that flow is impacted by the condition of the portal. Nevertheless, the enduring pattern of the fractal is beneath the chaos, and that suggests that, if loving is part of the nature of Godding, that this loving pattern may be called forth, especially as Humanings serve as portals to transpose the immensity of the Alternate into the realm of the Predominant.

The condition of the portal is reflective of the individual's attitude toward it. Several factors might condition that attitude: a willingness to "own" the portal; emotionally and spiritually turning toward or away from the Alternate; one's rigidness or insecurity about change; achieved levels of self-compassion. When we apply the concept of negative and positive dialectics to the notion that we are portals, then we can see that the negative dialectic would lead to a restricting of the portal because the negative dialectic increases the differentiation between our self-image and the Godding image. A positive dialectic would open the portal more widely and allow a more abundant flow of Godding energy into and through the individual. "The Divine, by whatever name you prefer, creates every human being, who is, therefore, a Divine experience walking." (Eldon Taylor, *Choices and Illusions: How Did I Get Where I Am, and How Do I Get Where I Want to Be?* p. 160. Hay House, Inc., Kindle Edition.) That idea points to what happens when the open portal allows Godding energy to flow from the Alternate into the Predominant. The portal is a passage, not a destination. Our portal nature exists to facilitate the flow of Godding energy into and among the Humanings. Each of us is a vortex of a swirling of Godding energy that creates a portal in the universing through which loving may flow into the world.

My thinking about the portal is conditioned by the metaphor of the iris in the eye or the iris diaphragm in a camera lens. The iris dilates, opening and closing, to regulate the amount of light flowing through it. If the iris in our eyes did not constrict, there would be occasions when our visual apparatus would be overwhelmed by light so bright we could not see. If the eye were permanently constricted and could not dilate in the darkness, then there would be much detail we would not be able to see. Our visual apparatus would be relatively useless if the iris in the eye wasn't adjustable. If we dismantle the camera lens system, we discover that the diaphragm or iris of the camera is an apparatus that adjusts the size of the hole through which the camera lens will focus light. Another interesting characteristic of light is that the speed of light is constant, which means that light flowing through a constricted diaphragm or an expanded diaphragm travels at the same speed. In this metaphor, I equate light with energy, which reminds us that the diaphragm, while limiting the quantity of light passing through this hole, does not limit the quality of light. If we equate light with energy, then the quantity of the energy encountered by the portal does not affect the quality of the perceived energy.

Portals have other characteristics. One of those is that we have a variety of filters that condition both what we can observe and how we get observed. I would put those filters into two categories: for now, I'll call them primary and acquired. A primary filter refers to a variety of characteristics of the human biosystem. Included here is the understanding that things like our sight and our hearing are inherently limited. There are aspects of both the visual and auditory spectrum that Humanings can't detect. We might mention things like infrared light, ultraviolet light, subsonic and supersonic sounds. There are also ways we have of augmenting the filters; for example, we can use microscopes and telescopes to extend our ability to see, although these devices will not overcome some system limits like the ones on how much of the light spectrum is humanly visible.

Then there are what we might call acquired filters. Language is an acquired filter whether we speak only one or several languages. There are some rather sturdy components of acquired filters. These might include gender stereotypes, certain prejudices or preferences learned early in life, maybe some religious beliefs (depending on when they were acquired), etc. Then there is a collection of emotional issues which may have been imprinted via non-verbal or kinesthetic experiences. I am thinking here about various kinds of childhood abuse as well as efforts families may make to fashion their children in their own image. The abuse issue might show up if the child was abandoned, thus making it hard for the adult to risk anything that might lead to abandonment again. Some women who were sexually (and sometimes violently) abused by their fathers have a very hard time with the notion that God is a Loving Father because they don't know what that is. An experience like that could create a filter that would condition what the portal can experience with the Godding reality.

When we talk about opening the portal wider, we have to address filters, which seems to be what Huxley was talking about in *The Doors of Perception*. Using hypnosis and hallucinogenic drugs or the use of rapid breathing or hyperventilation as taught by Stan Grof, may indeed help us get around the filters and be inspired by spiritual and emotional experiences. But we still face the question of how to return to ordinary states of consciousness without losing what has been acquired. Every Holy Person (in whatever tradition) has faced the same issue. The prophet Amos, in the Hebrew Bible, reports he was just an ordinary man engaged in landscaping (a dresser of sycamore trees), yet he felt compelled to share his spiritually-energized insights. Might we consider the establishment's persecution of spiritual non-conformists such as Jeremiah and Jesus to be the inevitable consequences of living spiritually-coherent lives?

Huxley suggests that opening a portal requires doing something to distract or separate the individual from the details of ordinary life. Thinking about the portal leads to recalling Maslow's pyramid. The bottom two levels of that pyramid represent physiological needs and safety needs. The theory of this pyramid is that one can never move to the higher levels unless the issues represented at the lower levels are resolved. At the peak of the pyramid we find self-actualization. No one can reach that realm if they are not safe or if there are distracting physiological issues for them. Between the safety level and the self-actualization level, we find love/belonging and esteem.

One issue in the diagrams of Maslow's pyramid has to do with the concept of esteem or self-esteem. There is research which tells us that the efforts people make to raise self-esteem increases narcissism and fosters a competitive environment. There seems to be plenty of evidence indicating that the more narcissistic individuals become, the less they are in touch with feelings of loving and belonging. I wonder if Maslow's original thinking here about including esteem at that point in the pyramid was influenced by artifacts of inferiority feelings generated and sustained by certain Western religious practices. If we substitute "self-compassion" for "esteem" in the pyramid, then we see that the individual moving through the fundamentals to self-actualization would move from a sense of safety through feelings of love and belonging, and then through self-compassion, and thus flow upwards to the top of the pyramid. Research also shows that when people increase self-compassion, they also become more compassionate toward other people. I suggest that the image of the pyramid be edited and the term "self-compassion" be substituted for "esteem." Here are the levels in the pyramid from the top down:

1. Self-Actualization needs
2. Esteem (replace with self-compassion) needs.
3. Love/belonging needs.
4. Safety needs.
5. Physiological needs.

Humanings are genetically programmed to evolve, and this evolution is facilitated at the physiological and the safety levels at the bottom of this diagram. This would show that our biological need to evolve will interfere with achieving higher levels of personal development unless the organism feels that the need to evolve remains unfettered. This again would highlight the critical nature of Humanings feeling safe. Although it is not developed in this section, one of my theories about the origins of evil has to do with the biological necessity to evolve overwhelming any particular theories of morality or ethics. If a Humaning feels their need to evolve is threatened or constricted, then that might physiologically trigger the fight/flight/freeze response. This could lead an individual in a situation that feels like a danger to his/her need to evolve to act to oppose the constricting forces. One might think of this as applying to the Humanings constricted to certain social and economic enclaves such as Humanings trapped in an urban slum with severely restricted economic and educational opportunities. That also might help us understand what often feeds the violence amongst Humanings who are stuck in evolution-denying situations. This process would not be limited to the disadvantaged. Anyone who feels trapped may be reacting to an unconscious fear that their need to evolve is being threatened. Humanings might somehow feel that their genetic impulse to evolve is being thwarted even though they could not verbalize that. In the next section, are some thoughts about the internal, non-conscious impulse to evolve.

Don't Grow So Many Teeth

Most adults develop wisdom teeth, the third set of molars, which often arrive in the early twenties (when one is supposedly wiser than when the other adult teeth developed). I once had a dentist who told me that there were professors at his university dental school, who were up there in age, who reported routinely seeing another set of molars (a fourth set which are now known as supernumerary molars) in their patients. Some researchers think that in the distant past adult Humanings had larger jaws and more teeth which helped them to digest food. Evolution has reduced the number of teeth that Humanings now have. It occurs to me to wonder just how that works. If I took a four or five-year-old child to one side and said, "Your great-great-ever-so-great grandfather says you shouldn't grow so many teeth," I doubt that this youngster would have any idea how to implement this grandfatherly dictum. We may be able to document the effects of evolution, but the fact is that none of the techniques we Humanings use to communicate seem to be involved in how our bodies change in response to the forces of evolution. This suggests that there is some way unknown to us that Humanings have of passing along the information needed to trigger the changes caused by evolution.

If we have an unknown and undocumented technique that tells oncoming generations not to grow so many teeth, then there is certainly the possibility that there is a plethora of information passed from generation to generation in ways we do not understand.

There is a new telescope being built which will enable Humanings to see farther "back into the past" and see light that originated very early in the development of the universing. We have believed this to be possible, and so the effort has been made to demonstrate it. I am not a physicist and am not qualified to judge this matter from a scientific perspective, but I have no reason not to accept the conclusions of some eminent scientists. My question is this: if we can perceive light from ancient times, might we be able someday to perceive other "signals" from ancient times?

It makes sense, in considering this ancient light, to suppose that it has been shining on us for a very long time, but that we lacked the tools to identify it for what it is. I want to suggest that a plethora of ancient factors may have been with us for a long time. Some of these may communicate with us in the form of intuition, some might take the form of prenatal influences, and all of it may be bound up in what Assagioli calls the Self that is more than the individual self. Assagioli said: "We shall also discover the immense reserve of undifferentiated psychic energy latent in every one of us; that is, the plastic part of our unconscious which lies at our disposal, empowering us with an unlimited capacity to learn and to create." (Assagioli, 2000, p. 19). Jung also talked about this kind of self (collective unconscious).

[http://carl-jung.net/collective_unconscious.html]
Both men suggest that we Humanings are more than our

individual selves, that we, if you will, may be conduits or portals through which the wisdom of the ages may be channeled.

This perspective will not sit well with materialistic perspectives which suggest that Humanings are self-contained mechanisms. Locke's view that we are born with a "blank slate" sort of mind may be outmoded in philosophical discussions, but the materialistic view of the world seems to suppose that there could be no contact with our predecessors (which seems to accept the essential point of the blank slate).

We don't know how we got the message not to grow so many teeth, but it is obvious that we did get the message in a form that allowed us to carry out the instructions. My own experience might also offer useful details here. I had four impacted wisdom teeth; that is there wasn't enough room in my mouth for those teeth to develop normally, so they grew in horizontally instead of vertically. I was the victim of my body being at war with itself, and those teeth had to be extracted. Evolution does not proceed without pain and inconvenience. What else is going on outside our conscious awareness that impacts the way we live out our lives?

Here is a metaphor that might help you understand the impetus to evolve and Humaning reactions to it. There are two anecdotal reports about the effects of sub-audible sound on Humanings. In one situation, a group of college students attached a sheet of metal to an auditory tone generator. After dark on a college campus, they lowered the sheet, so it hung unseen outside an open window of a dormitory room and energized it with the tone generator, using a tone below normal Humaning hearing. Humanings in the room grew restless, upset and left the room. In another report from the days in which movie theaters had organs which were played during silent films, there was an organ with a subsonic sound on a pipe. It was played during horror films, and on at least one occasion the audience was reported to exit the theater when the tone was played. What was going on in these situations is that Humanings were reacting to an unpleasant stimulus which they couldn't identify. Might the need to evolve function similarly, operating outside of our conscious awareness? If that evolutionary impulse is blocked, might Humanings react with fear and anger to a stimulus they can't identify, and would that lead to a variety of projected interpretations as Humanings scramble to find an explanation for their discomfort? This could lead to blaming the Other for some unintelligible experience. This would link with our need to explain things. If we lack an explanation for the discomfort generated by a below-awareness stimulus, we are likely to attach blame to the available Other. If those Others are different in easily-identified ways, they will become targets. I am sure my reader can readily identify manifestations of this process in current events. Opportunistic leaders could take advantage of this even though they might not understand that Humanings were dealing with the pressure of the need to evolve. There is also another dimension to the need to evolve issue, and that is that we are being pushed at a nonconscious level to change. If we resent that pressure but don't understand what it involves we might get frightened, and the fear of change we cannot specify could also encourage us to identify the Other as a threat.

Humaning awareness regarding personal safety is most likely to differ greatly from one Humaning to another. What I feel I need to feel safe is quite different from what other Humanings feel they need to feel safe. I feel it is likely that my perceptions of what I need to be safe are much more elaborate than what my physiology feels it needs to survive and evolve. The physiological drive to be safe is centered in the gut-brain. Over time the interactions between gut-brain and the autonomic nervous system will draw on the rational thinking of the head-brain to create a more elaborate description of what I need to feel safe. If I am going to open the portal and allow more energy to flow into the Predominant from the Alternate, I must address my perceptions of what I need to feel safe; this would involve examining the details of how my head-brain has elaborated my understanding of what I need to feel safe. Sometimes this elaboration gets separated from the actual response of the gut-brain and leads to trying to feel safe by chasing false premises—premises based on an actual threat experienced years ago which persist even if the original threat no longer exists. Sometimes this elaboration persists long after the visceral experience has ended. One of the things which meditators talk about a lot is how to quiet the chatter of the monkey mind. A lot of this chatter is about illusions of safety that have been generated by an overactive head-brain.

Another individual, the psychologist Stan Grof, was also an early researcher into the properties of hallucinogenic substances, especially LSD. However, when it became illegal to pursue this work, Grof focused his attention on a specialized process of hyperventilation driven by very loud, energetic music, especially drumming. Eventually, he developed a protocol for how to arrange the sequence of the music. This protocol also involves an individual who sits with the subject. It appears that this was also a part of the protocol used when hallucinogens were involved. He advocates a three-hour session of this specialized breathing which he claims produces similar reactions to ingesting hallucinogenics. Grof would probably embrace Huxley's assertion, in *The Doors of Perception* that, "Our linguistic habits lead us into error. For example, we are apt to say, 'I imagine,' when what we should have said was 'The curtain was lifted that I might see.'" Spontaneous or induced visions are never our personal property. Memories belonging to the ordinary self have no place in them. "The things seen are wholly unfamiliar." (Huxley, *op. cit.*) The altered state of consciousness is an event during which the Alternate flows into the Predominant.

Grof reports many instances of Humanings remembering their own births, the issues encountered in the birth canal, and the way they felt while they were being born. Maybe the "memories" encountered in this process result from the activation of the autonomic nervous system which may have been conditioned early in life to respond to this kind of stimulation. Some recent research about language memory has documented that the brains of children born Chinese but adopted early, before they could speak, into French-speaking families will respond neurologically to the sounds of spoken Chinese; children who had French origins with no early exposure to Chinese did not respond this way. This suggests that there are nonverbal memories encoded *in utero* that cannot be voluntarily accessed. I wonder if the feelings engendered by the Grof process while listening to loud music that people can feel is activating similar memories. It could be that these kinds of memories have been described as kinesthetic memory which seems to refer to a process of eliciting nonverbal reactions that are triggered by nonconscious processes. If we apply a similar metaphor to the experiences of the Alternate flowing into the Predominant, we can be reminded of Wordsworth's poem, *Intimations of Immortality*, which was written 1803-1806. Stanza 5 of that poem reads:

> *Our birth is but a sleep and a forgetting:*
> *The Soul that rises with us, our life's Star*
> * Hath had elsewhere it's setting,*
> *   And cometh from afar:*
> * Not in entire forgetfulness,*
> * And not in utter nakedness,*
> *But trailing clouds of glory do we come*
> * From God, who is our home:*
> *Heaven lies about us in our infancy!*
> *Shades of the prison-house begin to close*
> * Upon the growing Boy,*
> *But He beholds the light, and whence it flows,*
> * He sees it in his joy;*
> *The Youth, who daily farther from the east*
> * Must travel, still is Nature's Priest,*
> *   And by the vision splendid*
> *   Is on his way attended;*

At length the Man perceives it die away,
And fade into the light of common day.

If we consider that we are portals through which Godding energy flows from the Alternate to the Predominant, then we might look at certain religious or spiritual practices as properly relating to the maintenance and management of the portal. Most of us have been long accustomed to visual images of prayer as involving folded hands and bowed heads. This image seems to be related to a medieval conception of God as a feudal lord. This attitude speaks of passivity, petitioning, placating and submission. This historic prayer-pose does not show us a Humaning prepared to act, but simply someone who is waiting. Apparently, early Christian folk saw the physical posture of prayer as a standing Humaning with head held high looking upwards, and arms extended something like one might see when an athlete is awaiting the opportunity to catch a ball. This pose suggests a Humaning who is engaged and ready to act. If we follow the lead suggested by Huxley or Grof, then we can see a useful spiritual practice as a much more active endeavor. A discipline of meditation could involve the use of music, poetry, perhaps visual stimulation and perhaps some form of hypnosis which might include drugs. Native North American Humanings used peyote to foster transcendental experiences. Research indicates this practice is at least 5,500 years old!

We might even wonder if there are contemporary forms of physical mortification/stimulation which might be part of a spiritual discipline. Fasting, which is a spiritual practice with a long tradition, might be considered. Expanding the concept of fasting along the lines of reducing selfishness might involve the giving up of certain material goods or self-indulgent practices. Christians often make a stab at this by giving up something for Lent. There are groups that have used various kinds of physical pain to open the portal. I am thinking of the flagellants in Europe and also of Native American customs of inflicting wounds. Flagellants are often practitioners of an extreme form of mortification of their own flesh by whipping it with various instruments. It could be that flagellants were trying to open the portal by using pain to help them ignore or escape the bottom two levels of Maslow's pyramid. Spiritual practices that focus on physical stimulation are telling us that Humaning spirituality involves a lot more than the machinations of the head-brain. Self-inflicted pain is probably processed first by the autonomic nervous system and then by the gut-brain. Presumably, this would stimulate the fight/flight/freeze reaction. In some cases, the pain of flagellation has been accompanied by some bondage process which would interrupt at least the fight/flight reaction. The mBraining perspective makes the heart-brain the center of the value system. Using physical pain or stimulation for spiritual purposes would stimulate a dialogue between the value system of the heart-brain and the self-preservation drive of the gut-brain.

The philosopher Georg Hegel (1770-1831) proposed a rational process for understanding how things (anything) change or evolve into a more complex reality. He saw each "thing" as a thesis and the opposite of that as an antithesis. The interactive tension between these two perspectives resulted in a synthesis or something new. The synthesis would eventually become a new thesis, and the process would repeat. At an abstract level, he proposed that thesis = being and antithesis = nothing and synthesis thus = becoming.

Using Hegel's thesis, antithesis, synthesis metaphor, mBraining suggests that a disagreement between heart-brain (thesis) and gut-brain (antithesis) might get appealed to the head-brain to create a synthesis. In this particular situation, if head-brain finds itself overwhelmed by the challenge presented to it, then the synthesis thus generated could result in an experience of transcendence *which may be mediated by the insular cortex in the head-brain.* Here is a relevant quotation from the Wikipedia article on the insula: "A common quality in mystical experiences is a strong feeling of certainty which cannot be expressed in words. Fabienne Picard proposes a neurological explanation for this subjective certainty, based on clinical research of epilepsy. According to Picard, this feeling of certainty may be caused by a dysfunction of the anterior insula, a part of the brain which is involved in interoception, self-reflection, and in avoiding uncertainty about the internal representations of the world by 'anticipation of resolution of uncertainty or risk.' This avoidance of uncertainty functions through the comparison between predicted states and actual states, that is, 'signaling that we do not understand, i.e., that there is ambiguity.' Picard notes that "the concept of insight is very close to that of certainty," and refers to Archimedes' 'Eureka!' Picard hypothesizes that in ecstatic seizures the comparison between predicted states and actual states no longer functions and that mismatches between predicted state and actual state are no longer processed, blocking 'negative emotions and negative arousal arising from predictive uncertainty,' which will be experienced as emotional confidence. Picard concludes that '[t]his could lead to a spiritual interpretation in some individuals."

There is research which indicates that people who practice meditation increase the volume of the anterior insulate. However, the research about meditation seems to lean toward emphasizing a network of brain structures impacted by such practices. Such networks do include the insula.

This above quotation suggests that the head-brain in such situations is confronted with ineffability, which indicates there is no language for the experience available. It has been pointed out that we often shift to apophasis in these situations which means that we describe something by saying what it is not because we cannot say what it is.

When the portal is restricted to a minimum opening, the dominant reality in the Predominant could very well be mostly involved with physiological and safety issues. Some of the early existentialists called our attention to our tendencies to obsess about physiological well-being and material safety. Dostoyevsky is a good example of this. This obsessing could also represent what happens when someone gets enmeshed in a system and has no outside perspective. Enlarging the opening of the portal and thus allowing more Godding energy to flow into the system will inevitably alter the system and introduce a detached perspective that would facilitate a more realistic perspective on physiological and safety issues. Spiritual practices that can open the portal might provide the individual with the same experience about which Huxley was talking. Huxley suggested that people who have been through the "door" and returned are changed by their experience. ". . . the man who comes back through the Door in the Wall will never be quite the same as the man who went out. He will be wiser but less cocksure, happier but less self-satisfied, humbler in acknowledging his ignorance yet better equipped to understand the relationship of words to things, of systematic reasoning to the unfathomable Mystery which it tries, forever vainly, to comprehend." (Huxley, *op. cit.*) Huxley suggested that such a Humaning would have a better understanding of the unfathomable Mystery.

A friend suggested that love might be a force that could open a portal. As I wondered about this, I was led back to my concept of self-compassion. It makes sense to see the individual as a portal. Thus, self-compassion could lead to a Humaning being more open to the reality of Godding energy and the resources of the Alternate. Some of the examples my friend cited about Humanings who seem to fit the old-fashioned description of being hard-hearted also point to the absence of love and self-compassion and could be indicators of a closed or nearly closed portal. Considering that Humaning is not only a portal but also a fractal of Godding, then a variety of experiences which resonate with the essence of the Godding nature would also resonate with the Humaning, and that resonance like a sympathetic vibration could expand the portal opening. Those experiences would include not only love (both giving and receiving) but also forgiveness, gratitude, generosity, and creativity. This also leads to seeing the spiritual giants of human history (Moses, some of the prophets, Jesus, perhaps St. Paul, the Buddha, and Mohammad.) as open portals.

We would need to keep in mind that a portal is an opening through which things flow, not a container in which things reside. Jesus himself talked about Pharisees who swallowed camels but only defecated gnats as being phony portals. Such folks might be said to be spiritually and ethically constipated. There is no flow! Perhaps Humanings who are nearly-closed portals are afraid of a couple of realities. They might lose what they have if the portal were to open and opening the portal could challenge their devotion to the manifestations of the Predominant. These folks might fear both loss and gain. To become an open portal would be to change one's identity. Perhaps that might be an example of denominalizing: one goes from being a healer to healing, from being a lawyer to justice-ing, from being a minister to ministering, from being an artist to arting, from being an author to writing.

The condition of the portal is reflective of the individual's attitude toward it. Several factors might condition that attitude: a willingness to "own" the portal; emotionally and spiritually turning toward or away from the Alternate; one's own rigidness or insecurity about change; achieved levels of self-compassion; and so on. When we apply the concept of negative and positive dialectics to the notion that we are portals, then we can see that the negative dialectic would lead to a restricting of the portal because the negative dialectic increases the differentiation between our self-image and the Godding image. A positive dialectic would open the portal more widely and allow a more abundant flow of Godding energy into and through the individual. That idea points to what happens when the open portal allows Godding energy to flow from the Alternate to the Predominant. The portal is a passage, not a destination. Our portal nature exists to facilitate the flow of Godding energy into and among the Humanings.

Let me suggest another metaphor. Consider the symbol for infinity. Imagine for the moment that the left-hand side of the symbol represents the Predominant, and the right-hand side of the symbol represents the Alternate.

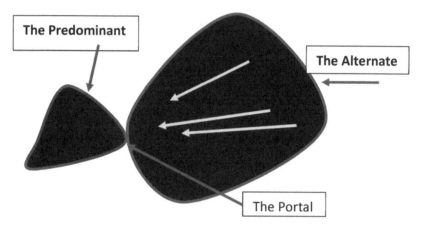

Then imagine that the left-hand loop is much, much smaller than the right-hand loop. The portal is where the two loops connect. It has been said that nature abhors a vacuum; perhaps in similar fashion nature might abhor an imbalance. This would suggest that there is a tendency for the energy in the Alternate to flow through the portal into the Predominant whenever the portal opens (see white arrows). This metaphor suggests that there is a constant challenge to the Predominant. This reality is referenced in various sayings which show that the only real constant is change.

If we think of a portal as an opening through which something (water, wind, energy) might flow, then we can easily understand that there would be a variety of ways of affecting the efficacy of that portal. It could be restricted by reducing its opening, incorporating various sorts of objects into the opening, screening stuff out, etc. On the outflow side of the portal, there could be a variety of conditions that would inhibit further flowing from the portal—like trying to save the effluent or taking the time to bottle it. Opening the portal wider, removing obstacles from it, and expediting the movement of the effluent would result in the portal performing more effectively.

If we consider that the Humaning portal is a two-way opening, then we can understand that from the Predominant reality of Humaning's portal there could flow gratitude, celebration, appreciation back into the Alternate. The flow either way through the portal enhances the quantum entanglement metaphor of both the Godding and the Humaning fractals. When Humaning owns the gifts bestowed, celebration happens. We cannot help but celebrate when we consider the giftedness of our fractal nature.

I would like to add a comment and some information about the use of quantum entanglement in this book. The reality of quantum entanglement has been demonstrated scientifically at a very small scale. However, physicists do not think entanglement works the same way involving large collections of particles, whether that collection is a person or a parrot. I think of quantum entanglement as a metaphor suggesting that something like that which happens at the particle level could happen on a different scale. There is also some research suggesting that life is an effect of the quantum state maintained in microtubules in human cells. It appears to me that the manifestation of energy in microtubules is something that happens on a very small scale and may approach the particle scale where quantum entanglement has been observed.

This suggests there could be the entanglement, which I have labeled as a metaphor, at the cellular level in Humanings. These microtubules contain information which is shared with the universe via dissipation when the individual dies. This would fit with the theory advanced in the biocentrism literature that the principle of conservation of energy makes it impossible to destroy life. The apparent destruction of life is a change in the form that expresses eternal energy.

Here is a quotation from an article about life (or soul) in those microtubules:

"It turns out that the human brain could be similar to a 'biological computer,' and that human consciousness may be like a program which is run by a quantum computer within the brain. What's even more astonishing is that after someone dies, their soul comes back to the universe, and it does not die.

"This is all according to American physicist Dr. Stuart Hameroff and mathematical physicist Sir Roger Penrose, both of whom argue that the soul is maintained in micro-tubules of brain cells. The two scientists refer to this process as 'Orchestrated Objective Reduction,' or 'Orch-

OR.' Allegedly, when human beings are 'clinically dead,' microtubules in the brain lose their quantum state but are still able to retain the information inside of them. . . . Hameroff's words suggest that human souls are much more than mere 'interactions' of neurons in the brain. In fact, this theory indicates that these 'souls' could have existed since the very beginning of time itself." (irelease.org)

It seems possible that the microtubules could, via entanglement theory, function as couplers connecting Humaning and Godding. The report of Hameroff's and Penrose's work ends: ". . . with all of the recent discoveries pertaining to dark energy and dark matter—substances which humans cannot see or interact with, but substances which we know exist, nevertheless—this theory could end up explaining things that are even more mysterious and fascinating."

Eugene Wigner said: "When the province of physical theory was extended to encompass microscopic phenomena through the creation of quantum mechanics, the concept of consciousness came to the fore again. It was not possible to formulate the laws of quantum mechanics in a fully consistent way without reference to the consciousness." It appears to me that the reality of microtubules which contain information validates the view that the concept of consciousness is related to a quantum view of reality whether we're talking about existent realities requiring observation or aspects of reality connected via quantum entanglement. Furthermore, since the microtubules appear to exist in cells throughout the human body, the notion that consciousness is a whole-body reality and not just a head-brain phenomenon is supported, as are the mBraining theories being advanced by Soosalu, Oka, and others.

I wonder if, as we get deeper into the details of Humaning life at the microscopic level, whether we may also find ourselves getting closer and closer to the Godding connection. Perhaps Mark Twain was right about Godding being hidden in the depths of Humanings.

There is another important lesson to be learned from the use of metaphors. The English poet, Alfred, Lord Tennyson (1806 to 1892) wrote:

For I dipt into the future,
* far as human eye could see,*
Saw the vision of the world,
* and all the wonder that would be;*
Saw the heavens fill with commerce,
* argosies of magic sails,*
Pilots of the purple twilight,
* dropping down with costly bales;*
Heard the heavens fill with shouting,
* and there rain'd a ghastly dew*
From the nations' airy navies
* grappling in the central blue;*

These lines are a metaphor for air travel and warfare—a vision, if you will, of airplanes. Tennyson was ahead of his time with his insights. This vision of his is in the poem *Locksley Hall* written in 1835. The Wright brothers first flew a controllable heavier-than-air aircraft at Kitty Hawk, North Carolina in 1903. It would be 1914 before planes began to function as fighter planes—nearly 80 years after Tennyson envisioned them. His poetic metaphor was a vision of the future. We might say that metaphors empower imagination which often leads to discoveries about our perceptions of reality and inspires scientists to explore uninvestigated aspects of the world.

We might take note of the truth voiced by Richard Rohr in his book *Falling Upward.* He says, "Mystics often intuit and live what scientists later prove to be true." (p. 167) Might we classify the physicists who think of the universe as Mind mystics? Would Tennyson be found among the mystics? Will we?

Meister Eckhart, the 12th century mystic proclaimed, "We are all meant to be mothers of God, for God is always needing to be born." That sentiment also might point toward entanglement between Humaning and Godding fractals.

The Critical Concept of Self-Compassion

It is important to take a bit of an excursus to consider the topic of self-compassion because this perspective has an enormous impact on the condition of the portal and helping to maintain an open and accommodating portal to facilitate the flow of Godding energy from the Alternate into the Predominant. Western theological thought has been heavily impacted by the concept of original sin which seems to legislate against the validity and social acceptability of self-compassion. This concept could interfere with the idea that Humanings are called to be portals which facilitates the development of the avatars.

Self-compassion could facilitate access to the "undifferentiated psychic energy" that Assagioli referenced. Self-compassionate Humanings would be more open to manifestations of Godding energy.

In the middle of the 20th century, Eric Berne developed a psychotherapy system which he called Transactional Analysis. He published a book in 1958 called *Games People Play* which provided a number of illustrations of how transactions between people played out. About ten years later, Thomas Harris brought out a popularized self-help book based on Berne's theories and the work of a neurosurgeon named Willard Penfield. This book, described as the most popular self-help book ever written (it's still in print), was titled *I'm Okay, You're Okay*. In this book Harris suggested that there are four basic transactional styles or positions: "I'm Okay, You're Okay;" "I'm Not Okay, You're Okay;" "I'm Okay, You're Not Okay;" and "I'm Not Okay, You're Not Okay." He felt that the vast majority of adults find themselves in the "I'm Not Okay, You're Okay" position. There has been some debate as to whether that is the position Humanings occupy from birth on or whether Humanings are born into the "I'm Okay, You're Okay" position which is then corrupted by social interactions.

The theology of original sin seems to go rather well with the more modern concept that Humanings by nature are Not Okay. Some might call this a biologically-transmitted feeling of inferiority. The concept of original sin became a mainstay of the concept of substitutionary atonement in a lot of Christian theology. In the late fourth century, Augustine of Hippo (known to some as St. Augustine) gave clear expression to the concept of original sin, which had been developing amongst Christian theologians for hundreds of years. In his view, all of humankind was a mass of perdition and inherited their sinful nature as a result of biological transmission from Adam and Eve, the original Humanings, who were portrayed as breaking God's rules. The Protestant reformers of the 17th century had a field day with this theory. Early Puritans converted some of this theology into mantras to instruct children; e.g., "In Adam's Fall, we sinned all." Some authors have proposed that the negative image of Humanings projected by those reformers motivated Humanings to do good and do a lot to demonstrate that they were among Godding's chosen (the "elect") instead of accepting a role as inadequate creatures.

Theological and philosophical enterprises are efforts to make sense of things and thus to explain why things are the way they are. While modern efforts in these fields try to take advantage of current scientific understanding (see Harris' use of Penfield's neuroscience), many of these historic systems are completely disconnected from modern science. When Augustine advocated for inherited sin, we had no understanding of the dynamics of modern genetics and concepts of what is heritable. Probably most people could only occasionally observe that a man's son looked like the father or that all the men in a particular family had oddly-shaped ears. Some of the most important original research in genetics was done by Gregor Mendel in 1865 (about 1500 years after Augustine)—interestingly enough he was an Augustinian monk!

Our current generation of Humanings can easily assume that what we know has been known for a very long time. We might be a bit startled to discover that the concept of the human brain being a constellation of inter-connected nerves is a little more than 100 years old and the anatomical drawings made by the discoverer of this reality are still in use in medical textbooks. Dr. Ramon y Cajal received the Nobel Prize for medicine in 1906 for his work in mapping the nervous system. Those of us who were living in 2015 were able to celebrate 150 years of modern genetics.

Many people who do not accept the concept of original sin (which would include most Jews, probably Buddhists and adherents of Islam) suppose that feelings of inferiority are results of poor parenting, educational deficits, negative experiences, etc. Against that background is a plethora of self-help books which advocate that because Humanings are basically good from birth and that they have simply lost the ability to believe "I'm Ok, You're Ok" it will take a change in one's attitude to get over those feelings of inferiority. Usually these amount to some system about raising one's self-esteem.

It seems to me that some recent developments in the study of the brain may offer us some important insights into the persistence of low self-esteem. In order to explain this, I need to give my readers a brief overview of brain morphology. Our brains, which are thought to be the product of eons of evolution, clearly show older, more primitive areas and more recent, more sophisticated areas. Deep within the brain is the limbic system (which includes the amygdala) which seems to be responsible for much of our emotional life. A part of the more primitive brainstem is called the Reticular Activating System. The abbreviation for this system is RAS. The more primitive aspects of our brains are driven by forces that want to preserve life and reproduce life. The conscious mind can only focus on a few things at any given time. If we had to be totally aware of everything that is stimulating our physical bodies, we wouldn't be able to function. The RAS acts as a filter to screen out background stimulation and does respond to some degree to directions from the higher cognitive functional areas of the brain. For example, my RAS screens out the feeling generated by my wedding ring or my watch band; however, if I ask what either of these things feels like, the RAS will allow that information to make it to my conscious awareness. Since the primitive brain is survival-driven, the RAS will forward any alarming stimulation to the amygdala which triggers the fight/flight response. Robert Cooper points out that the RAS ". . . has evolved over millennia with an inherent tendency to magnify negative incoming messages and minimize positive ones." (*The Other 90%: How to Unlock Your Vast Untapped Potential for Leadership and Life,* Kindle Locations 421-422. The Crown Publishing Group.) Cooper also points out that a ". . . few well-intended words of criticism—not a life-threatening communiqué, to be sure—are nonetheless amplified by the RAS into a simple message: Danger! Danger! We bristle up and get anxious and defensive. Conversely, a genuine compliment is usually deflated by the RAS to not much more than a whisper. Which is why, at the end of a typical day when a hundred things have gone quite well, and one has gone slightly wrong, nearly all of us become preoccupied with the one thing that went slightly wrong." (*Ibid.,* location 426-429) I would suggest that we often are confused by the way the negative bias of the RAS contradicts our more logical observations. We don't know what to make of this confusion, and so we allow it to generate those feelings of low self-esteem which make it easy for us to suppose that we are Not Okay. That RAS background feeling that all is not well finds fluent explanation in the doctrine of original sin. Humanings who embrace this concept have a way of blaming Godding for the way they feel and to confuse this even more, end up believing that they are supposed to feel bad about themselves. This gets complicated by the fact that both the RAS and the amygdala don't seem to know when or how to turn off the alarms, so any and all danger is felt to be mortal danger. These systems are like a home smoke detector which cannot tell the difference between burning toast and burning curtains. Perhaps this biology is the background for the familiar assertion that "I am a mistake" instead of the honest, "I made a mistake."

To many Humanings, it has seemed that the way to deliver us from this plague of self-defeating dynamics is to raise Humanings' self-esteem. When Garrison Keillor talked about the mythical city of Lake Wobegon and described all the children there as "above average," he was teasing us a bit about our notion that we can raise everyone's self-esteem. Indeed, some researchers are asserting that our efforts to raise self-esteem have resulted in record high levels of narcissism in our society. Narcissism is the attempt to look good and usually develops at the expense of emotional awareness or authenticity. I once knew a little girl (about 12 years old) who described her narcissistic father to me as like ". . . one of those super-fancy Easter eggs that look great on the outside but have all the insides blown out." My readers might remember those expensive, fancy Russian Easter eggs bedecked with expensive jewelry which are preserved because the contents of the eggs have been blown out. When everyone is trying hard to be above average, competition gets encouraged, and Humaning relationships really take a nosedive. I wonder if our efforts to maintain high levels of self-esteem put us into a perpetual battle with the RAS. Hear what Cooper has to say here: "Let's assume you're getting angry at one of the many things that may cause you to become frustrated or off balance. It's likely that deeply set habits or patterns are at work. The RAS is primed to magnify feelings of impending threat or lost control, instantly priming you for an outburst or, if you manage to suppress that reaction, increased tension or resentment." (*ibid.*, Kindle Locations 439-442). It is clear from current research that efforts to resolve issues of negative self-esteem by raising self-esteem are a failure.

If we look at the multiple brain theory advanced by Soosalu and Oka (*mBraining - Using your multiple brains to do cool stuff*), we don't find high self-esteem as a characteristic of the aligned, integrated personality. Instead, we discover that the highest expression of the heart-brain is compassion. We are discovering that self-compassion is the cure of choice for low self-esteem. The usual attempts to raise self-esteem seem to foster the notion that the individual is in competition with others and that s/he is winning. That takes us to the un-sane conclusion that it is possible for everyone to be above average. Self-compassion allows us to admit our mistakes (from which we will learn), affirm that we are valuable and acceptable the way we are, and celebrate the notion that other Humanings' successes don't detract from our own. Several studies tell us that self-compassion does not foster narcissistic perspectives but instead helps Humanings to be more compassionate toward others. We have learned that we all have specialized neurons called mirror neurons. Those neurons enable us to understand how other Humanings are feeling. It seems logical that developing and improving self-compassion would help those mirror neurons to decipher what's going on with the others that we encounter and make it even easier for us to be compassionate.

V.S. Ramachandran has speculated that mirror neurons may provide the neurological basis of Humaning self-awareness. In an essay written for the Edge Foundation in 2009, Ramachandran gave the following explanation of his theory: "... I also speculated that these neurons can not only help simulate other people's behavior but can be turned 'inward'—as it were—to create second-order representations or meta-representations of your *own* earlier brain processes. This could be the neural basis of introspection, and of the reciprocity of self-awareness and other awareness. There is obviously a chicken-or-egg question here as to which evolved first, but the main point is that the two co-evolved, mutually enriching each other to create the mature representation of self that characterizes modern humans." (From Wikipedia entry on Human Self-Awareness.)

Here is modern neuroscience telling us what Jesus and Buddha said a long time ago: that it is important to love others the way we love ourselves. The theological systems which have specialized in emphasizing original sin have made us unlovable in our own eyes—which makes it much more difficult to love other people. Many religions which focus on negativity often get violent. Those judgmental religions which seem to emphasize what is wrong with other Humanings are not far from the horrid practices of the Taliban and the ancient Christian crusaders! Such focus seems to be linked to focusing on the alarms from the RAS instead of the self-compassion the higher parts of the brain understand and promote.

Loving ourselves actually impacts our neural wiring and the ways our brains function. This will affect our perception of reality: compassionate Humanings are more likely to see the universe as a positive, life-friendly reality. Self-compassion improves our ability to be compassionate to others. Andrew Newberg has learned, through his brain research efforts, that positive spiritual practices alter the neurochemistry of our brains and ". . . bestow a sense of peace, happiness, and security while decreasing symptoms of anxiety, depression, and stress." (Newberg M.D., Andrew. *How God Changes Your Brain: Breakthrough Findings from a Leading Neuroscientist* (Kindle Locations 975-977). Random House Publishing Group. Kindle Edition.)   Dr. Gail Ironson, a professor of psychiatry and psychology at the University of Miami who studies HIV and religious belief says, "Here's what's surprising: a growing body of scientific evidence suggests that faith may indeed bring us health. People who attend religious services do have a lower risk of dying in any one year than people who don't attend. People who believe in a loving God fare better after a diagnosis of illness than people who believe in a punitive God. No less a killer than AIDS will back off at least a bit when it's hit with a double-barreled blast of belief even accounting for medications" ("Spirituality predicts for better disease control," *Time*, February 12, 2009).

Research is also showing that fear-based beliefs can be hazardous to one's health, leading to shortening of the lifespan, increasing of a variety of illnesses, prolonging of recovery rates, etc. Fear-based belief focuses on that old, reptilian brain and promotes fearful and angry responses. The more we focus on that aspect of our physiology, the more we will configure a brain that is involved with fears constantly and which as a result may even exhibit a fair amount of paranoia. We are discovering that the brain likes a balance and resists anything that will disturb that balance.

If we have a fear-filled brain, we will have a brain that specializes in maintaining a fearful balance. That will require us to get better and better at identifying enemies, to be supersensitive to threats, and to use our logical ability to explain all this turmoil. That will leave less and less energy to develop self-compassion as well as enhancing resistance to compassion.

Changes in how our brains are configured will change the way we perceive reality. Developing self-compassion will help us see things differently. Jesus assumed that people do actually love themselves when he asked us to love others as we love ourselves. To me, this means that Jesus is promoting self-compassion and is suggesting that developing self-compassion is the right thing to do. The self-compassionate person will see more good in others and indeed in the universe.

We have learned over generations that an orderly society requires us to modify the expression of many primitive brain mechanisms. We might consider the biological drive to reproduce. The rather primitive urge to copulate runs head-on into our awareness that Humaning babies have a very long period of dependence on parental care. We have devised particular social customs to limit copulation to chosen mates and keep the resulting marriages together to care for children. While I certainly would not argue that society's interest in restricting the number of sexual copulations has been overwhelmingly successful, it does seem to me that we have an example of how social interactions, pressures and individual needs have modified the basic biological reproductive urges. If we can develop customs to modify the primitive drive to reproduce, then we can also develop practices and customs to minimize the self-defeating elements of the RAS. Amongst healthy adult Humanings, there is a nearly universal success at toilet training—which is a process of teaching the primitive brain not to defecate or urinate whenever it feels like it.

There have been a plethora of articles (complete with graphs) which show that the rate of change in society has been accelerating for some time. We are being told that change is happening at an exponential rate. This rate of change is probably contrary to the "speed" with which components of human physiology change. Our amygdala has evolved over hundreds of years, and it is not likely to change quickly to accommodate the realities of 21st-century life. This means that we have to be deliberate and intentional about how we manage our physiology in order to make sense of contemporary life and to avoid making messes by reacting like our primitive ancestors needed to react in order to avoid the dangers of the saber-toothed tiger.

"Compassion is not religious business, it is human business, it is not luxury, it is essential for our own peace and mental stability, it is essential for human survival." Dalai Lama

Emma Seppala crafts a compelling summary of the science that shows why compassion is healthy. Seppala points to leaders in the positive psychology field, Ed Diener and Martin Seligman, who suggest that connecting with others in a meaningful way helps us enjoy better mental and physical health and speeds up recovery from disease. Further, research by Stephanie Brown at Stony Brook

University and Sara Konrath at the University of Michigan shows that experiencing compassion may even lengthen our lifespans. With the intention of answering the big question of why leading compassionate lives is good for us, Seppala reveals:

"The benefits of self-compassion, soft as that concept may sound, is backed up by hard data—much of which has been compiled by pioneer researcher Kristin Neff, author of the book Self-Compassion. Self-compassion has been linked to a host of benefits. Self-compassion means treating yourself as you would a friend in times of failure or pain—with more understanding and kindness. It means remembering Alexander Pope's quote 'to err is human' —we all make mistakes. And it means being mindful of your emotions and thoughts without over-identifying with them. Self-compassion doesn't mean being overly self-indulgent, but it also doesn't involve beating yourself up to no avail." (Emma Seppala, website, February 17, 2016)

It appears that increasing self-compassion also increases overall compassion toward others. Given the benefits of being compassionate, it is in our best interests, both personally and socially, to become more self-compassionate. ". . . one of the most important applications of compassion is with yourself. Your relationship with yourself is the platform from which you relate to others." (Soosalu, Oka, *op. cit., p. 232*)

There is plenty of research from, among other sources, the positive psychology movement which indicates that self-compassion is key to resolving the nearly innate self-criticism most Western Humanings harbor. Readers are invited to review the Wikipedia entry about self-compassion where they will find multiple citations about the topic.

Kristin Neff is a major researcher in the study of self-compassion, and she tells us that "Mindful Self-Compassion [MSC] combines the skills of mindfulness and self-compassion, providing a powerful tool for emotional resilience. A randomized controlled trial demonstrated that MSC significantly increased self-compassion, compassion for others, mindfulness, and life satisfaction, as well as decreased depression, anxiety, and stress" ("Center for Mindful Self-Compassion," www.self-compassion.org).

The unidentified editor of another website on the RAS has this to say about how we can utilize the filtering nature of the RAS to make changes: "Over 30 days, if you think about it and imagine yourself experiencing something new, or affirming an additional, recent belief like 'the world is full of amazing and incredible people', slowly but surely you are molding your filter so that this new statement is having access to your mind and a new mindset is taking place. As you give access to your mind for new convictions, new thoughts are making their way in your subconscious. We all know that no matter [what] our beliefs [are], especially where they normally deal with other persons, there are plenty of opinions to prove one right or wrong out there in the world. If you believe people are jerks, there will be plenty of people around that can prove you right. If you believe people are great, there are just as many people out there waiting to prove that belief right. In the end, it is about what belief you choose to embrace and impress upon your subconscious."

The author, Tschannen-Moran, writing about making changes in our brains, estimates that it takes six months of combined "unlearning" and "learning" to make permanent changes in neuronal firing patterns.

Most of us will have to get rid of old filters to change the RAS successfully. Mindfulness can help us get rid of those filters. If we insist that the only reality is NOW, that yesterday is NO LONGER, and that tomorrow is NOT YET then we can rightfully assign those old, negative and dangerous filters to the day that is no longer. The affirmations we use to make the changes probably will be more effective if they begin with the phrase "right now." "Right now, the world is full of amazing and incredible people." "Right now, I am loving myself and celebrating my gifts." "Right now, I am doing amazing things (like reprogramming my brain!)." We can also avoid passing the buck to tomorrow and refuse to say things like "tomorrow I will be more powerful or better or smarter or more creative." Any time we are tempted to delay the action to the NOT YET; we can restate those actions in terms of NOW.

Kristen Neff also invites us to: "Think about the times you've been lost in the throes of self-criticism. Are you self-focused or other-focused in the moment? Do you have more or fewer resources to give to others? Most people find that when they're absorbed in self-judgment, they actually have little bandwidth left over to think about anything other than their inadequate, worthless selves. In fact, beating yourself up can be a paradoxical form of self-centeredness. When we can be kind and nurturing to ourselves, however, many of our emotional needs are met, [it leaves] . . . us in a better position to focus on others." (October 2015, *Greater Good* e-newsletter.) Neff enumerates five common ideas about why self-compassion is often said to be a bad thing and is able to offer solid research reference in each case to refute these assumptions. The refuted assumptions are: (1) self-compassion is a form of self-pity; (2) self-compassion means weakness; (3) self-compassion will make me complacent; (4) self-compassion is narcissistic; (5) self-compassion is selfish. (See the above-cited newsletter.)

Soosalu reminds us that: "Dr. Robert Ornstein, a noted Psychologist and Neuro-Scientist, makes the point in his many pivotal books, that we become what we repeatedly do. Our personalities and identities are influenced by repeated behaviour and experience." This statement suggests that developing exercises and mantras to use regularly can help us to become more self-compassionate.

". . .there's now an impressive and growing body of research demonstrating that relating to ourselves in a kind, friendly manner is essential for emotional well-being. Not only does it help us avoid the inevitable consequences of harsh self-judgment—depression, anxiety, and stress—it also engenders a happier and more hopeful approach to life. More pointedly, research proves false many of the common myths about self-compassion that keep us trapped in the prison of relentless self-criticism."—Kristin Neff, *op. cit.*

Thich Nhat Hahn, the Buddhist teacher and activist, makes the point that compassion does not stop with letting our hearts feel the suffering of others. "Compassion is a verb," he stresses. "Compassion and action go hand-in-hand. When we're motivated by a true spirit of generosity, we benefit as much as those on the receiving end." Jesuit priest Anthony de Mello says it this way: "Charity is really self-interest masquerading under the form of altruism. ... I give myself the pleasure of pleasing others." In the same vein, the Dalai Lama playfully speaks of working to benefit others as "selfish altruism." "Psychologists have identified a typical state of euphoria reported by those engaged in charitable activity. They call it 'helper's high,' and it's based on the theory that giving produces endorphins in the brain that provide a mild version of a morphine high. Research at the National Institutes of Health showed that the same area of the brain that is activated in response to food or sex (namely, pleasure) lit up when the participants in the study thought about giving money to a charity. At Emory University, a study revealed that helping others lit up the same part of the brain as receiving rewards or experiencing pleasure." (These last three quotations are taken from the email newsletter of the Greater Good Science Center, October 2015)

If we follow the suggestion of Thich Nhat Hahn that compassion is a verb, then we'll need to start talking about compassioning. It is probably easier to do compassioning than to focus on becoming a compassionate being. It might be difficult to decide how much compassioning it takes to turn one into a certain kind of being and it is probably irrelevant. If I were indeed to be a compassionate being, then, of course, I would be doing a lot of compassioning. It seems less complicated to just decide to do compassioning. As has been said here and elsewhere, behavior transforms self-concept. If I do angering, then I'll become an angry man; if I do loving, then I'll become a loving man, and if I do compassioning then I will become a compassionate man. If I own compassioning as a goal, then it is easy to act my way into achieving that goal.

Avatars of Being

"God said, "Let us make humankind in our own image, according to our own likeness."
(Genesis 1:26)
"When I look at your heavens, the work of your fingers, the moon and the stars that you have established, what are human beings that you are mindful of them, mortals that you care for them? Yet you have made them a little lower than God and crowned them with glory and honor. You have given them dominion over the works of your hands, you have put all things under their feet." (Psalm 8:3-6a)

The word "avatar" is derived from Sanskrit. It refers, early on, to the incarnation of a Hindu god in Humaning form. The Sanskrit behind this means "he crosses over," and it might make a lot of sense to use the word "avatar" to describe how Humanings manifest eternal consciousness. The English definition of avatar tells us an avatar is the embodiment of some known model or category.

If individuals are seen as open portals through which eternal consciousness can flow, then Humanings might be drawn to becoming avatars of eternal consciousness. If we consider that Godding is eternal consciousness and is linked to various manifestations of energy (keeping the conservation of energy in mind), then we can look at the concept that we can all become avatars of Godding. We are each potentially an avatar through whom the Godding energy crosses over into the Predominant. The experience of Humaning consciousness (and eventually self-consciousness) would be the result of interaction between the physical Humaning and the Godding energy. Berman and Lanza (*Ibid.*) claim that consciousness as a form of energy cannot be destroyed even by the death of individual Humanings.

I suggested we use the term "Humaning" to refer to the living out of the avatar reality. This term gives us an opportunity to make distinctions between energy expressing itself through Godding and Humaning and also emphasizes the active nature of humans. There are clearly differences in our common understanding of how Godding and Humanings differ. Much religious thinking has emphasized the differences here and not taken seriously the two Biblical quotations I placed at the beginning of this section. The energy which makes Godding and Humaning alive is not different in its essence, but the vehicle of its expression shapes the reality thus revealed. Humaning limitations (for example, the physical aspects of our persons) point to a limit on how much of the Godding energy can be expressed in Humaning form. It appears to me that for Humanings to be Humanings, there must be some differentiation between Creator and creation. One very clear and obvious fact about Humanings as avatars is that there are certain limitations which seem to be part of the Humaning condition. For example, physically and usually psychologically, an individual is one of the two sexes, not both simultaneously. The essential Godding energy or consciousness encompasses all genders. While there are considerable differences among Humaning regarding both knowledge and understanding, it is not a Humaning trait to be all-knowing. For the essential Godding consciousness to manifest itself in an avatar (or to be incarnate), it must be self-limiting. Think of the impossibility of putting five gallons of water (or wine!) into a quart bottle.

In Mark Twain's story, *Letters from the Earth*, the archangels are deciding where to hide Godding. It is suggested Godding be hidden on the moon or deep beneath the surface of the sea, and so forth. Each suggestion, however, eventually leads the archangels to conclude that humankind is too smart to be fooled— sooner or later they would find Godding. So where do they decide to hide Him? Within every Humanings— for, ". . . the last place mankind will look is within," they conclude." (Taylor, *op. cit.*, Kindle Locations 623-627).

Certain historical Humaning figures have been "larger" or perhaps "more nearly complete" avatars of the Godding consciousness-- Humanings like Buddha, Moses, Jesus and Mohammad as well as more modern figures like Dietrich Bonhoeffer, Martin Luther King, Jr., the Dali Lama and Nelson Mandela. Of course, there is a wide range of folk who are powerful and awesome avatars of the Godding consciousness. This seems consistent with the understanding that everyone is an individual and that talents and abilities differ amongst the Humaning family. Huxley had an important understanding which suggests our ability to be aware of Godding consciousness is limited by our very Humaning and each individual needs to attend to the details of life in the world which requires us to often focus on basic needs (the stuff at the bottom of Maslow's pyramid). Huxley suggested Humanings needed to use special techniques to embody more fully the Godding consciousness. He was interested in psychedelic drugs and hypnosis as ways of becoming more fully aware of the Godding consciousness. He also thought once a person had experienced this level of incarnation, they remained changed individuals. The changes which Huxley suggested are consistent with the changes Humanings often associate with spiritual enlightenment, whether this is a gradually developing process or a more dramatic, intense personal encounter with the Godding consciousness. Huxley also understood we all have an intense desire for self-transcendence, related to an implicit or intuitive awareness that the Godding reality is within us. Might such an awareness relate to the innate need to evolve? It seems clear enough that the famous (or perhaps spectacular) avatars expected others could attain to the enhanced self-transcendence they achieved. The Buddha and Jesus both invited Humanings to make changes that would bring them closer to enlightenment or to the Kingdom of God. They seemed to expect anyone could have experiences like their own and, so they affirmed the inborn potential in all Humanings.

Much of organized religion has equated the appearances of the Godding reality with a transcendent energy that is above and beyond mere mortal reality. However, there has also been a less vocal tradition claiming there are immanent manifestations of the Godding reality. We owe a debt to existential theology and to Paul Tillich who in the last half of the 20th century helped us to develop a metaphor compatible with the immanent manifestations of the Godding reality. He talked about the Ground of Being which is beneath us and supportive of our being. Godding, for Tillich, was the Ground of Being without which nothing would exist. [See website religiousnaturalism.org/god as ground of being.]

It seems to me that his concept of Godding as the Ground of Being is quite compatible with the notion of the Godding Consciousness as the ultimate energy reality in the universe. It should also be noted in the Eastern Chakra systems, energy is described as flowing from the Root Chakra at the base of the spine up to the sixth or seventh chakra at the top of the head (there are two notions about the number of chakras, some systems count seven and others six). The Root Chakra is placed in contact with the earth in the classic yoga meditation posture. This suggests there is a certain similarity between Tillich's Ground of all Being and the yoga insistence that the root chakra is in an energetic connection with the earth which sustains life and supports us.

Huxley's notion of a hunger for transcendence is provoked by an intuitive awareness of the immanent presence of the Godding Consciousness which is always pushing us to become more extensive and elaborate avatars of what we might also call Divine Energy. We might think of the potential of entanglement involving the Godding Consciousness and the Humaning avatars wherein what affects one affects the other. There is a certain interchangeability between Consciousness and Energy here with both words designating the same or similar reality. If we respond to the invitation to become more elaborate avatars disclosing Godding reality to the world, we may eventually find ourselves becoming dissipative structures. The significance of becoming dissipative structures in response to the "push" to become more extensive and elaborate avatars is related to the dissipative structure's drive toward transcendence (or escaping to a new order of being) to avoid collapse from over-elaboration. The collapse from over-elaboration might be illustrated with the rise of fundamentalism. One of the places we see this is the vigorous and often well-funded denial of scientific discovery in the name of an outmoded theological perspective which seems to manifest itself in all religions.

There is also the issue of Humaning freedom: I am curious about how seeing each of us as avatars of the Godding consciousness would relate to the concept of Humaning freedom. For example, would some restriction on the perception of Godding Energy be necessary to ensure Humaning freedom of perception and thus decisions?

Is there a reciprocal relationship between Godding incarnate and Godding "essential" or "absolute"? Mirrors give us an opportunity to see reflections, but it is the nature of mirrors to degrade the image some. Mirrors not only flatten three-dimensional reality, but they also can distort color and the image itself when viewed from an angle. The outside rear-view mirror on the right side of my car warns me of the mirror's distortion and tells me images in the mirror may be closer to me than they appear. When we see ourselves as Godding avatars, we are beholding the essential power/energy of Godding in a limited or even distorted form. Perfection is not a Humaning attribute.

We might even take this a step further: if quantum physics is right and consciousness is required for the potential to become actual, does Godding create Humaning (Genesis 1:26: "Let us make humankind in our own image.") to provide a differentiated consciousness which, by beholding Godding, makes Godding actual? The metaphor which comes to mind now is for me to understand myself as a father, I must have children (somewhat made in my image). Hegel's dialectic comes to mind as I consider this perspective. Perhaps Godding and the avatars are entangled systems. Quantum physics insists, in entangled systems, that what affects one part of the system affects other parts of the system.

It may be useful to draw a couple of other perspectives into this discussion. The book of Genesis in the Hebrew Scriptures contains more than one account of the creation of the world. The more popular one is the first one but the second one may be more helpful here. The second creation account is essentially a reverse of the first one. In the first account, human beings are created last, but in this second account, Godding creates Humanings before other creatures are created. Then Godding involves the Humanings in naming the creatures created subsequently to the creation of Humanings. Even though this is a very ancient and primitive piece of literature, it may contain a perspective that fits well with modern physics. The Humanings become the observers of the reality which emerges after their creation. Another perspective that may be helpful is considering the images of the African-American poet James Weldon Johnson. In the first stanza of his poem, *The Creation*, we read that Godding stepped out on space, looked around and said he was lonely and so he would make himself a world. Subsequent stanzas of the of the poem describe Godding as creating other parts of the world. Then the poet tells us "... God said I'm lonely still." The poet depicts Godding as thinking for a while and deciding "... I'll make me a man!" This poem seems to have been written in the mid-1920s. Behind the rather literal imagery of this poem seems to lurk the reality of quantum physics which tells us that there must be an observer for probability to become actual reality. While a lot of Christian theology has made a major production out of the inadequacy and fallibility of the human race, there is an alternative perspective embedded in the Hebrew-Christian tradition. We see that in Psalm 8. Verse 5 of that Psalm tells us Godding created Humanings a little lower than divine beings and crowned them with glory and honor. The same Psalm goes on to describe Humanings as being given dominion over the earth. The Biblical creation stories declare that Humanings are made in the image of Godding which fits with the concept of Humaning avatars mirroring Godding.

There are reliable traditions within Hebrew-Christian history which justify suggesting that Godding and Humanings exist in a reciprocal relationship. In this relationship, the two realities observe each other and thus bring the other out of probability into being. When Johnson speaks of the loneliness of Godding, he is suggesting a common human experience which is also Godding's experience: a reciprocal togetherness is necessary for existence to arise out of probability.

Certain Humaning experiences, especially loss and its attendant grief, also underscore this dynamic reciprocity. We have a friend whose wife of some 60 years died. He speaks eloquently of his grief but also talks about a year-long journey visiting old acquaintances and places he and his wife visited or lived. We had a chance to talk with him while he was on this journey. His journey became a quest seeking to answer the question, "Who am I without the one who was my life-long reciprocal partner?" We are hearing some resolution of all this now as he is finding his way into a new relationship. This will not be the same as his marriage, but it will provide reciprocal validation of his being. Similar experiences go with divorce, with children growing up and leaving home, with retirement, with loss of job, etc. We often talk about these things in terms of our need to be in community. Being in community is not simply associating with other Humanings: dwelling in reciprocity enables us to be more than probabilities. The same dynamic applies to our being in relationship with the Godding consciousness. Compassioning is a key to dwelling in reciprocity because compassioning makes reciprocity safe. If we understand that, then we also understand that we actually can't exist without compassioning! Without compassioning, we are reduced to probabilities.

The Reciprocity Effect

Quantum physics insists that nothing can exist unless it is observed. That fundamental declaration is accepted in this discussion.

I am an observer. I observe a field of probabilities and choose to focus on one particular element in the field and so the "object" of my focused observation comes into existence for me. For example, the kitchen in my house is a field of probabilities when I'm not in it. When I choose to go there, I might decide to focus my attention on the probability that there could be an apple in the refrigerator for me to eat. This focus will eventually put the apple in my hand. Whether the apple observes me, I cannot say.

I am aware that I am observing (and eating) the apple. Self-consciousness permits me to observe myself observing the apple. There seems to be an internal reciprocity within my being: I observe, and I observe myself observing. This self-observation, when consciously acknowledged, is an important—perhaps even critical—element in the creation of self-awareness. Self-awareness grows out of a field of probabilities.

If I observe out of the field of probabilities around me another Humaning, then (like the apple) the Humaning becomes an existent reality. In this case, as soon as conversation between us begins, we are engaged in reciprocal observations. This gets a bit involved, so bear with me for a while. There are at the moment two Humanings (and each one is a system) engaged in reciprocal observations. I observe my colleague, I observe myself observing my colleague, and I observe my colleague observing me and my observation of my colleague may also tell me my colleague is involved in observing her own self observing me. The reciprocal nature of the observing has multiple layers. If I observe my colleague involved in her own self-observing of me, I am most likely to be making inferences based on non-verbal communication. Facial expressions, tone of voice, various gestures, shifts in the content of communication, etc., all cue emotional responses in me initially below my level of consciousness, but which rise into consciousness through my continued self-observations of myself observing. While we might make a case for reciprocal observations beginning before any communication exists between us, such reciprocity could only exist at a non-conscious level until some form of communication begins. Reciprocity is the factor that creates, builds and sustains relationships. Similarly, another outcome of the reality of reciprocity would be a rupture in communication, an end to observing and thus the reality of the "other" returning to the field of probability and ceasing, in my mind, to exist. It will be important to be specific as to whether the reciprocity is positive or negative. Positive reciprocity will tend to enhance the reality of the relationship between observers, while negative reciprocity tends to disestablish the reality originally observed. There would be a regular dialectic of various realities moving toward being or toward nonbeing as the focus of our observation changes. Now we see why abandonment has enormous power: *our refusal to observe un-creates the reality our observation has established.* Quantum physics tells us that one of the three pillars of reality is relationship:

"All events of a system occur in relation to another system" (Rovelli, p. 137).

Reciprocal interactions would involve the functions of our mirror neurons. Mirror neurons are specialized to "decode" other Humaning's actions in a way that helps us to anticipate as well as to understand what is going on with another individual. Here is a very basic example. If several Humanings are sitting in a room together and there is a pitcher of water on a table in the corner, when one Humaning stands up, takes a drinking glass in hand and starts walking across the room, we all know he is going to get water from the pitcher. He didn't announce his intention, but our mirror neurons "mirror" his actions in our own minds and we know that's what we might do and, so we know what he is going to do. This process works for all sorts of complicated scenarios and also for emotions. At the same time, if someone reacts atypically in response to a particular stimulus, our mirror neurons would encourage us to scratch our heads and wonder why that person's reactions are not like our own would be in such a situation.

If we are attentive to what our mirror neurons are telling us, this information will enhance reciprocal relationships because it will help us to know as we observe ourselves observing, what the content of the other Humaning's self-observation is. The longer these relationships endure and the more positive affirmations we get that our observations are useful, the more intuitive the reciprocity becomes. Scott Peck was once asked what Godding does when people do evil things, and Peck said, "God weeps." (Cf. *People of the Lie*, 1983) I believe Peck got this insight from his own mirror neurons and his experiencing of weeping when encountering similar events. If we are sensitive enough to our own self-observations and willing to commit to developing reciprocal relationships, then we too may be able to intuit the self-observations of the Godding-Self.

We are learning from quantum physics that nothing exists unless it is observed. It seems to me that human speech is observation reporting. We are familiar with how speech may change how things are observed. There have also been several reports that when we attach names to objects or events, we also limit or fix the reality of that particular object or event. Ancient literature, such as the creation stories in Genesis, refer to Godding creating via speech. Thus, we have reports of, "God said . . . and it was so." Insofar as our ability to observe is linked to our need to speak or to translate experience into language, self-talk is linked with observation. I do not think that there is any observation without self-talk. Even hard-to-explain experiences, like surprise or pain, get expressed with words like "Wow" or "Ouch."

Much of contemporary psychology focuses on what effect self-talk has on people. There are a variety of theories about how Autonomic Negative Thoughts (known as ANTs) interfere with successful living. I think we can equate "thoughts" here with "self-talk." Things change for Humanings if they replace the ANTS with PLANTs (Positive, Loving, Autonomic Nurturing, Thoughts). Here again, we're looking at speech as a creative force.

Godding needs to be observed in order to exist and so do Humanings. Thus, we have a reciprocal relationship between Godding and Humaning. Conversation between

Godding and Humaning enhances and empowers both. The capacity for self-observation is inherent in the Godding-Humaning fractal. Given that Godding is the more comprehensive, extensive manifestation of the fractal, it makes sense to suppose that Godding comes into being through self-observation. The poem which describes Godding as saying he is lonely assumes that self-observation not only brings Godding into being but also makes Godding aware of the opportunity to more fully manifest the Godding-essence by making Humanings. The metaphoric entanglement of Godding and Humaning elaborates the fractal components which might lead to the discovery that through the portal connection the giftedness of reality flourishes and flows—perhaps with all reality dancing to the sound of love.

If communication is disrupted, all suffer. There is a rather nasty side to this: there are some religious communities which shun people who have gotten into conflict with the community mores. The effect of this on the shunned individual can be devastating because their very existence is being negated and ignored. I once knew a man who was raised Amish but left the "church" to marry and work in the non-Amish world. He was shunned by his birth community including his family of origin; the shunning was a powerful influence in helping him become a practicing alcoholic.

This reality asks us to consider what we are creating with our self-talk. If our autonomic self-talk has a negative bias, it will encourage us to be more sensitive to the negative probabilities within us and in our environment. This sensitivity would result in a creature who featured the worst about us and ignored (and thus denied) the reality of positive probabilities. We might wonder if this kind of situation would result in disrupting any reciprocal relationship between Humaning and Godding. I have suggested that the creation by Godding of the Humaning world is an expression of Godding's need to be observed in order to exist. In order for the observer to be authentic and legitimate, the observer has to be free. For example, if someone holds a gun to my head and tells me that I can see flying saucers hovering over my backyard, I am likely to agree. Of course, almost anyone would notice the inaccuracy of my observation and would explain that my invalid observation resulted from my being held hostage. In order for the observer to create a legitimate manifestation of the probabilities, that observer must be free. If free Humanings not only fail to observe Godding but also fail to observe the probabilities of loving (which seems to be part of the Godding character), then we need to ask what the observer is now creating. This might suggest the deficiencies in the observer could become the vehicle which creates evil. Positive self-talk in this perspective would also become an important factor in creating and enhancing the Godding reality. A reciprocal relationship between the self and Godding would result in patterns of communication which enhance the positive qualities of the participants. However, if the observer has elected to focus on the negativity which denies the Godding reality, then the observer enters into a reciprocal relationship with his own negative projections. Active reciprocal relationships tend to amplify and extend the very things which create the reciprocal bond. This leads me to conclude that we need to consider the ontological implications of self-talk.

There is a recent clinical report indicating that depressed people lose their ability to remember or to be in touch with positive aspects of their own history. The researchers concluded that depressed people don't know what it's like to feel good. This raises the question of how we choose to talk to ourselves and how that choice might compromise the ability to observe probabilities outside our ordinary frame of reference.

We are familiar with the phenomenon of psychosomatic illnesses. We have tended to discount the reality of these conditions. In this discounting process, we have often discounted the Humaning with such jargon as, "It's all in your head." Sometimes when what we described as the psychosomatic illness has turned out to be a more vociferous illness such as cancer, we have had to backtrack some and suppose our original diagnosis of psychosomatic illness was wrong. If we begin to see that self-talk has an ontological function in creating reality out of the realm of probabilities, then we will probably have to take another look at what we mean by psychosomatic illness.

Eldon Taylor's idea that "The Divine, by whatever name you prefer, creates every human being, who is, therefore, a 'Divine experience walking,'" was referenced earlier. The reciprocity between an individual and Godding reality would suggest that there is ontological feedback from the Divine experience talking to the Divine creator. We might even suppose that the ontological feedback in reciprocal relationships changes all who are involved in the relationship.

Many of the more traditional, serious spiritual practices involving meditation, prayer, and so on, may be the enactment of the reciprocal relationship that brings the individual and the Godding into Being. We can begin to modify the concept of Being and refer to Being as "Being-In-Relation." The new physics would suggest that there is no such thing as pure isolated Being but perhaps the notion of Being-In-Relation would speak to both scientific and spiritual traditions.

There is another dimension to this shared reciprocity. We see a rather dark and foreboding development when we realize that when Humanings become negative about themselves, the Godding they imagine they observe becomes an angry and judgmental power. If I look at things through a lens distorted by dirt and mud, then everything I see is festooned with dirt and mud—even Godding. Usually, Hegel's process is envisioned as one that moves upward toward a better day or better Humanings. But the opposite could be true. The dynamic interaction of thesis and antithesis could lead to ever blacker syntheses and then more depressed theses. Such a negative dialectic would make it increasingly difficult to discern good and evil, health and disease, hope and despair. This negative dynamic appears in the self-talk of depressed people. We may also see the influence here of the reticular activating system (RAS) which is part of our brainstem. This system, which functions as a warning system to protect us, has a negative bias, as previously discussed. Practicing interoceptive self-observation may help us to evaluate the negative bias of the RAS and shift our observation elsewhere. The quantum perspective suggests that such a deliberate change in the self-observing would change our understanding of what exists and what does not exist. If we allow the RAS to link with the theological conception of original sin, we make ourselves to be bad. This suggests a natural, internal self-critic that needs to be accepted and managed so that it won't manage us. However, if we challenge the RAS with Matthew Fox's concept of original blessing, then who we think we are will shift.

Quantum physics suggests the existence of things is dependent on their being perceived. There are two or three things that seem to be involved with this. First, we might consider the fact that there is no such thing as two identical Humanings; this means each person's perception is individual and unique. For example, if two Humanings report seeing an apple, we would have to understand that they did not see the same apple. Another factor is that Humanings appreciate being perceived. I am personally glad that certain individuals have done things to make it possible for me to be alive. I share the reality with every other Humanings that I had parents who gave me life. I had a unique experience of being saved from a critical illness by certain individuals, some of whom I know and some whom I do not know. I very much appreciate the fact that these people gave me back my life.

Andrew Newberg, who has written extensively in the field of neuroscience, indicates that the mind is not to be equated with the operations of the brain. (See, *Principles of Neurotheology*, Newberg, 2010) He seems to concur with others who see the brain as an instrument giving us access to mind. The issue with quantum physics and perception creating the reality suggests that mind could be a creation of our perception. This very quickly gets us into the sticky issue of mind perceiving itself. We might wonder if the universing that I bring into existence through my perception rejoices at being perceived. We might ask the same question about mind. If the relationship between Humaning parents and their offspring can serve as a viable metaphor, then we can wonder if the universing and mind rejoice at being perceived. If we could go there, then we might understand that the fundamental relationship between people and the environment they perceive, including mind and the universing, is one of gratitude.

It is obvious there are many people in the world whose fundamental relationships with others are more likely to be based on anger than on gratitude. Newberg reminds us that anger is related to the evolutionarily primitive brain which is also the center of the fight/flight response. The same theory which relates anger to the primitive brain relates gratitude and compassion to the newer parts of the brain. Newberg contends the primitive brain never goes away and it needs to be managed by those brain structures where compassion and gratitude are manifested. (Newberg, *How God Changes Your Brain,* Kindle location 248) I wonder if Humanings who are dominated by the primitive brain find it difficult to conceptualize a gratitude-based relationship with the universing. These might be people whose anger is related to an awareness that their need to evolve is being frustrated. If we use Humaning experience as a metaphor, then when we consider people having an anger-based relationship with the universing, we might be dealing with elements brought into existence by perception but not appreciated. We are familiar with the reality of underappreciated family members causing lots of trouble in the family in their attempt to get positive recognition. We describe these families as dysfunctional and expect Humanings from these families will become problem-makers. What happens to Humanings whose anger drives their connections to both the universing and the Humaning community? It seems to me if I were to be at war with the universing, I would be at war with myself. If I am at war with myself, which means my various "parts" are incoherent, my behavior is likely to generate unhealthy conditions. It appears that most people know lots of folks who are optimistic and lots of folks who are pessimistic. It also seems that pessimism is the enemy of healthy living. Maintaining either optimistic or pessimistic attitudes will certainly result in doing things and thinking things that will get involved in brain programming.

The quantum physics concept of the interdependence of who observes and what is observed is more than an exercise in mental gymnastics. There is an ontological dimension to this. We create via observation. It seems to be instinctive for us to attach names to what we observe. In fact, there may be a Hegelian dialectic to this in which we move back and forth between observing and naming and thus refine or recreate what we observe. This suggests that the familiar reality of psychosomatic illness is indeed much more than a way of telling people their problem is in their head. My self-descriptors will create the reality they claim to discern. There is a potentially huge difference in what happens if I observe a pimple on my cheek and say either, "This is the start of cancer," or "This proves I still have an adolescent lurking in my body." It literally could be the difference between saying, "I'm beginning to die," or, "I have lots of life yet to live." This thinking might be extended to consider what is going on when I observe myself. Most of my self-observation involves self-talk, and that could become either a positive or negative dialectic. The old caution, "Be careful what you wish for," might be connected to this reality. Perhaps the ontological aspect of self-talk (which is a process of self-creation) would help us to understand why it is quite difficult for most people to change their self-talk even when they see a good reason to do so. Hebrew-Christian thought emphasizes the creative power of the word. While tradition usually attributes this to God, the reality is that the power which we all have to name objects and processes is a creative process. Therefore, it is not surprising that in one of the Hebrew creation stories, God brings objects to man and asks the man to name them. Avatars of Godding engaged in creating are (via the entanglement theory metaphor) also manifesting the creating reality of Godding. The reality of an ontological dimension to observing/being observed means that the reciprocal relationship between Godding and Humaning would be described as a co-creative relationship.

Some scientists suggest that the universing is not an object but is a vast field of data. The act of observing the data in this field creates holograms, which are what we see when we behold the universing. These holograms bring actuality out of possibility. It seems obvious that each Humaning would see this data field differently and thereby yield different holograms. Thus, it would seem that even at the ontological level your reality and my reality are not the same.

Consider electricity as a metaphor for energy. When you apply electrical current to a light bulb, you get light. There are many forms of bulbs (incandescent, fluorescent, CFL, halogen, LED) and each kind of bulb yields different light—different in intensity, color, etc. If you apply electrical current to a motor, you get motion. There are, of course, all kinds of motors and they range in size from huge to tiny, but all do the same thing—turn electrical energy into motion. We harness light and motion in many ways: there are reading lamps and traffic lights; there are motors to open the garage door and run the elevators at the hotel. If you apply electrical current to certain devices you get heat: you can boil water on the electric range or heat up your soup in a microwave. If you apply electrical current to other kinds of devices, you might get cold as in a refrigerator or freezer. The power of loose electricity is tremendous: it can kill you or start a forest fire. The expression of electrical energy depends on the medium or vehicle through which or into which it flows. Light bulbs don't move, motors don't light up the night, my kitchen range won't freeze my food. We might think of these objects as conduits for the energy, helping it to manifest itself in useful ways. At a fundamental level (where we talk about energy neither being created or destroyed), there is no real difference in the energy itself as it is applied to different structures. In other words, energy is energy. This opens the door to speculations about the paradox of the unchanged changing. Or perhaps I should say the changing unchanged. What we're talking about here is that morphology changes, but essence, which is energy, does not.

When Godding energy connects with Humaning reality, considerable power is displayed as the Humaning avatar becomes a portal for the Godding reality to enter the ordinary world (the Predominant reality based on Humaning experience). When Humaning avatars become portals or more accurately "own" their portal nature, then the Godding energy has a conduit through which to flow into the world. The teachers of ancient wisdom, whether we reference the Buddha or Jesus, insist that the flow of Godding energy into the world manifests itself as love. They all seem to insist that the Godding energy doesn't just flow into the individual avatars and reside there—it turns the avatars into portals and flows through those portals into the larger world.

Music as Metaphor

Music is another rich metaphor. It seems to have a nearly infinite variety, and yet it is composed of certain identifiable and discreet elements such as: pitch, tempo, intervals. It can be rendered on or through an enormous variety of instruments and through the Humaning voice. If we use music as a metaphor for the Godding energy, we might think of individual Humanings voicing or sounding the Godding energy. Avatars voice Godding as they open themselves to be portals of the Godding energy. This celebrates the fact that each individual gives different expression to the ontological reality. Just as a choir or an orchestra gives fuller expression to music, so a reciprocal community of avatars may voice the Godding reality more powerfully and more persuasively. Variety may indeed enrich our awareness of the complex beauty of the Godding reality.

The quantum concept of entanglement, which holds that related but distant particles maintain a dynamic connection, can be illustrated by the concept of dancing. Humanings dance together when music links them. Dancing could even be described as synchronized vibrating. If one Humaning changes their step, their partner will change as well. Dancing doesn't usually go well if the participants are listening (perhaps via earbuds) to different music and the result would be chaos.

It would be delightful if a musician who composes would write music called, "The Dance of the Avatars."

The authors of *A General Theory of Love* write about limbic resonance. They said: "Because limbic resonance and regulation join human minds together in a continuous exchange of influential signals, every brain is part of a local network that shares information." This resonance might be described as reciprocal resonance. This reciprocal resonance would be reinforced by the overlapping electromagnetic fields emanating from the hearts of Humanings who are in close proximity to each other. The vibration of music is a metaphor for reciprocal resonance.

Humanings are fractals of Godding. Our fractal nature predisposes us to vibrate together. This "dance" promotes the potential for self-consciousness contained in the fractal reality. Chaos theory suggests that feedback will influence the development of individual self-expression of the fractal reality which can either promote or interfere with the development of self-consciousness. Humanings come into being as portals through which Godding Self-conscious energy <u>may</u> flow into the Predominant, but it may or may not follow that individuals will allow themselves to become avatars of the Divine. The process of becoming an avatar involves developing coherence with the Godding energy. This works at the individual level as detailed by the mBraining concept. The theory advocated by the mBraining perspective sees the multiple human brains becoming coherent in their reciprocal relatedness and sees that coherence as facilitating the flow of wisdom through the Humaning system. The same dynamics might apply to groups/communities.

With regard to quantum theory's assertion that "things" can only exist if/when they are observed, it would be important to look at mirror neuron functions. Could mirror neurons be the source of non-conscious intuitive comprehension? If intuition is a function of mirror neurons, then might there be mirror neurons in heart, gut and pelvic-brains? Alternatively, might mirror neurons in the head-brain be responsive, via the vagus system, to gut, heart and pelvic reactions to events? It does appear that it would be important to look at how mirror neurons and all the multiple brains interact. It seems obvious from the perspective of meditation practices (in all religions) that perception of Godding is not a function of logical observations. There has been experiential validation of a link between orgasm and a perception of transcendence. Poetry and music, which in some forms conform to logical rules and in other forms do not, would seem to be other ways in which the experience/involvement of all the brains with Godding reality gets expressed.

The mBraining concepts of prime functions and highest expressions are concordant with the concept of Humanings as Godding fractals. Authentic fractal development and expression would put the individuals, families, and communities in harmony with Godding which might be expressed via musical metaphors. The concept of mBraining Wisdom fits into all this. Wisdoming is a distinction of the avatars. This suggests that avatars would be in reciprocity with Godding self-consciousness and thus experience resonance. It appears that mBraining is at least hinting that integrated coherence of the multiple brains, which facilitates the development and manifestation of Wisdom, is related to the nature of things. In other words, the ontological perspective of mBraining sees Humaning as coherent with Godding. That would also suggest reciprocity with Godding via the portal nature of Humaning as Humanings manifest as avatars.

There is some recent research which demonstrates that the autonomic nervous system (ANS) couples resonantly with changes in solar and geomagnetic fields which sounds like an example of the entanglement theory metaphor, suggesting that the so-called "rhythm of the spheres" is correlated with the rhythms of Humaning physiology. This is also related to research showing that individual heart rates are influenced by the heart rates of others who are close enough (3 to 6 feet) so that there is a sharing of personal electromagnetic fields.

There are issues about the relationship between self-consciousness and self-expression. The choices we make about what to observe will be determinative of what comes into being in our lives. This would have a major impact on whether an individual portal will become an avatar of Godding. There could be forms of self-expression that are consistent with or inconsistent with self-consciousness. Self-expression is a manifestation of the chaos theory that feedback could block self-consciousness. The Humaning who has self-awareness, but no self-consciousness is sleepwalking through life. We might consider whether the portal is either open or closed to the call of Godding energy. What distinctions might we make between self-awareness, self-expression, and self-consciousness?

Roberto Assagioli's ideas about the self seem to be pertinent here. Roberto Assagioli (1888-1974) was the founder of a school of psychotherapy called psychosynthesis. He believed Sigmund Freud did not go far enough in understanding the spiritual aspect of human life. He had views often compatible with those of Carl Jung, especially with regard to creativity and the collective unconscious. Here is a diagram of his system.

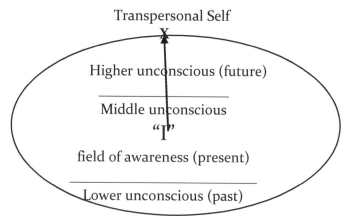

This is all surrounded by the Collective Unconscious
(See *Psychosynthesis*, Assagioli, 1965)

Assagioli saw the transpersonal self (X in the diagram) as rising from the conscious self (I) and moving through three fields of consciousness/unconsciousness until it connected with the Collective Unconscious. mBraining sees Wisdom as rising through the coherent multiple brains. The flow of Wisdom in this model is similar to Assagioli's concept of the transpersonal self rising or flowing from "I" to merge with the Collective Unconscious (which I am calling the Alternate reality). While there are certainly some differences between these two systems of thought, it does appear that they are both referencing similar realities. Both systems share lots of similarities with the Eastern chakra concepts. I believe that mBraining could benefit from a more intentional articulation of its ontological components. I would expect this process to show in some detail how mBraining does embody and reflect what Soosalu calls Ancient Wisdom. His idea of the personal self would seem to equate with self-awareness and would then suggest that the super-conscious concept he described is related to self-expression and that Assagioli's transpersonal self is coherent self-consciousness. The Wisdoming concept from mBraining would correspond to this transpersonal self.

The idea of the call of Godding energy might be likened to the sympathetic vibrations of musical strings. If one string of an instrument begins to vibrate, other strings may vibrate sympathetically unless the other strings are restricted in some form or other. Sympathetic vibrations may mirror the source vibration or vibrate in tune with the source (in which case the vibration might sound different than the original source). Thus, the call of Godding energy moving through a portal into the Predominant might inspire a sympathetic response that would help transform the portal into an avatar.

If I consider what mBraining calls the prime functions of heart and gut-brains, I see there aspects that would relate to Godding. The heart includes values and relational affect, and the gut includes core identity. These are aspects of our Humaning that would connect with the Godding reality. Of course, the compassion of the heart would get involved here as well. I find that intuitive knowing makes the probability of Godding real for me. These heart and gut aspects are, for me, like the tuned strings of a harp, piano, violin, cello, and bass. Those strings sympathetically vibrate when the notes to which they are tuned waft through the air. They will even respond to vibrations too delicate to reach the human ear. As fractals of Godding, we share many of the essential attributes of Godding and so the presence of Godding will set us tingling. Perhaps the presence is mediated by another person (even the covenantal community), or perhaps it moves up and into our bodies through that chakra system when it is in tune with nature. As a fractal of Godding, I am known by Godding before I know Godding—I have to learn the language to label my feelings. Before I know, I am—created, invited, summoned—it is, for me, about the call of Godding which resonates with my being. I have never felt disconnected from Godding, even when I used different terminology to describe the reality I currently call Godding. In my core—which would be gut—I feel the connection. I felt it that night alone in the hospital when sepsis threatened my existence and I loudly declared "Maybe Not!" Godding resonates with my essential values. Grant Soosalu describes the highest expression of the pelvic-brain as co-creating and links that with the creativity of the head-brain. He suggests that together we create and nurture ideas and understandings that are metaphorical children. I would amplify that and say that when we are at our best, our co-creative nature links with and manifests the creative power of the Godding energy. Through the portals that we are, Godding energy makes its way into the world, and we become avatars of the Divine. Obviously, we are free (more or less!) to ignore or even deny these realities, and that compromises our openness and thus the openness of the portal. I hear and feel those Godding vibrations in the teaching of Portal Masters like Jesus, Buddha, Amos, Isaiah, and more modern figures like the Dalai Lama, Martin Luther King, Jr., and Nelson Mandela. Those teachings validate my perceptions, and because of that, I find some of the often-ignored Holy Writings of the first and second centuries to amplify what I hear Jesus saying. When I can feel my many brains in mutual coherence, then my whole self is in sympathetic vibration with Godding energy and that energy is, for me, what Soosalu describes as the Wisdoming that flows through that coherent system.

The development of self-consciousness could be compromised by choices made via the self-expression process. This suggests that inauthentic living (violating, compromising or ignoring prime functions and highest expressions) results in missing the mark (aka "sinning") regarding the self-consciousness being expressed as avatars.

Thinking about time: if we can understand that time is a verbal device and not an actual "object" out there, then we can also look at the fact that length of life is irrelevant in assessing anything (good or evil) about the life-ing. Sagan's comment that, "We are made of star-stuff," when coupled with the notion that energy cannot be created or destroyed, and when combined with the understanding that all time is NOW, is another way of connecting Godding and Humaning into a reciprocal oneness.

Why bother with remythologizing? Because if we don't, we are going to be stuck with rigid thinking that results from nominalizing (objectifying) Spirit. If we accept the time-tested view of the Spirit, like the wind, going wherever it chooses, then refusing to demythologize and remythologize is to oppose the movement of the Godding Spirit, and that might become a problem. There is an issue regarding authentic and inauthentic observing of the Godding energy: if the observation is obscured by primitive myths that have been nominalized into objects (e.g., God as Father), then the mutual observation is static, and the person is nominalized into an object. If I see Godding as a thing, then I will see myself as a thing; the result will be a mechanical, lifeless (aka dead) construct (I can't say relationship because objects can't relate.) This now lifeless attempt at spirituality will become a collection of rules and pronouncements about history and will be frozen as an artifact of another era. The artifactual spiritual life will be incapable of engaging actual contemporary events and issues without resorting to "interpretation according to the artifacts." Thus, possible events like a nuclear holocaust get discussed according to the artifact of Armageddon. Ancient allegations which see Armageddon as an act of Godding then get linked via artifactual interpretation to a nuclear holocaust which then gets described as Divine judgment.

Here is a comment about mirror neurons pointing to the potential of the authentic observing of the Godding energy—a process consistent with our biology: "Our neurobiology— our mirror neurons— commits us to others. Mirror neurons show the deepest way we relate to and understand each other: they demonstrate that we are wired for empathy . . ." (Marco Iacoboni, *Mirroring People*, p. 268).

Mirror neurons may communicate with the viscera via the face's connection with the parasympathetic system. This would mean, for example, that when I see someone smile and smile in return my "smile" is also linked with gut, pelvic and heart-brains via a link between the face-parasympathetic-vagus system. This would be one way to at least symbolize the way mirror neurons interact with gut, heart and pelvic-brains.

Iacoboni, lays the groundwork for the significance of the mutual observing of Godding and Humaning. "How can we even think of 'self' except in terms of the 'other' that the self is not? Without self, it makes little sense to define an 'other,'"and without that other, it does not make a lot of sense to define the self. How could mirror neurons not play a role here? These are the very brain cells that seem to index (with their neuronal firing pattern) this unavoidable relationship between self and other, the inevitable interdependence." (Ibid., p. 133) This interdependence described here might also be described (via quantum physics) as a form of entanglement, which would also suggest that once an interdependent relationship has been established, any distance between those involved would be irrelevant. This would also explain the intuitive ability of some individuals to be aware of what those within their interdependent world are experiencing.

When the portal opens to facilitate the influx of Godding energy, then the stage is set for a Humaning to be transformed into an avatar. Avatars have the ability and the power to restrict or enhance their own portal nature as they respond to their own experiences and the challenges of living out their avatar-hood and feeling the power of the flow of eternal consciousness moving through them.

Jesus As a Godding Portal

(Who Manifests as the Avatar Called the Christ)

Spong raises the issues about the lack of hard data regarding the beginning of Christianity and the lack of details about the life of Jesus. I have been looking at the idea that the universing is a hologram which human observation assembles from a vast field of data. We might consider that a similar process could be used to create a credible story about the life of Jesus; to do that requires two basic efforts. The first of those is to ignore the extensive versions of the stories about Jesus that have been composed and proposed since the Council of Nicaea (325 CE). The second major effort would be to include all documents about the life of Jesus that antedate the Council of Nicaea and intentionally regard them all as equivalent factors in the data field from which a new hologram can be constructed. This means, for example, that the Gospel of Matthew and the Gospel of Judas would be given equal footing. We would have to disregard the church's tendency to canonize particular literature and give it a special status while ignoring or discounting the literature labeled as non-canonical.

In every era, theologians and scholars have constructed stories about the beginning of Christianity. Those constructions have taken seriously the science and worldviews of the dominant society in which these authors lived. It is of course very helpful to give names or labels to objects and events we wish to discuss. However, once we provide a name, we rule out at least as much as our rule includes. The names we choose tend to persist over time and to resist efforts to change them. If we choose to describe an event in history as a miracle, we can predict a couple of results from that. The label will invite Humanings who deny the reality of miracles to ignore this event, and in that process, alternate analysis or understanding of the event will elude us. The label will also encourage Humanings who believe in miracles to ignore other aspects of the original event. Most of the stories we have about the life of Jesus come to us from a non-scientific age. These stories reflect such things as a three-story universe, a tendency to attribute miraculous status to things that were not very well understood, and a habit of comparing God with a medieval monarch or perhaps even Caesar (who was worshipped as a god). It is not likely that in the 21st-century people would easily equate divine being with a king or emperor. If we suppose that democratic styles of government are about 300 years old, then we are faced with the idea that most of the history of modern religions transpired under various kinds of dictatorships and monarchies. The political realities of that long history guarantee that metaphors being used to describe spiritual realities are steeped in nondemocratic experiences. That history will reinforce the notion of original sin and the inherent corruption of everybody because it fits with a monarchical style of governance.

It will be necessary for Christians working to incorporate the Godding concept into their perspective to do some demythologizing and remythologizing about the central figure in Christianity, namely Jesus himself. Tillich taught us that "Christ" was not Jesus' last name as we often seem to think it is. "Christ" is a Greek word used as a title and means anointed"; it is used to translate the Hebrew word "Messiah."

The gospels, particularly the Synoptic Gospels, (Matthew, Mark, and Luke) were written to respond to the liturgical year by offering a synopsis of the life of Jesus, which has led to the impression that the ministry of Jesus lasted for a year. That does not fit with the facts. The ministry of Jesus lasted between three and three and a half years. It included many trips from Galilee to Jerusalem and back and got him familiar with Samaria.

In constructing a story of the life of Jesus that can be used to inform current beliefs and practices, we must deal with what I call glorious backwash. We might consider the main narrative of the Synoptic Gospels to be like a piece of rope that is composed of tightly woven fibers. The beginning of these gospels and the ends of these gospels appear more like a frayed rope; in other words, there is a lack of agreement about the beginning and end of these works. These frayed narratives have been influenced by Humanings' belief in the amazing qualities of this man.

The author of the Gospel of John is quite clear about his writing. He states, "Jesus did many other signs in the presence of his disciples which are not written in this book, but these are written so that you may come to believe." (20.30-31) He also says: "There are many other things that Jesus did. If every one of them were to be written down, I suppose that the world itself could not contain the books that would be written." (21:24-25) John is the only gospel writer that tells us why he has written his book. He also is acknowledging the existence of many other stories and details, presumably known to his contemporaries. Perhaps it would be a useful way to study the gospels if we allowed ourselves to wonder what motivated the authors and what criteria affected their decisions about what to include and what not to include. We cannot come to any absolute truth about this, but we might be better able to appreciate the idea that there are other perspectives on the life of Jesus than those offered by the canonical gospels. There are other interesting variables also in play here. For example, apparently in the first century you could go to a shop and buy a blank scroll just like we can buy a ream of paper. Those scrolls apparently came in a standard length. There seems to have been an intent to get the story on one scroll. Luke, the apparent author of both the Gospel of Luke and the Acts of the Apostles, wrote a two-volume work: the gospel is the Jesus story, and the Acts is a history of the early church.

It will be important for people trying to reconstruct the life of Jesus to take into consideration non-canonical materials. The Gospel of Thomas, the Gospel of Mary, and the Gospel of Judas are examples of the materials which need to be considered. Elaine Pagels and Karen King, in their book *Reading Judas* (Penguin Group, 2007), remind us that there is no common agreement within the early Christian community about a number of things that present-day Christians seem to take as established truth. This would include ideas about the resurrection of Jesus and ideas about the purpose of Jesus' death as well as acknowledgement that there was substantial disagreement early on about things now considered to be established facts. The attribution of the virgin birth was common in the biographies of famous people in that era. It could also be that the attribution of the virgin birth was propaganda to counter the notion that Jesus was conceived out of wedlock.

Although Spong doesn't say so (see p. 243 above), Jesus' bloodline flows through the personage of a bastard. Bishop Spong's reminder that the female lineage leading to Mary the mother of Jesus included several women of questionable repute also makes me wonder about the church's need to make Mary respectable. Perhaps what is at work here is also the influence of non-Jewish Humanings in the construction of the narrative. Orthodox Jews would have known the stories about the ancestral women and perhaps would not have been bothered by Mary being another non-conformist in that tradition. Perhaps the story that Joseph struggled about breaking off his relationship with Mary when he discovered she was pregnant was included in the narrative by Humanings who did not know the whole back-story.

Jesus seems to have lived most of his life in Galilee, in the north of Palestine which was known to be a home base for terrorism. The terrorists seem to be descendants of the Hasmoneans who moved into Galilee during the time the Hasmoneans controlled the government of Israel. That was before the birth of Jesus. These folks continued to make trouble for Herod the Great even in Jesus' time. Their involvement in politics would have made the government in Jerusalem sensitive to things going on in Galilee— perhaps including the fact that Jesus was reported to have gathered some large groups of people there. The presence of Simon the Zealot amongst the disciples may reflect connections between Jesus and his terrorist neighbors. This might also apply to Judas. From Wikipedia: ". . . the revolt by Judas of Galilee, arising from the census of Quirinius in 6 AD, was the ultimate origin of the Jewish freedom movement, which developed via the 'Fourth Philosophy' group into the Zealots, even by the time of Jesus. . . [R]esearchers suggest that 'Simon Zelotes' was indeed a Zealot belonging to this movement, and perhaps that other disciples were also."

It also seems that the church needed to make Judas out to be evil or perhaps a demonized individual because of his role in the arrest and subsequent crucifixion of Jesus. I have some questions about the role of Judas. One piece of historical data which appears to be accurate is that Judas was the treasurer of the band of disciples. Part of the attempt to "black-wash" Judas was the allegation that he stole money from the treasury. It seems reasonable to me to suppose that Judas was the treasurer of the group because he had some administrative skills. The narrations about the Last Supper make it clear that Jesus sent Judas on a mission that the other disciples did not understand. This mission was to arrange for the arrest of Jesus, which may have been part of a plan which Jesus had. Some of the evidence of that planning can be seen in the fact that during the last week of his life, while he was in Jerusalem, he made sure he was out of town each day by the time the gate would have been closed for the night. The exception to this was the night of the Last Supper. Jesus also instructed his disciples to follow a man carrying a jar of water through the city, so the man could show them a place where he and the disciples could have that Last Supper. It was apparently not common for men to carry water, but perhaps it was something that could be done without attracting too much attention from the Roman authorities. The water jar could have been a secret code that Jesus had set up with the man who carried it. Jesus' instructions to the disciples to follow this man certainly implies that he was involved in detailed planning, including arranging for a venue, for the events of what Christians now call the culmination of Holy Week. The attribution of the name Iscariot to Judas could be a historical anomaly. The Iscari were terrorists who apparently sidled up to their victims in crowds and stabbed them. It does appear however that the Iscari appeared on the scene later and were not involved in current events at the time of Jesus arrest. Perhaps the reason for calling Judas by this name was part of an intentional campaign to discredit the man. Spong proposes that Judas was a late addition to the list of disciples and was part of a deliberate effort to advance anti-Semitism amongst the Christians. Spong's idea that the Judas story, as we have it, could have been used to advance anti-Semitism is possible, but that doesn't necessarily mean that there wasn't a different Judas behind the one portrayed in the gospels. Amongst the ancient documents discovered in recent years is a brief one titled, "the Gospel of Judas." This document makes Judas out to be a hero. The author of this document offers a radical interpretation of the meaning of the crucifixion. When Jesus tells Judas to ". . . sacrifice the human being who bears me," he is asking Judas to help him demonstrate to his followers how, when they step beyond the limits of earthly existence, they, like Jesus, may step into the infinite – into Godding. Time and again in the literature of this period, we find beliefs that the Divine is contained within Humanings and that death, as the Gospel of Judas puts it, ". . . the death of the body is not the end of life, but only a step into the infinite." Pagels and King tell us: "[that]Those who hear this message [of the Gospel of Judas] recognize that rather than being simply physical bodies with complex psychological components, we are fundamentally spiritual beings who need to discover what, within us, belongs to the spirit. This gospel suggests that our lives consist of more than what biology or psychology can explore – that our real life begins when the spirit of God transforms the soul." (op. cit. p. 97) There is a good deal of criticism in the Gospel of Judas of common practices in the early Christian community especially about the celebration of the Eucharist. This document, along with things like the Gospel of Mary, shows us that there was a good deal of conflict in the early church and that the idea that there was something called common, consistent beliefs is bogus. We are reminded again that the concepts of orthodoxy and heresy are all about winners and losers.

Most of the efforts to describe the life and ministry of Jesus have failed to place him firmly in his historical context. We now have evidence that points to the idea that his father was not a carpenter, but a peasant who had lost his land and thus was technically a homeless person. Jesus may indeed have had a homeless family. The story of his being born in Bethlehem, spending time in Egypt and then living in Nazareth and finally making Capernaum his "home base" might indeed be the story of a landless, homeless, wandering family. In Matthew 8:20 [also in Luke 9:57] there is a report of Jesus telling a man who wants to follow him that ". . . the Son of man has no place to lay his head." That could be the honest reality of being homeless. One can make the case that Jesus was a troublemaker. Perhaps all this stuff about Jesus being illegitimate is related to defining him as a rebel. The concept of legitimacy is created by the establishment. A case could be made for the idea that from the Jewish perspective Jesus was a heretic. He is the only person that I know who nearly got killed over a sermon he preached in his hometown. He apparently associated with Samaritans and confronted his audience with what they would have seen as an oxymoron by talking about a good Samaritan. He broke with convention in speaking to women and having female friends which would have been unusual for a religious teacher of the time. He also had an especially close relationship with Mary of Magdala. He apparently had some connections outside of Galilee. One could make a case for the idea that his father may have traveled North and West of Nazareth to find work, especially in the community of Sepphoris. It makes sense to suppose that such commuting to get work would have produced social connections and friendships outside Galilee and perhaps with non-Jewish folk.

There are a lot of questions about the role of Mary Magdalena in Jesus' life. We have remnants of a gospel written by this woman in which she is reported to set the Apostle Peter straight. We know that it would have been highly unusual in that time and culture for Jesus not to have been married. It also seems obvious that we have several centuries of church doctrine that apparently needs to see him as a single man. One can only guess at the difficulties that would arise if it could be demonstrated that Jesus was married and indeed had children. Perhaps one-dimensional figures are easier to manipulate theologically.

The early church, including Paul himself, was generously supported by women. Paul's *pièce de résistance*, the letter to Rome, was taken to Rome by a woman. I wonder if this grew out of women's appreciating Jesus' willingness to include them, respect them and befriend them. I have also wondered if women were less likely attract the attention of the Roman authorities.

There has been substantial agreement among scholars for some time that the Gospel of Mark is the first canonical gospel to have been written. Some feel that the Gospel of Thomas is older than Mark, but it is not considered to be canonical. It is interesting that the Gospel of Mark has no details about Jesus' life before he began to teach. It is also interesting that there are no accounts of the resurrection in the Gospel of Mark. There are some versions of Mark that seem to have resurrection accounts tacked on, but these are considered to be pious edits from a later date. It has frequently been noted that the writings of St. Paul don't include any details about the life of Jesus. One could say that Paul is not interested in Jesus' life but is focused on his function as the Christ. The details of Jesus life and even of his teachings seem to be irrelevant to Paul's determination to promote a theology that focused on salvation by grace and not by works. It is difficult to date Paul's work, but there is some hard evidence about his being in Corinth, Greece in the mid-50s CE. He was supposedly killed in a Neronian persecution in Rome around 64 or 65 CE. There is some indication that Paul was at the stoning of Stephen, the first Christian martyr, around

29 or 30 CE. There is also a story that Paul disappeared for several years after he encountered the transcendent Christ on the Damascus Road. It is further supposed that one of the first letters we have from Paul is the letter to the Galatians which is often dated in the mid-40s CE. The Gospel of Thomas, which comes from a similar time, is composed entirely of sayings or teachings of Jesus and is not at all interested in the details of his life or in promoting a salvation theology. This would also indicate that Paul's theology wasn't the only one around.

I wonder if Paul, who was both a Roman citizen and a Pharisee, anticipated the destruction of Jerusalem, which happened in 70 CE. Was he concerned that Judaism, which was closely linked at that time to the sacrificial system in the Temple of Jerusalem, might be destroyed when the temple was destroyed? We also know that in various Roman cities where there were synagogues, there were people attracted to Judaism who avoided conversion because of the practice of circumcision. These people were known as "hearers," and it appears that Paul was interested in cultivating their support and convincing them that the Christ that Paul proclaimed would offer them the benefits that make Judaism appealing without the necessity of circumcision. It seems to me that Paul's efforts to reach out to the hearers would be consistent with his concern for the future of Judaism. So, I pose an interesting question: was Paul trying to spread Christianity or was he trying to save Judaism? Suppose for a moment that Paul focused on freeing Judaism from its connection to the animal sacrificial system associated with the temple in Jerusalem. There was in the ancient world substantial resistance to the concept of animal sacrifice. Animal sacrifice was common among many different religions, and there were also Humanings who thought it was a barbaric practice. Paul was an educated man who was thoroughly cognizant of traditional Jewish practices. He might have had several reasons to urge Judaism to forsake animal sacrifices. This would mean that Paul's intention was not what many conservative (i.e., evangelical) Christians suppose: namely that Paul was trying to promote a theology of substitutionary atonement which requires the faithful to believe that Jesus died for our sins. One of the problems with the substitutionary atonement theory is that it requires God to be both loving and angry and unwilling to offer forgiveness just because forgiveness is a good idea. Regardless of Paul's motive, it seems clear enough to me that there is nothing in the teaching of Jesus that supports the notion of substitutionary atonement. Amongst contemporary evangelical Christians, there are even some who claim that the teachings of Jesus are secondary to the concept of substitutionary atonement. There was an interesting piece in the NY Times ("Am I a Christian, Pastor Timothy Keller?" by Nicholas Kristof, 12/23/16) in which an evangelical pastor claimed that Jesus' teaching was ". . . not the main point of his mission." In this article, several major premises of historic Christianity are discussed, and Keller keeps coming back to what the Bible says. It appears that for him what the Bible says is the final authority. Of course, the Bible says a lot of things and many of them are contradictory. The reality is that the People of the Way (aka "the Church") existed for a long time before the Bible as we know it was assembled (probably in the early fourth century of the common era). The gospels were all written years after the end of Jesus' life—anywhere from 30 to 90 years later. The earliest material in the New Testament is found in Paul's letters which were written between about 45 CE and 64 CE. Jesus is believed to have been crucified in 29 CE. We can make a much better case for the concept that the Bible is the Church's book than we can for the notion that the Bible tells us how to do church. Lots of conservative thinkers point out that Revelation is the last book in the Bible as if it was the final word on many things. It is at the end of the Bible because when the Church voted about what to include, it got the fewest votes. There is a book called "The Shepard of Hermas" which nearly beat Revelation for inclusion.

Keller makes the whole point of Jesus' life to be one of substitutionary atonement to appease an intolerant, angry God. In my opinion, much of the early discussion of substitutionary atonement amongst the People of the Way was to help first century Jews, who lost their temple and the center of a sacrificial system in 70 CE, understand that Godding didn't require atonement. In other words, what was originally an attempt to appeal to Jews has gotten turned into the whole rationale for Christianity. Paul focused a lot on the "hearers" group and helped them to understand that religious sacrifice (the slaughter of animals) was not needed for Humanings to commit to the ethical concepts of both Judaism and the Way. All the emphasis on substitutionary atonement strikes me as a classic example of the tail wagging the dog; in this case, we might spell tail as tale!

All the gospels are thought to have been written after Paul's death. There is some speculation that there was some urgency in the early church to get some written records of things as the principal players in the life of Jesus began to die. It is thought that Peter was martyred at the same time that Paul was killed. Perhaps this order of things encourages Humanings to read the gospels through the lens of Paul's teaching and thus to play down the significance of Jesus' teachings and his life example of living as a foil to authority.

I'm also interested in the implications of the role of Judas in the life and ministry of Jesus. The rejection of Judas in the gospel narratives could well be part of the early church effort to make Jesus "respectable." Did Jesus befriend a terrorist? What did Jesus think of the terrorists of his time? Humanings of the 21st-century need to understand how outside the system Jesus was and is. I see Jesus as someone that very few established middle-class Humanings would enjoy meeting. Jesus was an in-your-face advocate for societal change and personal transformation. I'll say it again: Jesus was a heretic.

Let's consider an alternative perspective on the last few days of Jesus' life. We know that he came and went in and out of Jerusalem for several days and that he intentionally stayed in the city the night he was arrested. We know that he gave his disciples instructions about how to find the room for the Last Supper. Jesus was deeply involved in managing events that week. There was apparently a demonstration in the city linked to Jesus' arrival in Jerusalem. That demonstration, which is known to church history as Palm Sunday, seems to have been planned by Jesus himself. He rode into the city on a donkey which his disciples obtained following his instructions. I can't imagine this demonstration would have gone well with the authorities. Jewish authorities were hypersensitive to the moods and preferences of the Roman government. They would have known that any wrong steps on their part could bring down the wrath of the occupying powers. Pilate was notorious for antagonizing the Jewish establishment— in fact sometime after the crucifixion of Jesus, Rome recalled Pilate probably for his ineptitude which was demonstrated by deliberately antagonizing the Jewish establishment. We know that the gospel narratives are compact descriptions of events. The gospels were written to make a point, and like any written work they would subject the factual details to the purpose of their narrative. We may want to revisit the question of why the Apostle Paul says so little about the kinds of details to be found in the gospels. What we do have in the gospels about the Last Supper is an indication that Jesus sent Judas on a mission. It is implied that the other disciples didn't know why Jesus did that. It would appear that we have a few sketchy details of a rather elaborate scenario which may indeed have been orchestrated by Jesus himself. We might wonder if the enthusiasm of the Palm Sunday demonstration encouraged Jesus to suppose that a broader protest could be linked to the celebration of Passover which would, of course, have brought many pilgrims into the city. If I want to be seen as being a really energetic heretic, I could suggest that the crucifixion was either the result of a failed demonstration plan or an intentional act to complete his ministry and release his spirit from his worn-out body while attempting to maximize the effects of his teaching.

I consider that Jesus made several trips to Jerusalem during his ministry and that he aroused the suspicion of the Jerusalem authorities by the sorts of crowds he may have attracted in Galilee. One way to go and come from Jerusalem to Galilee would be to go up the west side of the Jordan River which would have put you in Samaria. Samaria was not governed by the same authorities as was Jerusalem. Of course, Samaria was also considered to be heretical by Orthodox Jews. It appears that Jesus' conversation with the Samaritan woman at the well took place in Samaria. Such a conversation would have been an illustration of at least two contradictions of Jewish orthodoxy: it would have shown a Rabbi (teacher) talking to a woman which was very unconventional, and it would have shown that same Rabbi consorting with heretics. If Jesus used Samaria part of the time as a route between Galilee and Jerusalem to ensure safe passage, it might also be an indicator of how savvy Jesus was about political realities. If Jesus indeed made that trip through Samaria more than once, he might even have had some connections there. Walking through Samaria going between Galilee and Jerusalem would probably have taken nearly a week so, presumably, the traveler would have to arrange for places to sleep and eat. Jesus' story of the good Samaritan indeed describes such a place to which the Samaritan took the victim and arranged for his care. That parable, which we know as the story of the Good Samaritan, would have been aggravating to most Jewish citizens who saw the Samaritans as heretics. Galilee was a hotbed of opposition to the Roman establishment that was controlling Jerusalem. We probably also need to take seriously the question, asked by Nathaniel, "Can anything good come out of Nazareth?"

I see Jesus as a rebel who practiced and taught nonconformity to the stultifying customs of society. If we get hung up on substitutionary atonement, we actually discount the significance of this man, his life, and his teachings. I see Jesus as a wisdom figure who was a portal through whom the energy and wisdom of the Godding Presence flows and who thereby became the Avatar we call the Christ. I see Jesus as dwelling among other distinguished and excellent portals of wisdom, including the Buddha, Moses, many Hebrew prophets, Mohammed and more contemporary figures like Martin Luther King, Jr., the Dalai Lama, Bishop Tutu, Nelson Mandela, and others. Interesting to me is the fact that many of these people have taught much the same essential truths.

All of this raises some questions about whether we see Jesus as typical or atypical of his culture. The church has done a thorough job of sanitizing the life of Jesus. We could have some fun with the tradition that church art shows Jesus with a halo around his head, not to mention artwork showing a pretty Jesus and even a white (!) Jesus. Jesus' comment about swallowing a camel and straining out a gnat is a blunt, earthy saying which refers to digestion and elimination. Jesus' choice of metaphors here underscores the very human, down-to-earth nature of the man. In this metaphor, he invites us to wonder about the story as pointing to the failure of a whole system to function effectively. Perhaps Jesus was concerned that love did not flow through the religious system. It would be interesting to look at the teachings of Jesus through fresh eyes and to ask ourselves how earthy and revolutionary much of this content would be. We might even end up with a version we couldn't read in church. Perhaps we could stimulate people's interest with the phrase: "The Jesus you think you know is a phony."

The term "Christ" means anointed and, as Tillich pointed out, should be affixed to Jesus (in English) by turning what appears to be a name (Jesus Christ) into a title: Jesus the Christ. Behind the scene in this vocabulary discussion is the concept of Jesus as God incarnate. "Incarnate" means "in the flesh," which is usually interpreted as pointing to Jesus as unnatural and not Humaning, which makes the usual descriptions of Jesus as a Humaning phony. Much of the conventional theology about incarnation is an assumption that Humaning nature is degraded, unholy and trash. It is, therefore, necessary (from a logical perspective) to insist that the Holy Jesus isn't really a Humaning.

If we see Jesus as an earthy, outspoken rebel, who transformed his portal nature into an Avatar of Godding energy, we are free to set aside the usual verbiage about his supernatural nature. We are free to give him credit and admiration for the unusually magnificent Avatar he became and to appreciate the way in which he facilitated the flow of Godding energy into the Predominant without needing to separate him from the rest of humanity. If we go at it this way, we will celebrate the potential goodness in Humaning nature and allow Jesus the Christ Avatar to join with other heroic avatars who have all brought hope to humanity.

Bibliography

Armstrong, Karen, *The Battle for God*

Assagioli, Roberto, *Psychosynthesis*

Berne, Eric, *Games People Play*

Berne, Eric, *Transactional Analysis*

Borg, Marcus *Jesus and Buddha*

Brooks, David, New York Times article dated December 27, 2016

Cooper, Robert K., *The Other 90%: How to Unlock Your Vast Untapped Potential . . .*

D'Aquili, Eugene and Newberg, Andrew *The Mystical Mind*

Fox, Matthew, <u>*Original Blessing,*</u> 1996

Fractal Foundation website

Fredrickson, Barbara, *Love 2.0*

God's Plan for All, a free, online book

Greater Good Science Center e-newsletter October, 2015

Grof, Stanislav, *Healing Our Deepest Wounds*

Harris, Thomas. *I'm Okay, You're Okay*

Henry, R. C., "The Mental Universe"; Nature 436:29, 2005

Heyward, Carter, *When Boundaries Betray Us*

Huxley, Aldous, *The Doors of Perception and Heaven and Hell*

Iacoboni, Marco *Mirroring People*

Ironson, Dr. Gail, Time magazine, 2/12/2009

Kak, Subhash et al, *Quantum Physics of Consciousness*

Kenney, Bradford, *Shaking Medicine*

Kierkegaard, Soren, *Fear and Trembling/Sickness Unto Death*

Kristof, Nicholas "Am I a Christian, Pastor Timothy Keller?" NY Times, 12/23/16

Lanza, Robert and Berman, Bob *Biocentrism*

Lanza, Robert, *Beyond Biocentrism*

Lewis, Thomas et al, *A General Theory of Love*

Mandelbrot, Benoit, *Fractals*, 1977

Markova, Dawna *I Will Not Die an Unlived Life*

Neff, Kristin, "Center for Mindful Self-Compassion" (website)

Newberg, Andrew, *How God Changes Your Brain*

Newberg, Andrew *Why God Won't Go Away*

Newberg, Andrew, *Principles of Neurotheology*

Newberg, Andrew, *The Metaphysical Mind*

Oka, Marvin and Soosalu, Grant *mBraining. Kindle edition*

Pagels, Elaine and King, Karen L., *Reading Judas*

Peck, Scott, *People of the Lie*, 1983

Ramachandran, V.S., Wikipedia entry on Human Self-Awareness

Ribeiro, Carlos and Haberl, Cristina, *Biocentrism 28 Questions and Answers*

Rohr, Richard, *The Divine Dance*

Rohr, Richard, *Falling Upward*

Rosenblum, Bruce and Kuttner, Fred, *Quantum Enigma*

Rosenblum, Bruce and Kuttner, Fred, *Quantum Physics of Consciousness*

Rovelli, Carlo, *Reality is Not What it Seems*

Russell, Peter, *From Science to God*

Spong, John Shelby, *Biblical Literalism: A Gentile Heresy*

Spong, John Shelby, "Charting the New Reformation," in his e-Newsletter, April 7, 2016

Taylor, Eldon, *Choices and Illusion*

Thomas, Andrew, *Hidden in Plain Sight 7*

Tillich, Paul, *Systematic Theology*

Index